CERTIFICATE

FUNDAMENTALS AND PRACTICE OF MARKETING

First edition 1991
Third edition September 1993

ISBN 0 7517 4000 4 (previous edition ISBN 0 86277 470 5)

British Library Cataloguing-in-Publication Data

A catalogue record for this book
is available from the British Library

Published by
BPP Publishing Limited
Aldine House, Aldine Place
London W12 8AW

**Printed in England by
DACOSTA PRINT
35/37 Queensland Road
London N7 7AH
(071) 700 1000**

We are grateful to the Chartered Institute of Marketing for permission to reproduce past examination questions. The suggested answers have been prepared by BPP Publishing Limited.

We would also like to acknowledge the important contribution made to the preparation of the first edition of this text by Professor Geoffrey Lancaster of Huddersfield Polytechnic.

©

BPP Publishing Limited
1993

CONTENTS

PREFACE

The examinations of the Chartered Institute of Marketing are a demanding test of students' ability to master the wide range of knowledge and skills required of the modern professional. The Institute's rapid response to the pace of change is shown both in the content of the syllabuses and in the style of examination questions set.

BPP's experience in producing study material for professional examinations is unparalleled. Over the years, BPP's Study Texts have helped thousands of students to attain the examination success that is a prerequisite of career development.

This Study Text is designed to prepare students for the Certificate in Marketing examinations in the Fundamentals of Marketing and the Practice of Marketing. It provides comprehensive and targeted coverage of both syllabuses (reproduced on pages (vii) to (xii)) in the light of recent developments and examination questions (analysed on pages (xii) to (xvii)).

BPP's Study Texts are noted for their clarity of explanation. They are reviewed and updated each year. BPP's study material, at once comprehensive and up to date, is thus the ideal investment that aspiring marketing professionals can make for examination success.

The September 1993 edition of this text

This Study Text has been updated to take full account of recently examined topics.

BPP Publishing
September 1993

If you wish to send in your comments on this Study Text, please turn to page 261

INTRODUCTION

Syllabus

Fundamentals of marketing

This subject is designed to provide students with the grounding and theoretical marketing framework on which they will be able to build throughout the rest of their studies.

It is strongly advised that this paper is studied early in the course and prior to the *Practice of Marketing* and *Behavioural Aspects of Marketing* papers.

Aims and objectives

● To ensure students have a basic understanding of the concept of marketing and its impact on the organisation.

● To introduce students to the activities and tools of marketing.

● To provide students with an understanding of the terminology and techniques used by marketing practitioners in the application of the marketing concept.

By the end of their study students should be able:

(i)   to explain the development of the marketing concept and its relevance to different types of organisation;

(ii) to appreciate how the marketing function is organised and how it relates to other functions in the company; and

(iii) to demonstrate an understanding of the value and limitations of each of the tools of marketing – marketing research and the elements of the marketing mix (product, price, promotion and place).

Content

(a) *Origins and development of the marketing concept*

    The changing philosophies of management
    Product, sales and consumer orientations ✓
    The impact of consumerism and environmental factors ✗

(b) *The role of marketing*

    Discovery and delivery of user values
    Providing customer satisfaction at a profit

    The marketing function
    As a bridge between producers and consumers
    Influencing the flow of goods and services from the suppliers to the customers
    In non-profit making organisations

    Controllable and uncontrollable factors
    The controllable factors in the marketing operation: the marketing mix
    The impact of the uncontrollable, macro environmental factors (political, economic, social and technological)

INTRODUCTION

(c) *Marketing organisation*

The marketing department
Co-ordination of marketing with other management functions
Allocation of functions and responsibilities
The need to adapt the company's structure to serve the requirements of the company's markets

(d) *Scope and value of marketing research*

The importance of accurate marketing data as a basis for management decision-making and action
The need to monitor customer/consumer behaviour
Importance of and methods for segmenting the market

Research options
Distinction between market research and marketing research
Types and sources of information available
Methods for data collection (primary and secondary data, quantitative and qualitative data)
Research limitations (cost, accuracy, timing, security and compatibility)

(e) *The marketing mix*

Product planning, design and development
Concept of the product life cycle
    Maintaining a product mix
New product development
    Stimulation of evaluation and innovation
    Variety reduction

Distribution
Cost vs control issues of distribution decisions
The development and structure of distribution channels
    Changes in the distribution systems
    Development of mail order selling and direct marketing
The wholesaling and retailing functions
    Relationships between producers, distributors and customers

Pricing
Pricing methods
    Pricing structures
    Price competition
Administration of price changes

Promotion
Communication objectives
    Communicating product benefits and unique selling propositions
Elements of the promotional mix
    The role of conferences and exhibitions
Using specialised agencies

INTRODUCTION

Hints and tips from the examiner

The *Fundamentals* examination paper is designed to examine basic textbook knowledge. Marketing is taking place all around, so there is no need to stick to strict textbook answers, use illustrations from your own experience and observations. Those who show a basic understanding of the fundamentals of marketing should achieve a pass, but those who can demonstrate the following will score high marks in the examination:

● Appropriate use of relevant practical examples

● An ability to think creatively or originally about a topic or problem, rather than just relying on a 'textbook-type' answer

● Adherence to the question asked, producing answers in a clear, concise and objective way

Practice of marketing

This is an optional Certificate subject. You may choose to study for either this paper or the *Practice of Sales Management* paper. If you successfully take both, the extra paper will be credited to you on your Certificate. For those choosing to take this paper, you will find that it builds upon the foundations of marketing principles already gained in the prerequisite papers *Fundamentals of Marketing* and the *Behavioural Aspects of Marketing*.

Aims and objectives

● To provide students with a level of knowledge and skills to allow them to perform adequately in any single functional area of marketing

● To provide students with an understanding of the principal systems and institutions relevant to the marketing process and marketing systems

● To encourage students to examine the issues of applying marketing theory in practice

By the end of their study students should be able:

(i) to demonstrate a sound, practical application of marketing theory to business scenarios;

(ii) to use real life experience and marketing theory to illustrate and justify practical marketing solutions to given questions;

(iii) to handle all the tactical aspects of the marketing function in a competent and convincing way; and

(iv) to demonstrate how a company's overall resources are directed to meeting marketplace requirements.

INTRODUCTION

Content

(a) *The information input*

Market research
Management of research
 Defining objectives
 In-house research or agency
 Responsibilities of agency and client
Information sources
 Secondary data
 Primary data
Management of a survey
 Sample selection
 Questionnaire design
 Managing data collection
 Data analysis
 Reporting findings

Marketing research
Objectives, organisation and methods of:
 Retail audits
 Motivation research
 Readership and viewership research
Internal analysis of the effectiveness of
 Sales
 Distribution
 Advertising
 Promotional activities
 Market and marketing research activities
Test marketing
 Objectives, organisation and methods
 Problems and pitfalls

Sales forecasting
Applications, objectives and alternative methods
Sales force composites
Opinion juries
The need to state the degree of uncertainty in forecasts

(b) *The promotional output*

Selling and sales management
Variety of roles and contexts for selling activities
Sales management activities
 Recruitment
 Selection
 Training
 Organisation
 Motivation
Organising to support the sales force
 Role of the sales office
 Sales manuals
 Meetings and conferences

INTRODUCTION

Advertising
Variable roles of advertising in different product/market contexts
Relationship between clients and agencies
Organisation of agencies
Client's role in advertising
    Relating advertising to other marketing activities
    Specifying themes, messages and objectives
Agency's role in advertising
    Media selection and buying
    Creating the communication vehicle
    Measuring and evaluating the results

Below the line activities
Sales promotion
    Common types of promotional activity
    Integrating promotional activity with the marketing mix elements
    Role of promotions in relation to sales force/clients
    Attempting to correlate 'selling out' with 'selling in'
Public relations
    Role
    Methods
Package design
    As an aspect of the marketing mix

(c) *Marketing internationally*

The special problems of marketing abroad
Distance
Unfamiliarity
Local regulation and protections
Cost of obtaining market information

The alternatives
Agencies
Sales office
Full international operation

(d) *Marketing management*

Planning
Statement of objectives
Mobilisation of the marketing mix
Budgets as a key component of the marketing plan
Use of forecasts, market information and internal management
Control information for the production of marketing budgets
Profitability (contribution) and actions

Evaluation
Using qualitative and quantitative methods to evaluate
Marketing strategies and plans
Appropriate quantitative measures for the long and short run
Evaluation for internal consistency

INTRODUCTION

Organisation
Organisation round a marketplace focus
Organisation around project or processes
Role of product and brand managers as integrators
Development of matrix-type organisations

Control
Review of performance against plan
Importance of quantitative measures as control criteria
Measuring the effectiveness of marketing activities
Modifying plans and information for next year's planning cycle

Hints and tips from the examiner

The examination for this subject places emphasis on the practice of marketing and whilst the theoretical base is important, it is the sound practical application of this theory to practice which is essential to achieving a good pass.

The examination will consist of two sections:

1   A mini-case study, which you will have to assess in the examination room and on which you will then answer two compulsory questions.

2   Section B, worth 60% of the marks and offering you a choice of three questions from eight.

The examiners are seeking evidence of students who can:

●   effectively communicate ideas both in language and in numbers;
●   show a common sense understanding of people;
●   demonstrate evidence of a year's study of marketing institutions and practices.

Analysis of past examination papers

Fundamentals of marketing

The paper comprises ten essay type questions, each worth 20 marks, from which any five must be attempted.

June 1993

1   What is the marketing concept and why is it becoming more fashionable?
2   Marketing theory and consumer behaviour
3   The marketing mix and non-profit organisations
4   What is market segmentation? Describe four different bases, with examples
5   Outline and explain the stages in the product life cycle
6   Distribution channels, channel intermediaries. Direct marketing
7   Distinguish the separate stages of a sales interview
8   Brief notes on three of: test marketing; product testing; recognition and recall tests; product screening
9   What is the intended purpose of a marketing information system?
10   Outline three different methods of sales forecasting

INTRODUCTION

December 1992

1 What is the marketing concept and why has a marketing orientation become more common?
2 Why are the four Ps described as 'the controllables'?
3 Explain the difference between selective, intrinsic and exclusive methods of distribution
4 Outline four different bases upon which markets can be segmented
5 Justify the use of exhibitions in business to business marketing
6 Explain the term secondary data, with examples of sources and usage
7 Define: cost plus pricing; penetration pricing strategies; market skimming and differential pricing
8 Explain the changes that can occur in promotional strategy at each stage of the product life cycle
9 Explain product positioning, with examples of FMCGs
10 The consumer movement and marketing decisions

June 1992

1 The appropriateness of production orientation
2 Should 'People' be the fifth P in the marketing mix?
3 How is the marketing channel a system of exchange?
4 How do undifferentiated market coverage strategies achieve profit objectives?
5 Explain why industrial product exhibitions are effective
6 Distinguish between market research, sales research and product research
7 How do trade promotions and consumer promotions achieve market share increases and how are they inter-related?
8 Marketing information systems
9 Explain the concept of a market
10 Why do marketers need to be environmentally aware?

December 1991

1 Marketing v production orientation
2 Change and marketing mix decisions
3 Push and pull promotion and distribution flows
4 Distinguish market segmentation and product differentiation
5 The use of PR for company communications
6 Research proposals to examine potential market for new product
7 Above-the-line advertising media
8 Limitations of the product life cycle concept
9 Methods of sales projection
10 What is a market?

June 1991

1 Marketing and sales orientations
2 How the main elements of the marketing mix are associated
3 Direct marketing
4 Market segmentation
5 In-store merchandising
6 Advantages of market research
7 Effective sales persons: born or made?
8 Functions of product packaging
9 Markets' duties to society
10 Limitations of the product life cycle concept

INTRODUCTION

December 1990

1 The marketing concept and non-profit organisations
2 Marketing mix: differences between industrial and consumer product markets
3 Collecting market data
4 Role and functions of physical distribution management
5 Forms of marketing organisation
6 Stages in product life cycle
7 Merchandising: use by retailers
8 Public relations and company communications
9 Consumer movement's influence on marketing
10 Notes on cost plus pricing; market skimming pricing; marginal cost pricing; market penetration pricing

June 1990

1 Marketing orientation and product orientation
2 Elements and formulation of the marketing mix
3 Distribution in UK of consumer goods
4 Notes on above the line media activity; below the line activity and direct marketing
5 Relationship between market segmentation and product differentiation
6 Marketing department's co-ordination with other management functions
7 Value and limitations of the product life cycle concept
8 Mail order selling: why has it grown?
9 Value of marketing research
10 Product screening, positioning, mix and elimination

December 1989

1 Marketing concept and orientation
2 Achieving a balanced marketing mix
3 Selective, intensive and exclusive methods of distribution
4 Marketing fast moving consumer goods
5 Market segmentation
6 Use of exhibitions in marketing industrial products
7 Direct marketing methods
8 Market research and marketing research
9 Influence of consumer movement on marketing decisions
10 Notes on four of: unique selling proposition; promotional mix; point of sale display; publicity; above the line media advertising

Practice of marketing

The paper is divided into two distinct sections. In section I, you are given a mini case study on which you must answer two compulsory 20 mark questions. In Section II you must choose three 20 mark essay style questions from eight.

INTRODUCTION

June 1993

Section 1
1 Advise holiday company on market information needed to decide locations of retail outlets
2 Suggest what form of local promotion should accompany opening of new retail outlets

Section 2
3   The product life cycle and the Boston Consulting Group matrix
4   The value of market research data
5   Reduction in advertising expenditure during recessions
6   The difficulties of entering overseas markets outside Europe
7   The importance of public relations
8   The use of forecasts in the marketing planning process
9   Disagreements between advertising agencies and their clients
10 'Marketing means business'. Why?

December 1992

Section 1
1 Tyre manufacturer: market research to improve understanding of consumer attitudes, purchasing behaviour and brand awareness
2 Tyre manufacturer: recommendations for maximising promotional effort

Section II
3   Marketing practice and adaptation to changing conditions
4   The marketing mix and pricing strategy (fast food)
5   The value of the diffusion of innovation model
6   How is brand personality established?
7   Sample surveys, census surveys and quota sampling
8   Sales forecasting and corporate financial objectives
9   Marketing planning and the marketing information system
10 Can Europe really be considered as one market place?

June 1992

Section I
1 Market research to explain non-use of an exercise sandal
2 Proposals for increasing repeat purchases of the sandal
Section II
3   The market environment and growth through customer satisfaction
4   Why are there disputes between advertising agencies and their clients?
5   The limitations of the product life cycle concept
6   The hierarchy of effects and marketing communications
7   The structure of a market research plan
8   The difference between the promotional mix for FMCGs and for legal services
9   Outline the annual marketing plan to a client and explain how it should be monitored and controlled
10 How is export marketing influenced by culture?

INTRODUCTION

December 1991

Section I
1   Selection of an advertising agency to handle the image problem of a holiday camp
2   How can the holiday camp use direct marketing to widen appeal?
Section II
3   Can marketing orientation work in practice?
4   Action to achieve growth using the Ansoff matrix
5   How should FMCG marketing managers respond to the green movement?
6   Distinguish between objectives and tactics of push and pull promotional strategies
7   Test marketing as a means of risk reduction
8   Problems of organisations which overstate their annual sales forecast
9   Can banks be marketed like FMCGs?
10 Short talk on problems of small businesses entering the Single European Market

June 1991

Section I
1   SWOT analysis
2   Short-term tactical proposals to build sales in retail chain
Section II
3   Adjustment from production to marketing orientation
4   Penetration and premium pricing strategies
5   BCG matrix
6   Pre-testing and post-testing to measure effectiveness of advertising
7   Formulation of market research questions to eliminate bias
8   Importance of motivation of purchase
9   Corporate mission statement and marketing
10 Marketing and bringing about change

December 1990

Section I
1   Setting advertising budget for launch of cosmetics range
2   Appointing an advertising agency to handle this new account
Section II
3   Accuracy of marketing research
4   Primary and secondary research
5   Preparing a sales forecast
6   Effective workload planning to achieve sales
7   Implementation of financial services corporate advertising campaign
8   Effectiveness of public relations at a time of corporate crisis
9   Expansion through overseas market entry
10 Budgets and the annual marketing plan

June 1990

Section I
1   Information needed for three year plan
2   How to achieve three stated marketing communications objectives

INTRODUCTION

Study guide

Using this text

In order to obtain full benefit from this text in every area, you may find it helpful to adopt the approach set out below.

(a) *Read* the chapter you are tackling to get a flavour of the topic, perhaps several times.

(b) *Identify the main principles* and attempt to understand their significance and application.

(c) *Learn* the points contained in the text. As you proceed slowly through the chapter, pause at the end of each paragraph or set of paragraphs to ensure that you can remember the details.

(d) *Make short notes* if you find this helpful, but try to avoid the temptation to write out the text in full!

(e) *Move on* to another topic once you have learnt a point - but try to recall it again later to see if the knowledge is really there.

(f) *Test your knowledge questions* appear at the end of every chapter to help you in this process. Attempt these when you have finished your work on the chapter, and write down your answers. Then refer back to the paragraph number noted in the question, and see how much detail you have recalled. If you are not satisfied with your performance - study the topic again until you are!

INTRODUCTION

Examination technique

The best way to acquire and improve exam technique is to *practise* doing exam questions. Attempt some at first without timing yourself, to consolidate your studies and to practise the technique of writing long essays. You ought, however, to aim to get in some practice under exam conditions - completing questions *in the time allowed*.

(a) You can then develop your sense of how much you are consistently able to read/think about/write in the 30 minutes or so available for each question.

(b) You will also develop a sense of priorities: what depth of detail can you go into in the time, and how can you recognise which points are essential, important, marginal or irrelevant?

To obtain the greatest benefit from the use of this study material you are recommended to proceed as follows.

(a) Complete a thorough preparation of each subject before attempting the questions on that subject. Answering questions is a test of what you have learnt and also a means of practising so that you develop a skill in presenting your answers. To attempt them before you are ready is not a fair test of your proficiency and the result may discourage you.

(b) Write answers to exam-style questions in examination conditions without referring to books, manuals or notes. Then refer to the suggested answer in this text. The suggested answers have been written to give a full coverage of the points from which you might take a selection in composing an answer. If you have included the main points in your answer and presented your material in a clear, logical fashion you have achieved at least a pass standard. The subsidiary points, if you know them and have time to include them, earn bonus marks - very useful to have but not always attainable.

The suggested answers are only suggestions. They are correct and complete on essentials but there is more than one way of writing an answer.

(c) If you find that your answer is basically incorrect or lacks essential points do not be discouraged. This result indicates that, while you still have time, this part of the syllabus requires further revision.

The questions in this text have been chosen to provide a wide coverage of the syllabus. By working through the questions, you should therefore be going over all the topics you ought to learn, and assessing your ability to answer examination-style questions well.

Answering questions in the exam

As many marks will be lost through poor exam technique as through lack of knowledge. The following points may be helpful.

(a) Every question, including really difficult ones, has some easy marks available. You must not panic on being faced with a complex question and as a result throw away these marks. Remember that everyone else will find the question difficult.

(b) Keep strictly to the time limit for each question and resist the temptation to overrun just to finish an answer. Remember that you are more likely to pick up the easy marks at the start of a question than obtain the last few marks at the end of one in the same amount of time.

(c) Read the question carefully and underline the key words and phrases. Note what the examiner requires and resist the temptation to give the answer to a question you would prefer to have been asked!

(d) Don't feel that you have to spend your three hours scribbling furiously: pause for thought whenever you need to.

(e) Draw up an answer plan. Quickly jot down the key points you are able to recall. Then list what you expect will be the main points in each paragraph and make sure the answer will be properly structured.

(f) Don't be afraid to state the obvious. It is worth marks, and the examiner can't *assume* that you know something if you don't make it clear.

(g) Write neatly and precisely. The examiner is more likely to reward short, neatly written essays which keep to the point than lengthy scrawled ramblings. Try to keep handwriting neat: if it is large or difficult to decipher, write on every other line.

(h) Use spacing, point-numbering and sub-headings to get your line of thought across more effectively. Use underlining to give emphasis to important headings and points. Note format (provided it still offers a coherent discussion) is acceptable.

(i) Ideally, you will have time to go back and read over your answers. Correct them if you find errors. You may even be able to pick up some extra marks by adding points you left out.

Keeping up to date

Use your common sense and judgement to evaluate the ideas put forward in your study materials, but be receptive to those that you have not met before in your own experience.

A notable feature in recent examinations has been the requirement that students *give examples* of the subject under discussion. You must, therefore, be alert to what is going on around you.

You will need to keep up with your reading in trade journals such as *Marketing Week* and the management sections of the quality press. Look out for example, for the latest on the 'demographic downturn', on new applications of technology, on fresh marketing initiatives in particular sectors, such as retailing and mass market consumer goods, and on the implications of the Single European Market. Keep a file of relevant press cuttings and articles.

It is essential to read the CIM's invaluable publication *Marketing Success* which is free to students and is published quarterly. It is designed to help you obtain up to date reference material in a readily digestible form.

INTRODUCTION

Study checklist

This checklist is designed to help you chart your progress through this Study Text and thus through the Institute's syllabus. You can record the dates on which you complete your study of each chapter, and attempt the corresponding illustrative questions. You will thus ensure that you are on track to complete your study in good time to allow for revision before the exam.

	Text chapters	Illustrative questions
	Ch Nos/Date Comp	Ques Nos/Date Comp
Marketing overview	1	1, 2
Marketing research	2	3-5
Distribution	3	6-8
Product	4	9, 10
Price	5	11
Promotion	6	12-15
Buyer behaviour	7	16
Sales management and sales forecasting	8	17, 18
Planning, evaluation, organisation and control	9	19, 20

Chapter 1

MARKETING OVERVIEW

This chapter covers the following topics.

1. History of marketing
2. The marketing concept
3. Marketing orientated strategy
4. The business system
5. What is marketing management?
6. Marketing and the environment
7. The marketing mix

---

1. HISTORY OF MARKETING

1.1 The concept and practice of marketing is centred around putting the customer first. To be successful, this consumer orientation should infiltrate the whole organisation from top management down to shop floor workers. Marketing can be thought of as a philosophy that business organisations should adhere to. It can also be a functional area of management located within a departmental structure. The techniques of marketing include the 'marketing mix' variables of product, price, place and promotion which will be discussed throughout this text. This chapter aims to give an overview of the marketing concept including the various marketing environments and the scope of marketing. It will also investigate, in detail, the organisation of marketing within the company structure but first, it is worthwhile to look at the historical development of marketing.

1.2 Marketing has its roots in trade and exchange. When a society becomes capable of producing a surplus (that is, more than is necessary for its own subsistence), this surplus can be traded for other goods and services. In early societies this trade was direct, using a barter system, exchanging goods for other goods. As societies develop trade takes place using an agreed medium of exchange, usually money.

1.3 Production before the industrial revolution was usually local and small scale. During the industrial revolution production became organised into larger units. Towns developed and trade increased as people became more dependent on buying goods for their consumption rather than on producing these goods themselves. There was much greater geographical divergence of buyers and sellers. Before the industrial revolution buyers had direct contact with sellers and so producers then knew their customers' needs and wants. Later when buyers lived some distance from producers it became necessary for producers to find out what products buyers wanted and what product attributes were desired.

1: MARKETING OVERVIEW

1.4 Mass production techniques, such as the division of labour, also meant that the number and types of goods increased dramatically. This industrialisation also increased productivity and so reduced unit costs. With new cheaper products on offer to the public, demand was such that marketing was not formally recognised and so until very recently many business problems centred on production and selling rather than marketing.

1.5 This was exacerbated in the UK because of its historical pre-eminence in industry and trade. Great Britain had predominance in world trade up until the First World War. Since then other countries have emerged to compete in the world marketplace. The United States, Japan and Germany have taken much of Britain's share in the market for manufactured goods. Present day UK organisations therefore have to rely on marketing to identify customer needs and to find products that satisfy those needs.

1.6 Production is no longer the main problem facing business concerns. Indeed, for most products and services, it is excess supply rather than excess demand which is the problem. In these circumstances, the focus of attention has switched from 'how to produce enough' (supply factor) to 'how to increase demand' (demand factor). Often marketing techniques have been developed as a result of this switch in orientation.

1.7 Initially marketing techniques were applied in the area of fast moving consumer goods such as washing powder, toothpaste and groceries because these types of good benefited earliest from the use of mass production techniques. Subsequently, marketing methods have been applied in addition to industrial goods and, more recently, to services (both public and private sector). It can be said, then, that marketing techniques have grown in importance as a response to competitive pressure. Marketing methods are seen as a means of competing with rivals.

1.8 Some services and industrial markets are only now becoming marketing orientated. However, what is marketing orientation? The next section aims to answer this question and to discuss the marketing concept in more detail.

2. THE MARKETING CONCEPT

2.1 There are many definitions of marketing. Here we will consider two which each give a useful insight into how marketing can be used in practice.

2.2 *Definition 1*

'Marketing is the management of exchange relationships'.

This definition emphasises the role of marketing in relating to the world outside the organisation. All relationships which cross the boundary between the organisation and the outside world, especially when they relate to customers, need to be managed. Looked at from the outside, the organisation will be judged by customers, suppliers, competitors and others according to their personal experience in dealing with it. How often have you been put off an organisation by the bored and haphazard way in which communications are dealt with? Having an efficient telephone operator and receptionist are often really important in creating a positive image with people contacting the organisation for the first time.

2.3 *Definition 2*

'Marketing is concerned with meeting organisation objectives by providing customer satisfactions.'

This definition is important because it stresses the importance of the customer, and more particularly, customer satisfaction. When people buy products or services they do not simply want the products, they also want the benefits from using the products or services. Products and services help to solve a customer's problems. It is the solution to these problems that customers are buying.

2.4 A market orientated organisation will possess two key characteristics.

(a) Firstly, there will be a commitment to meeting the needs of customers more successfully than the competition.

(b) Secondly, the organisation will need to operate in a fashion that will achieve this aim. It is not sufficient that the company employs a marketing manager or has a market research department. It is necessary that all of the company's activities are co-ordinated to ensure that the needs of the customer are considered when making decisions about what to produce and subsequently how and where the product or service is to be made available.

Underlying all of this is the belief that adopting a market orientation will maximise the long term profitability of the company.

2.5 In summary the marketing concept has three elements :

(a) customer orientation;
(b) a co-ordination of market led activities; and
(c) profit orientation.

2.6 We will now contrast the activities and philosophy of market orientated companies with production orientated and sales orientated organisations.

Peter Doyle provides a useful distinction between these viewpoints:

'A *production orientation* may be defined as the management view that success is achieved through producing goods of optimum quality and cost, and that therefore, the major task of management is to pursue improved production and distribution efficiency. A *sales orientation* is the management view that effective selling and promotion are the keys to success.'

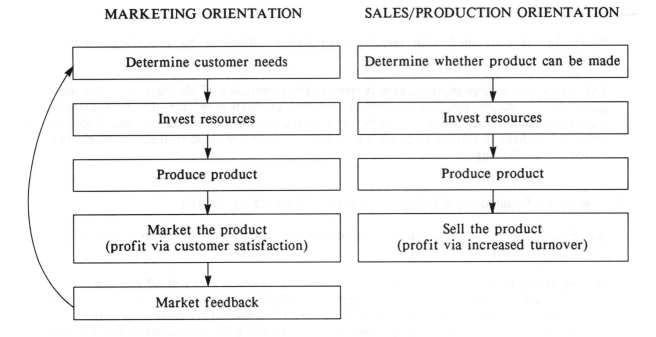

MARKETING ORIENTATION   SALES/PRODUCTION ORIENTATION

Customer orientation

2.7 It is an old truism that 'without customers, you don't have a business.' This, in essence, remains the logic for maintaining a customer orientation where satisfying customers' needs at a profit is the central drive of the company.

2.8 In contrast to following a market orientation many companies follow what can be described as a sales orientation. In such sales orientated companies the tendency is to make the product first and then to worry about whether it will sell. Underlying this philosophy is a belief that a good sales force can sell just about anything to anybody (the refrigerators to Eskimos syndrome).

2.9 Professor Levitt distinguishes between sales and marketing orientations in terms of the place of the customer in the marketing process:

> 'Selling focuses on the needs of the seller; marketing on the needs of the buyer. Selling is preoccupied with the seller's need to convert his product into cash; marketing with the idea of satisfying the needs of the customer by means of the product and the whole cluster of things associated with creating, delivering and finally consuming it.'

2.10 The marketing concept suggests that companies should focus their operations on their customers' needs rather than be driven solely by the organisation's technical competence to produce a particular range of products or services.

2.11 A quotation attributed to Charles Revlon describes the customer orientation of a marketing led organisation:

'In the factory we make cosmetics. In the store we sell hope.'

2.12 If new products and services are developed with an inadequate regard for customer requirements, the result will be the need for an expensive selling effort to persuade customers that they should purchase something from the company that does not quite fit their purpose.

2.13 As the management theorist Peter Drucker says, 'The aim of marketing is to make selling superfluous.' Thus, if the organisation has got its marketing right, it will have produced products and services that meet customers' requirements. If these are readily available at a price that customers accept then relatively little or no selling effort will be needed.

Co-ordinating marketing activities

2.14 A true marketing orientation requires a co-ordinated marketing effort. This covers market research to identify customer needs, market-led product development, sales promotion and advertising to ensure that customers know of the existence of the product and its benefits, effective distribution and delivery to ensure availability, and market-based pricing.

2.15 It follows that marketing orientated companies will need to exhibit some key organisational characteristics if an integrated marketing effort is to be achieved.

The following two organisational features are present in market orientated companies.

(a) Marketing tasks are recognised and co-ordinated under a single executive (market research, product-market planning, advertising and promotion, sales and distribution).

(b) Clear formal communications are established between the chief marketing executive and executives responsible for development, design and manufacturing, and finance. This ensures that a linkage exists between market needs and production decisions.

2.16 If a company's marketing effort is directed at making long run profits the whole organisation clearly benefits. However, at least in the short run, many companies will set sales maximising objectives to the sales force. High *sales* don't necessarily guarantee high profits, as we will see below.

2.17 These two positions can be represented in the following diagrams.

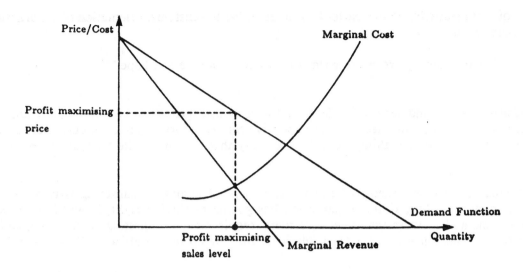

PROFIT MAXIMISATION : Where marginal revenue = marginal cost

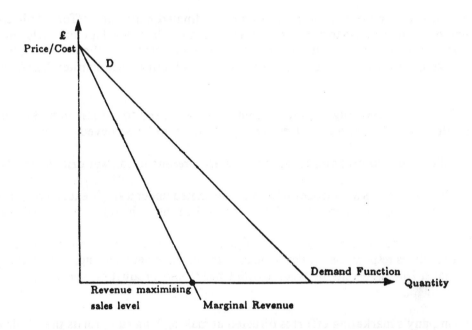

REVENUE MAXIMISATION : Where marginal revenue = zero

2.18 If the sales force is motivated solely to maximise revenue (sales), then it may wish to reduce prices or attempt to offer speedier delivery. There will be a greater incentive to reduce prices and disrupt planned production at the cost of overall profitability. Under these circumstances there is likely to be frequent and unhelpful conflict between production and sales departments with an inevitable loss of customer service. Profit margins will fall.

2.19 However, when the sales force is motivated to maximise profit rather than sales, it will only wish to make extra sales if this is profitable for the company. The impact on profits will be weighed before securing a sale by offering a price cut. Similarly, the costs of disrupting production will be born in mind when deciding whether or not to make a delivery promise that would involve rescheduling production of the next batch of the product.

2.20 Thus, marketing performance should be judged by profit and return on investment – not by volume of sales. This ensures that the wider implications of marketing decisions are recognised, avoiding the possible conflict with the production department if sales are an end in themselves.

2.21 There may be the need for clear administrative decrees to ensure that the marketing department and in particular the field sales force acts in a manner that increases corporate profits. As an example, the UK subsidiary of Landis and Gyr, the Swiss multi-national, has a rule whereby the sales department can make changes to the production plan without penalty for up to six weeks before manufacture but after this date the sales department's budget must carry all the costs of disrupting the line. The six week period was determined as being a reasonable lead time within which an efficient production system should be able to accommodate change without incurring significant extra costs. Naturally, the appropriate length of such a lead time will be determined by the particular technology being employed in the manufacturing process.

2.22 The establishment of profitability as the benchmark for performance within the company also acknowledges the role of the market place as the ultimate arbiter of success.

The marketing concept in practice

2.23 The term marketing has only become widely used since the 1960's in the United Kingdom. Before this time, most companies had a sales department but not a marketing department. However, it is by no means certain that the increasing use of marketing rather than sales in job titles necessarily means that all such companies are becoming more marketing orientated. A study by Professor Peter Doyle, funded by the Chartered Institute of Marketing in 1987, concluded that:

> 'British chief executives increasingly recognise the need to make their companies more marketing orientated. But boards of directors are still dominated by a financial outlook and most lack a professional approach to strategy and market innovation.'

2.24 Doyle's study went on to give a good indication of the degree of acceptance of the marketing concept within British industry. The survey was based on a detailed questionnaire mailed to the chief executives of all the Times 1,000 companies. 365 companies responded. Of these, 92 were in consumer manufacturing, 119 industrial manufacturing, 54 industrial services, 41 consumer services and 59 retailers.

CORPORATE PHILOSOPHIES

	%
Production orientated	10
Sales orientated	21
Marketing orientated	50

Doyle concluded that the remaining 19% of companies responding could best be classified as having a financial orientation, by which he meant:

> 'the management view that success is about using assets and resources to optimise profit and return on capital employed.'

2.25 However, in spite of the widespread acceptance of the need for a market orientation within companies that attempt to produce goods and services that match their customers' requirements, there will always be a need for a persuasive sales force. The need to convince the customer that they should buy the company's products arises because it is highly unlikely that their market needs can be exactly satisfied. The sales force will therefore have to overcome the following problems.

(a) The organisation is unlikely to be the only potential supplier. It will therefore be necessary to convince customers to buy from the company and not from a competitor who may also have attempted to match the customer's needs and wants.

(b) Customers may need to be reassured about the benefits of owning or using the company's product or service. In industrial markets buyers will require evidence that technical specifications and appropriate industry standards are met.

(c) It may not be economical or technically feasible to meet the exact requirements that in an ideal world are required by each specific customer. This is particularly true when mass production techniques are targeted at the average customer's requirements, for, as we all know, none of us are average.

(d) Customers' requirements might have changed since market led production decisions were made. In some markets such as basic commodities customer requirements are stable over considerable periods. Other markets are very dynamic in terms of changing consumer needs. This is particularly true of markets subject to rapid changes in taste or fashion such as designer clothing and the latest trends in leisure and entertainment. We have all heard apocryphal stories of the warehouses full of unsold skateboards or the like that were delivered a few weeks after another craze evaporated.

2.26 Whilst it is accepted that there will always be the need for a sales force, sales effort will be more successful if products and services have been developed in response to market needs. Such a market led approach will reduce the time and expense involved in trying to make what is on sale more acceptable to customers by attempting to persuade potential buyers to change their perceptions of what they need. The sales force can then be employed on more productive activities such as developing leads and providing better customer service and identifying changes in customer requirements to which the organisation needs to respond. Such sales force activities constitute a key element of any company following a market orientation.

2.27 All good sales presentations follow the maxim of a customer orientation. Instead of merely cataloging a series of product features, the intelligent sales force concentrates on promoting the benefits that will be derived by the customer using or consuming the company's product or service. The DIY enthusiast is not necessarily interested in the technical specification of a power drill's electric motor. Whilst this might be the pride and joy of the company's research and development team, the customer is only really interested in finding a solution to a particular range of DIY tasks. The customer may really be looking for a way of getting a series of 3/16 inch holes to fix some brackets. The good salesperson will ensure that the potential purchaser is assured that using the product will provide the particular benefits that the purchaser seeks. In industrial markets such benefits might include the cost reductions that can be achieved using the company's products, and the reliability of the supplier in terms of delivery and consistent quality.

3. MARKETING ORIENTATED STRATEGY

3.1 So far the discussion of the applicability of the marketing concept has concentrated on tactical issues - the day to day operations of a company's marketing activities. At this level it is possible to argue that under certain circumstances a sales orientation might be preferred. After all, it is undoubtedly true that people do buy things that they have little need of after being at the receiving end of some persuasive selling. The argument might develop that a particular company has a charismatic sales force that is highly effective but lacks any skill to comprehend or respond explicitly to customer needs. Such a company may well be profitable operating its sales orientation and would find it difficult and costly to change its direction towards a market needs focus.

3.2 However, when the argument moves on to the longer term consequences of ignoring market needs the case for adopting a marketing orientation appears to be overwhelming. Theodore Levitt published the seminal article *Marketing Myopia*, originally published in the Harvard Business Review in July-August 1960, on the imperative that a market orientation should provide the driving force that determines the longer term strategic direction of companies. He warned of the perils of perceiving the company's business solely in technical and production terms. Managers will then view products according to their physical properties. The company will be seen as operating in an industry where competitors share similar technical competences allowing them to produce similar products.

3.3 Levitt started by making the bold statement that :

'Shortsighted managements often fail to recognise that in fact there is no such thing as a growth industry.'

Levitt's argument is that there are clearly large numbers of growth *markets* in terms of society's needs. However, the *industries* that serve these needs at a particular time may decline if another industry's new technology better matches the growing market's needs.

3.4 Levitt goes on to illustrate his argument with examples of blinkered thinking that focuses on the production concept of competing for business in a particular industry. The following question is posed.

Q   :   Why did the American Railways not respond to the airlines and trucking companies that eventually took away the railroad's passenger and freight business?

The railways certainly had the available capital reserves built up over the years that 'rail was king'. The infant businesses that grew to be Pan Am, TWA and the national carriers struggled for their early existence. Levitt provides the following answer.

A   :   They let others take customers away from them because they assumed themselves to be in the railroad business rather than in the transportation business. The reason they defined their industry wrongly was because they were railroad oriented instead of transportation oriented; they were product oriented instead of customer oriented.

Whilst the railway industry went into decline, the transportation market continued to grow by leaps and bounds. By adopting an industry focus the railways did not take on the new enterprises because they were not seen as being any part of the railroad business.

3.5 Not all North American railways followed such a 'myopic' stance. Canadian Pacific had a very clear idea of its operations in the transportation market. The company expanded into trucking, shipping and airlines. Later it moved into telecommunications and telex to adopt the most suitable technology for transporting data. Canadian Pacific is today one of the world's largest transportation businesses.

3.6 The strategic message is clear. Adopting a marketing orientation concentrates the attention on the needs of the customer. If these needs change or a better technology emerges that more closely attends to these needs then the company will perceive such events as its business. Only by adapting to such changes is the company's future assured. Applying the marketing concept as the basic philosophy that underpins corporate strategy is therefore widely accepted as essential good practice.

3.7 Even if the need to respond to change is perceived, adherence to a production orientation can produce costly mistakes. In the late 1950's and early 1960's the American car market was under threat from import penetration, with the Volkswagen Beetle making the most significant inroads.

3.8 General Motors, the biggest American motor manufacturer, decided that it was time to react. Their reaction betrayed the production orientation followed by the company. GM has four main badges which are used to segment the market place. The super luxury market is catered for by Cadillac, the executive range by Pontiac, the middle range by Buick leaving the Chevrolet division to cover the value for money and young driver segment. It was left to Chevrolet to take on the invader.

3.9 If one was to identify the *physical* product characteristics of a VW Beetle the list might include:

(a) small (by US standards);
(b) rear engined;
(c) air cooled engine (therefore noisy);
(d) minimal instrumentation.

3.10 This was the product to which GM was losing sales. Chevrolet set about making just such a product. Naturally the new small car was to be powered by an air cooled rear engine and it would have very basic instrumentation. GM were ill prepared for this venture. Having at last decided to react to Volkswagen, the company was under pressure from senior management to produce the new car quickly. The smallest available engine block was a flat six cylinder that was still very heavy for a relatively small car. The new engine also needed to be air cooled as that was what the customers were buying. To achieve this, Chevrolet mounted a large fan that sat on top of the engine driving air vertically down on to the cylinder heads. To drive this large fan a long fanbelt was added that took the power from the crankshaft via a right angle pulley.

3.11 The new car was launched as the Chevrolet Corvair. Its design caused a number of serious problems. The stresses on the fan belt frequently led to either the belt braking or the bracket holding the right angle pulley fracturing. The car was so noisy that the sound of these mechanical failures could not be heard. Naturally, with minimal instruments the driver could not sense that the engine was now rapidly overheating until, as often happened, the engine either seized or caught fire. To compound these problems, the weight distribution on such a small car with a very heavy rear engine caused difficulties. For safe driving the rear tyres had to be pumped up rock hard whilst the front tyres were kept soft.

3.12 After a number of fatal accidents, Ralph Nader wrote his book *Unsafe at any speed*, which recounted the story of the Chevy Corvair. The book made little impact until General Motors, unwisely, sued and lost. Ralph Nader's name was established as the leader of the American consumer movement.

3.13 Think for a moment, just what would have happened if GM had followed a marketing orientation and had attempted to find out *why* people were buying the Beetle rather than looking at the Beetle's product features. The list of key consumer benefits might have included these points:

(a) reliability;
(b) economy;
(c) affordability;
(d) ease of parking.

The Japanese were to get this message right in the late 1960s and 1970s with Toyotas and Nissans that bore very little *physical* similarity to the Beetle.

The marketing concept: a critical review

3.14 Not all commentators accept that the increasing use of the term marketing rather than selling represents a real shift in the basic philosophy followed by organisations. Some suggest that the use of marketing simply reflects that the task of bringing in revenue is now more complex and that it is now rational to use advanced techniques in advertising and market research that were previously not available. Others argue that today's 'sophisticated' consumers are more critical and more aware than their forefathers. Companies therefore need a battery of so called marketing techhniques in order to continue the same old process of persuasion in order to sell products.

3.15 The most strident critic from this school of thought is the economist J K Galbraith who summarised his views as follows:

'So called market orientated companies have merely adopted more sophisticated weapons for selling the product.'

3.16 Approval of the marketing concept is not universal even amongst those who accept that the adoption of a market orientation represents a real change in philosophy and practice. Thus, the widespread and often uncritical acceptance of marketing orientation as the established wisdom within large elements of both the commercial and academic communities has, itself, been the subject of debate.

3.17 There are two main arguments against the influence of the marketing concept.

(a) A bias is introduced into the organisation that favours marketing activities at the expense of production and technical departments. This bias then directs insufficient energies into the development of technically superior products that subsequently offer better product value to customers.

(b) Secondly, in addition to attending to customers' current needs, organisations must focus on producing goods and services for anticipated changes in future customer requirements. Slavishly focusing new product development on satisfying immediate customer perceptions of what is needed can, the argument runs, stifle real innovation.

3.18 These points are forcibly made by Bennett and Cooper.

'A market orientated R & D strategy necessarily leads to low risk product modifications, extensions, and style changes. Product proliferation, a disease of the seventies, has been one result. Market driven new product ideas will usually result in the ordinary. Market researchers have become expert at encouraging consumers to verbalise their wants and needs, but people tend to talk in terms of the familiar, about what is around them at a particular moment. For example, ask a commuter what new product ideas he would like to see in the area of rapid transit and, chances are, he will list a number of improvements to his bus or subway system - tinted glass windows, air conditioning, better schedules, and the like. Rarely will he be able to think in terms of totally new and imaginative urban transportation systems. The latter are the domain of the engineer, scientist and designer.'

3.19 In defence of Levitt (see paragraph 3.2) one might consider the case of the collapse of Rolls Royce in the early 1970s. The reason for this failure is well documented. The company had embarked on the production of a new generation of large turbo-fan jet engines. All three major competitors in the international market for civil aircraft engines were producing such engines. The Rolls Royce response was the RB211. The RB211 differed from competitors' engines in its use of advanced carbon fibre technology in the manufacture of its turbine blades. The introduction and development of the new technology turned out to be an extremely costly business. Rolls Royce chose to show this expenditure as an asset on its balance sheets, rather than to adopt the prudent principle of writing off development costs against current revenues. Research and development expenses exceeded budgeted levels and Rolls Royce encountered severe cash flow problems resulting in the company's liquidation.

3.20 The focus on engineering excellence is a clear indication of the production orientation then being followed by Rolls Royce. Pratt & Whitley and General Electric appeared to follow a product development strategy that more closely accorded with a marketing orientation. The demand for the new generation of engines was generated by a change in airlines' requirements. The environmentalist lobby against aircraft noise in the late 1960s and 1970s had culminated with restrictions on night flying and regulations covering permitted noise levels from all new civil aircraft. The oil crisis and rising energy prices created the need for greater fuel efficiency. The new generation of wide-bodied jumbo jets created the need for a range of powerful jet engines.

3.21 The needs of the customers were therefore clearly defined. The airlines needed larger, more powerful, more economical, quieter jet engines. Provided that engines met this criteria then customers would be interested. The Rolls Royce engine was proving to be more expensive largely because they offered a product feature, carbon fibre technology, that airlines did not need. The American competitors gave customers what they wanted without having to develop a new metallurgical competence. In the event the technical innovation became a major impediment to sales of the RB211 as airlines became aware of teething problems with the carbon fibre turbines.

3.22   It would be uncharitable to accuse Rolls Royce of completely ignoring market conditions. All companies have to take risks, this being part of the justification of profits, and the RB211 project was on such a scale that failure would have inevitably jeopardised the company's future. However, the suspicion remains that with Rolls Royce the company's history of engineering excellence had produced too great a bias towards production and too little concern for the marketing concept. The Rolls Royce case illustrates the need for a balanced view. Whilst the technical competence and manufacturing skills of companies can not be ignored, it can be fatal not to follow closely what is required by customers.

3.23   General Electric, one of Rolls Royce's major competitors, made its commitment to the marketing concept as long ago as 1952.

> '(The marketing concept) ..... introduces the marketing man at the beginning rather than at the end of the production cycle and integrates marketing in each phase of business. Thus, marketing, through its studies and research, will establish for the engineer, the design and manufacturing man, what the consumer wants in a given product, what price he is willing to pay, and where and when it will be wanted. Marketing will have authority in product planning, production scheduling, and inventory control, as well as in sales distribution and servicing of the product.'

> 1952 Annual Report : US General Electric Company

4.   THE BUSINESS SYSTEM

4.1   We will now look at how marketing fits into business operations. We will consider three essential systems.

The distribution system

4.2   There is a flow of goods and services from producers through a distribution system to customers in exchange for payment. This flow has a large number of components, such as credit terms, delivery, insurance, price/discounts/margins and storage.

4.3   The distribution system can be *long* or *short*. For example, customised industrial goods are often supplied direct from producers to customers. But when international trade is involved, the distribution system may involve importers, exporters, agents, wholesalers and retailers.

4.4   The distribution system may be owned by the producer or may be independent. So, for example, a building society's distribution system is its branch network. This is a short system. A producer of low value plastic toys may export them in the first instance using a freight forwarder. The overseas buyer may be a wholesaler who then sells to shopkeepers who finally sell to the end consumers. This is a long system.

4.5   Customers may be final consumers of the product or service or they may be organisational buyers who in turn are producers of other goods and services for which the purchased item is a component.

The information system

4.6 Information flow is essential in marketing. Before a customer orientated producer makes and supplies goods and services, it will want to ensure that they meet customers' needs. In other words, it needs to understand customer behaviour first. If distributors are independent, the producer also needs to be aware of their needs in the business system. Thus, there should be a flow of information into the producing firm from its market and distribution system. This information should then be used by the producer to construct its product (or service) offering, expressed in terms of customer satisfactions.

4.7 The flow of information from the producing firm to its market is a marketing flow. The elements of this marketing flow are price information, product/service information, promotion/ advertising information, distributor information and selling information. Together these make up the *marketing mix* for the product or service. The art of marketing is to combine these elements into a unified whole which presents the market with a clear overall message, distinguishing the product from its rivals. This clear overall message is the product's USP: its unique selling proposition.

Flow of influence

4.8 The business flows thus far described do not operate in isolation. Each part of the process has influences on it.

(a) The actions of producers and distributors are influenced by competitors. Each competitor is striving for competitive advantage, trying to get ahead of its rivals.

(b) Customer behaviour is influenced by a whole range of factors since people are members of groups and members of organisations; such influences may be cultural, social, psychological and practical.

4.9 The whole business system must be considered in the wider context of its environment: influences on it may include the following.

(a) *Political and legal* influences such as employment legislation, advertising laws, legislation affecting sales and purchasing and credit controls.

(b) *Economic influences* such as income levels, employment levels, the rate of inflation and growth rates in the economy.

(c) Social influences such as healthy eating, 'green' issues and attitudes to war, and political influences such as voting intentions and attitudes to the EC, South Africa and the Commonwealth.

(d) Technological influences such as the growing capability of computer systems, automation, robotics and computer integrated manufacturing.

These PEST factors (from the initials of each influence) will be dealt with later in this chapter in more detail, as will the marketing mix.

What is the scope of marketing?

4.10 The table below (adapted from Neil Borden's) shows a list of the types of marketing decision with which an organisation might be involved. Clearly, it can only give a typical list for a 'typical' organisation. Different organisations operating in different markets will have different organisational structures and may have a particular sub-set of marketing decisions from this list.

Elements of the marketing mix

Marketing decision   *Policies and procedures relating to:*

Product planning

Product lines to be offered - qualities, design, detailed contents etc.
The markets in which to sell - to whom, where, when and in what quantity.
New product policy - research and development programme.

Branding

Selection of trade marks and names.
Brand policy - individual or family brand.
Sale under private brand or unbranded.

Pricing

The level of premiums to adopt.
The margins to adopt - for the trade, for direct sales.

Channels of distribution

The channels to use between company and consumer.
The degree of selectivity amongst distributors and other intermediaries.
Efforts to gain co-operation of the trade.

Selling personnel

The burden to be placed on personal selling.
The methods to be employed (1) within the organisation and (2) in selling to intermediaries and the final consumer.

Advertising

The amount to spend - the burden to be placed on advertising.
The copy platform to adopt (1) product image desired, (2) corporate image desired.
The mix of advertising - to the trade through the trade to customers.

Promotions

The burden to place on special selling plans or devices directed at or through the trade.
The form of these devices for consumer promotions, for trade promotions.

Servicing

Providing after sales service to intermediaries and to final consumers (such as direct mail offers).

4.11 It can be claimed (and often is by marketing managers) that marketing involves every facet of the organisation's operations. The philosophy of a customer orientation, central to marketing, can be argued to be a central business function which is a prerequisite to success. It is easy to get carried away with this argument and thus to understate the role of finance, production, personnel and other business functions. A strongly held conviction by the marketing department that customer orientation is all important can lead to conflict with other departments.

5. WHAT IS MARKETING MANAGEMENT?

5.1 To manage the marketing mix so as to achieve the aims of marketing management involves analysis, planning and control.

Analysis

5.2 As we have seen, a marketing orientation begins and ends with the customer. Thus analysis in marketing management involves identifying for example who are the customers, why do they buy and are they satisfied with it, having bought it? This process includes *market research* which is covered in more detail in the next chapter. The process can include quantitative analysis (How many customers? What is our market share? How many competitors?) and qualitative analysis (Why do people buy? What are their motivations, attitudes, personality?)

5.3 In sophisticated companies, sources of market information are integrated into a *marketing information system* which can be used by managers in making marketing decisions.

Planning

5.4 Marketing management also involves using the information gained from marketing analysis to plan the organisation's marketing response - *the strategic marketing plan.*

The strategic marketing plan will involve:

(a) identification of selected target markets;
(b) forecasting future demand in each market;
(c) setting the levels of each element of the marketing mix for each target market.

Control

5.5 The third main component of marketing management is to control the implementation of the marketing plan. Control involves setting measurable targets for the plan and then checking performance against these targets. If necessary, remedial action must be taken to ensure that planned and actual performance are brought into line.

5.6 We will now discuss how marketing can be organised within a company's organisational structure.

The development of marketing departments

5.7 Although every organisation is different, it is often suggested that common patterns appear in the structure of organisations. The position occupied currently by departments of marketing is widely recognised as having evolved from the existence of sales departments. Traditionally all dealings with a marketplace would have been the responsibility of a sales director who would typically report direct to senior management. At this stage a marketing orientation was probably absent and the organisation would usually have been production or sales orientated. When the need for a marketing orientated approach became more apparent a marketing director might appear in parallel to the sales director, but with two distinct functional departments.

With fuller recognition of the marketing approach to business, sales and marketing would become a single functional department, but with sales as a sub-group within marketing as opposed to marketing being a sub-group within sales.

5.8 Thus the emphasis within organisational structures has generally moved from a sales department to a marketing department as the business philosophy changes.

5.9 In its current format, the marketing department in any organisation plays a key role in co-ordinating marketing activities. The marketing manager in particular has to take responsibility for planning, resource allocation, monitoring and controlling the marketing effort. In fact, in order to ensure that the marketing effort has maximum effectiveness, this co-ordinating role is crucial, involving co-ordination of marketing efforts for different products in different markets as well as ensuring that individual marketing campaigns are themselves co-ordinated and consistent. As such, the marketing function tends to be thought of as a staff management function with a co-ordinating role, rather than a line management function.

Organising marketing departments

5.10 In the same way as the development of marketing within organisations has varied, so will the present organisation of marketing departments. There is no one format which can be described as 'best' or 'most effective'; rather the format chosen will depend on the nature of the existing organisational structure, patterns of management and the spread of the firm's product and geographical interests. Whatever the format, the marketing department must take responsibility for four key areas:

(a) functions (promotion, pricing etc);
(b) geographical areas;
(c) products;
(d) markets.

By considering these four areas of responsibility we can gain some insight into the different forms which a marketing department may take.

Functional organisation

5.11 The department is headed by a marketing director who is responsible for the overall co-ordination of the marketing effort. A number of functional specialists such as a market research manager and a sales manager are found in the second tier of management and they take responsibility for all activities in their functional specialism across all products and markets. This format has the benefit of great simplicity and is relatively straightforward in administrative terms. It allows individuals to develop their particular specialisms, but also imposes a burden on the marketing director who will be required to perform co-ordinating and arbitrating activities to ensure the development of a coherent marketing mix for elements of the product range.

5.12 With a limited range of products, the burden on the marketing director may not be a problem. However, as the organisation's range of products and markets expands it will tend to be less efficient. When this occurs there is always the danger that a particular product or market may be neglected because it is only one of a great variety being handled by a specific functional manager who will find it difficult to be a specialist for all products.

Geographical organisation

5.13 This is an extension of the functional organisation with responsibility for some or all functional activities being devolved to a regional level, through a national functional manager. This type of organisation would probably be more common in firms operating internationally where the various functional activities would be required for each national market or group of national markets.

Product-based organisation

5.14 Product managers take responsibility for specific products or groups of products. This type of approach is likely to be particularly appropriate for organisations with either very diverse products or with a large range of products.

5.15 The individual product manager takes responsibility for developing plans for specific products and ensuring that products remain competitive, drawing on the experience and guidance of functional managers. The product manager is effectively responsible for all the marketing activities relating to a particular product group and must therefore draw on and develop skills in relation to promotion, pricing and distribution. This approach allows the individual product managers to develop considerable experience and understanding of particular product groups and as such may be of particular importance in a rapidly changing competitive environment. At the same time because these managers have to undertake a variety of functional activities, there is always the danger that they will become 'jacks of all trades and masters of none'. In spite of this possible problem, the product-based approach is one that is becoming increasingly important because the benefits of managers with particular responsibility and experience for specific product groups is seen to outweigh the costs associated with a loss of functional specialisation.

Market management

5.16 This is a variant on the product management structure, but instead of individual managers taking responsibility for particular products they will instead take responsibility for particular markets. The advantage of this approach arises when an organisation sells a variety of different products into particular markets and the understanding of the product is perceived to be slightly less important than the understanding of the market.

Matrix management

5.17 In simple terms matrix management can be thought of as an integration of the product and market management approaches. In an organisation dealing with a variety of products in a variety of markets the product based approach will require managers to be familiar with a wide variety of different markets while the market-based approach will require managers to be familiar with a wide variety of products. In either case, however, expertise may not be fully or efficiently utilised. The matrix-based system combines the two with a series of managers dealing with markets and a further series dealing with products. The market managers will take responsibility for the development and maintenance of profitable markets while the product manager will focus on product performance and profitability. The system is interlinked with each product manager dealing with a variety of market managers and each market manager dealing with a variety of product managers.

5.18 Although this system may seem the ideal approach to resolving the dilemma about the most appropriate form of organisation for a marketing department, it nevertheless presents certain problems. The most obvious one may be cost because of the extension of the range of management. More importantly, there are also possible sources of conflict between product and market managers to consider and, particularly, the issue of who should take responsibility for certain activities. For example, should the sales force be product or market based and who should take responsibility for pricing?

Divisional marketing organisation

5.19 So far we have considered the organisation of marketing within a unitary organisation, but increasingly there are many organisations where the larger product groups are developed into separate divisions (what is often called a multi-divisional or 'M' form organisation). These divisions will have a high degree of autonomy, but ultimately are responsible to head office. Within this arrangement, marketing activity will often be devolved to divisional level as is shown below. This is not always the case, since some marketing activities will be the responsibility of corporate headquarters, but the extent of corporate involvement can vary from none at all to extensive. There is no obvious indication that any one particular level of corporate involvement is desirable; however, it is often suggested that corporate involvement will tend to be more extensive in the early stages of the organisation's development when the divisions are individually quite weak, but as divisions increase their strength, the extent of corporate involvement in marketing begins to decline.

6. MARKETING AND THE ENVIRONMENT

The micro environment: the market environment

6.1 The earlier sections of this chapter have highlighted the importance for an organisation of understanding its operating environment. This understanding is crucial in providing the opportunity to exploit changing market conditions which is the essence of a successful marketing strategy. We will now consider specifically that part of the environment which can be described as the micro environment. This environment includes all factors which impact directly on a firm and its activities in relation to a particular market or set of markets in which it operates. It also incorporates any internal aspects of the organisation such as corporate culture which will influence the development of a marketing strategy. We will consider the market environment and the internal environment in turn.

6.2 The nature of the market environment is outlined in the diagram below. In essence the market environment concerns itself with all aspects of a market which affect the company's relationship with its customers and the patterns of competition. The importance of the market environment should not be underestimated, not only because it will have a major impact on the operation of a business, but also because it is an aspect of the environment that the business can, in part, control and change. The understanding of suppliers, distributors, consumers, competitors and interest groups have been identified as key elements of the market environment.

6.3 By attempting to understand the interactions and the behaviour of these groups, the firm can use its marketing strategies to encourage loyalty, obtain preference from suppliers/distributors, and influence what competitors do and what consumers think. Equally, through the development of corporate image, it can influence perceptions held by various interest groups. In that sense the understanding of and reactions to the market environment can be a key factor in ensuring longer term competitive success.

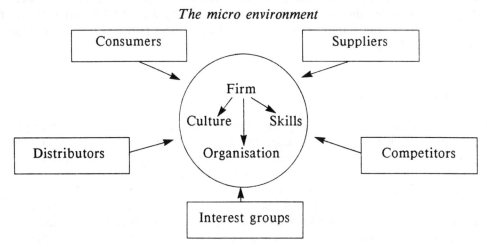

The micro environment

We will now consider each of the key elements of the market environment in turn.

Suppliers

6.4   For most organisations this would require some consideration of the number, size and bargaining strength of their suppliers; their ability to guarantee regular supplies, stable prices and quality.

Distributive network

6.5   Although the nature and structure of the distributive network is generally treated as a marketing mix variable which can be controlled by an organisation, it is nevertheless a feature of the market environment. There are few instances where an organisation can enter a market which is so new that there are no existing distribution systems. Where these systems are in place, as is normally the case, then they will impose some constraints on what an organisation can do. This may arise partly because of consumer familiarity with existing systems and partly because of the degree of market power which is held by the distribution network. A simple example arises from the food industry where the distribution decisions of food manufacturers are very much influenced by the market power of the large supermarket chains.

Consumers

6.6   Understanding consumers is clearly of considerable importance in terms of developing a marketing strategy and the behaviour and motivation of these consumers will be examined in more detail later in this text.

Competition

6.7   The importance of marketing as an aid to establishing a competitive position in the market place has already been stressed; clearly then there is a need for any organisation to develop an awareness and understanding of its competitors, their strengths and weaknesses and the essence of their strategic approach to their markets.

Interest groups

6.8   Finally, any analysis of the market environment must give some consideration to the role of interest groups (sometimes referred to in marketing literature as 'publics'). These refer to a variety of groupings whose opinions and attitudes will have some bearing on the success or otherwise of a bank. An understanding and awareness of the attitudes of these groups will enable the bank to consider how best to present itself to them.

The micro environment: the internal environment

6.9   Clearly, the internal environment is the area in which the firm can exercise greatest control and should possess the greatest knowledge. Nevertheless, as was emphasised above, it should not be overlooked because the internal capabilities of the organisation are a key factor in generating marketing success. At a very general level, the analysis of the internal environment requires an understanding of the nature of the *corporate culture* - the attitudes and beliefs of personnel at all levels. The strategies available and appropriate for an organisation with a culture orientated towards rapid innovation and risk taking may be quite different to those available to a company orientated towards high quality and an exclusive image, and different again from those which could be pursued by an organisation which sees itself as a low risk, market follower with a reliable, if traditional product range to offer.

6.10 Equally important is an understanding of the strengths and weaknesses of the structure of the company and of the personnel within the company. In many instances, internal structures are changing and reflect the increased pressures of a competitive market place.

6.11 The use of *marketing audits* is one technique which is of considerable use in helping an organisation (and the individuals involved in the planning process) to understand the internal environment. A marketing audit is simply a systematic analysis and evaluation of the organisation's marketing position and performance. According to need, it may cover all activities which are either directly or indirectly connected with the marketing function, or it can simply focus on specific products/markets or specific marketing functions. Further distinctions are often drawn between audits which take place at the corporate level, those which take place at the divisional level and those which take place at the level of the product/market.

6.12 Although a marketing audit will focus on all the relevant marketing activities, the following may be singled out as being of particular importance.

Marketing capabilities

6.13 This includes trying to identify the aspects of marketing in which the company may be considered to have particular strengths and weaknesses, such as. Questions to ask include the following.

   (a)   How flexible/responsive is the organisation of the marketing department?
   (b)   What is the company's image/reputation?
   (c)   How strong are particular product lines?
   (d)   What is the extent of brand loyalty among customers?

Although many of these are subjective assessments, their importance cannot be understated because they will often form the basis of future marketing campaigns.

Performance evaluation

6.14 This is essentially the process of comparing the actual achievements of marketing with what was expected – are sales meeting forecasts? Is advertising presenting the desired/planned message? Is the distribution system getting the product to consumers as anticipated? This evaluation will identify weaknesses and strengths of current marketing campaigns which can then be modified when reconsidering the campaign for that product and considering marketing campaigns to be used for new products.

Competitive effectiveness

6.15 Essentially this focuses on evaluating the source of an organisation's competitive advantage. This will require some analysis and understanding of competitors, the markets they are targeting and the particular features they use to their advantage.

6.16 There are a number of tools available for marketing audits; while not exploring these in depth, we should note that the marketing audit should be systematic, should canvass a wide variety of opinions and is frequently based on questionnaire analysis.

The macro environment

6.17 The macro environment concerns itself with broad trends and patterns which are taking place in society as a whole which will affect all markets, but will be more relevant to some than others. Many environment changes, if identified and carefully analysed, can provide invaluable assistance in the process of evolving marketing strategies, identifying profitable products and determining the best routes to reach consumers. Equally, careful monitoring of this environment can enable an organisation to identify developments which may be harmful to its business and will enable it to adopt a *proactive* rather than a *reactive* stance in the action it takes.

6.18 The macro environment can usefully be broken down into four key components: political/legal, economic, social/cultural, and technological (PEST factors). The diagram below shows these factors.

The macro environment

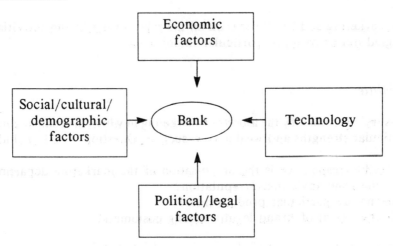

The political/legal environment

6.19 The political/legal environment concerns itself primarily with the interaction between organisations and government or regulatory bodies. It incorporates a variety of legal restrictions which governments impose to regulate the pursuits of businesses in a formal sense. Equally important are the less formal aspects of government relations with industry such as government attitudes to business and willingness to support initiatives. Increasingly, international developments, including the EC, need to be considered in the context of the legal environment.

The economic environment

6.20 Economic conditions are perhaps the key component of the macro environment. Attention is focused on developments within the economy which are likely to have an impact on businesses either directly or as a result of their impact on consumer spending. Key aspects of the economic environment usually include inflation, unemployment, economic growth, consumer income and wealth, interest rates, balance of payments and currency fluctuations.

The social/cultural environment

6.21 The social cultural environment concerns itself with a variety of factors including demographic change and changing attitudes and perception. The UK, like many other developed countries, has an ageing population, and this of course has many implications for organisations. The changing role of women may also have implications for the marketer. For instance, as more women work, more convenient shopping times have been developing.

Exercise

In recent years 'green' issues have come into considerable prominence. How have green issues affected the way in which products are marketed?

Solution

There are many points to make because every stage of a product's life is affected by environmental issues - how it is made, what is made of, how it gets to the customer, what it is used for, what is the effect of its use, and how it is disposed of. 'Green' issues have affected the *product* itself ('ozone-friendly', 'dolphin-friendly'), its *packaging* (recyclable), its *price* (organically produced vegetables are more expensive, for example), and its *promotion* (BMW got a good deal of mileage out of the appealing idea that their cars are almost totally recyclable for the next generation of car drivers).

The technological environment

6.22 This fourth component of the macro environment focuses on the way in which technology (both the level and the rate of change) will affect the way an organisation undertakes its business.

6.23 When developing marketing strategy the firm must look at both the micro and macro environmental factors. Ultimately a successful marketing strategy needs to be consistent with the external operating environment, but at the same time consistent with internal attitudes and capabilities. One trend that affects businesses is consumerism which will be looked into in further detail below.

Ethics/consumerism

6.24 A trend which has increased the importance of customer care is consumerism. A number of consumer rights have developed, including the following.

(a) The right to be informed of the true facts of the buyer-seller relationship, for example:

   (i) the true cost of loans (APRs must now be published in any advertisement for loans);
   (ii) truth in advertising (watchdog bodies vet any advertisement and consumers complain about advertisements to the Advertising Standards Authority).

(b) The right to be protected. Consumers' trust in organisations must not be abused. For example, the sale of mailing lists to third parties can lead to consumers receiving vast quantities of 'junk' mail.

(c) The right to ensure quality of life. This right is focused increasingly on environmental protection which should awaken suppliers to the social implications of their actions.

6.25 Suppliers need to take careful note of these consumerist pressures. Their reputations must be protected at all cost. This requirement may well militate against aggressive marketing tactics and so, despite competitive pressures, the need to consider the best interests of customers should be paramount in a marketing strategy. The long-term view is necessary rather than attempting to maximise short-term profits.

7. **THE MARKETING MIX**

7.1 The concept of a marketing mix, sometimes known as the marketing offer, was first used by Professor Neil Borden of Harvard Business School in 1965, who summarised the concept of the marketing mix as:

'a schematic plan to guide analysis of marketing problems through utilisation of:

(a) a list of the important forces emanating from the market which bear upon the marketing operations of an enterprise; and
(b) a list of the elements (procedures and policies) of marketing programmes.'

7.2 Borden went on to provide a check list of the market forces bearing upon the marketing mix. Changes in any one of these market forces should result in management reviewing its marketing mix and making any necessary adjustments in the face of the new market conditions.

1: MARKETING OVERVIEW

7.3 These market forces are:

(a) The *motivation* of users and their buying habits and attitudes towards products or services in the market.

(b) *Trade motivation* and attitudes, trade structure and practices.

(c) *Competition*
Is this based on price or non-price actions?
What choice is available to customers in terms of products, price and service?
What is the relation between supply and demand?
What is the company's size and strength in the market?
How many firms operate in the market?
Is market power becoming more or less concentrated?
Are there any substitute products or services?
Are competitors developing new products, pricing strategies or sales promotions?
Are competitors attitudes or behaviour changing?
How is the competition likely to react to any of the company's proposed plans?

(d) *Government controls*
Over products (eg government standards - BSI, prohibitions and health and safety legislation).

Over pricing (eg on government contracts, measures to control inflation).
Over competitive practices (eg referals to the UK monopolies and mergers commission, EEC rulings on fair competition, USA Sherman anti-trust legislation).
Over advertising and promotion (eg restrictions on advertising tobacco, gambling and alcohol, limits on the advertising spend on ethical drugs, cooling off periods after signing contracts for personal loans).

7.4 Borden's original very broad concept of the marketing mix encompasses both market forces which are not within the control of the company and management's response of changing the company's marketing activities.

7.5 The current, most common, definition of the marketing mix concentrates on the variables under the firm's control that the marketing manager manipulates in an attempt to achieve tactical marketing objectives.

7.6 Marketing mix variables are usually summarised into the four P's of product, price, place and promotion. These four variables are the heart of a marketing plan. It should be noted that the marketing mix variables are highly interactive. A decision with respect to one variable is likely to have an effect on other elements of the mix. There is a need for a highly co-ordinated approach if the company is to maximise profitable sales to its customers.

Example: marketing mix

7.7 In the spring of 1981 Hammerite, the all in one rust proofing paint, ran what appeared to be a highly successful advertising campaign. Timing was immaculate, the advertisements in both national press and the DIY magazines co-incided exactly with a break in the winter weather. All over the country avid do it yourselfer's were ready to go out into the garden to repair the ravages of rust that the British winter had wreaked on swings, wrought iron gates and the like.

7.8 The problem was that the campaign was too successful. Dealers rapidly stocked out. As a result shopkeepers, rather than lose a sale, recommended other perhaps inferior products. By not fully co-ordinating their marketing activities much of the benefit of Hammerite's promotion went to the competition. Their marketing mix lacked balance between promotion and place elements. Hammerite's distribution could not support the promotional policy that was in operation.

7.9 The four Ps of the marketing mix are often described as 'the controllables', to distinguish elements of marketplace operations that an organisation can influence as opposed to those that it cannot control. Examples of the latter are competitor's actions, government policy, general economic conditions and so on. The Hammerite fiasco referred to above was caused by factors that should have been entirely within the organisation's control.

8. CONCLUSION

8.1 In this first chapter we have looked at the marketing, sales and production orientations and discussed why the marketing orientation has graudally come to be accepted by most commentators as the most successful in the long term.

8.2 We have seen how this has resulted in the increased importance of the marketing department and we have looked at ways of organising the marketing function in an organisation.

8.3 Finally, we have looked in outline at the factors to be taken into account by the marketing department; the micro, macro and internal environments and the four Ps. In the remainder of this text, we will examine these issues further, beginning by looking at how marketers gather the information on which to base their decisions.

8.4 Later in this text we shall be investigating the elements of the marketing mix individually. However, before any marketing mix decisions are made marketing research should be carried out and it is to this we now turn our attention in the next chapter.

TEST YOUR KNOWLEDGE
Numbers in brackets refer to paragraphs of this chapter

1 Why did mass production lead to the development of the marketing orientation? (1.6)

2 Give two definitions of marketing. (2.2, 2.3)

3 What is a sales orientation? (2.6) How does it differ from a market orientation? (2.9)

4 Why might sales maximising objectives result in lower profit margins? (2.18)

5 Why did Levitt say 'there is no such thing as a growth industry'? (3.3)

6 Where did General Motors go wrong in developing the Chevy Corvair? (3.13)

7 What are the two main arguments against the marketing concept? (3.17)

8 Differentiate between long and short distributive systems. (4.3, 4.4)

9 What are PEST factors? (4.9)

10 What are the advantages of functional organisation for a marketing department? (5.11)

11 What are the disadvantages of matrix management? (5.18)

12 Why should a firm analyse its market environment? (6.3)

13 Name a technique useful in analysing a firm's internal environment? (6.11)

14 Why should a firm take note of consumerist pressures? (6.25)

15 List the market forces bearing upon the marketing mix. (7.3)

Now try questions 1 and 2 at the end of the text

Chapter 2

MARKETING RESEARCH

This chapter covers the following topics.

1. Why do we need marketing research?
2. Types of marketing research
3. Marketing research procedure: secondary data
4. Marketing research procedure: primary data
5. Marketing information systems

---

1.   WHY DO WE NEED MARKETING RESEARCH?

1.1   Marketing decisions are inevitably made under conditions of uncertainty and risk. The use of marketing research cannot eliminate risk but can reduce it by indicating the likely outcome of a certain course of action.

Markets are dynamic and competitive; success in business depends on greater investment and more frequent innovation so as not to lose ground to competitors. Important decisions have to be taken frequently, and in order to make decisions with confidence management needs relevant and comprehensive information. It is the task of marketing research to provide this information.

The categories of information needs

1.2   Marketing information needs can be classified into three broad categories:

(a)   information for strategic decision-making (such as product life cycle estimates, information to help with decisions about diversifying or to segment a market);

(b)   information for tactical decisions (such as planning sales territories, setting short term marketing cost budgets); and

(c)   information for a marketing database (such as for market share analysis, competitor analysis, substitute product analysis).

The information system for marketing is referred to as *marketing research*.

2: MARKETING RESEARCH

Definitions of marketing research

1.3 Marketing research is the investigation of the marketing activities of a company - the entire marketing mix - and should look into how far all these activities are consumer-orientated and should recommend how they can be planned in the future in order to sustain profits and customer demand.

1.4 'Market research' and 'marketing research' are often used interchangeably although there is a difference of scope.

(a) Market research refers to finding out information about the market for a particular product or service.

(b) Marketing research was defined more broadly by the American Marketing Association as 'the systematic gathering, recording and analysing of data about problems relating to the marketing of goods and services'. Thus marketing research includes research on the effects of pricing, advertising and other marketing decision variables.

2. TYPES OF MARKETING RESEARCH

2.1 Marketing research may include the following specific types of research.

(a) *Market research* includes:

   (i)   analysis of the market potential for existing products;
   (ii) forecasting likely demand for new products;
   (iii) sales forecasting for all products;
   (iv) study of market trends;
   (v)   study of the characteristics of the market;
   (vi) analysis of market shares.

(b) *Product research* includes:

   (i)   customer acceptance of proposed new products;
   (ii) comparative studies between competitive products;
   (iii) studies into packaging and design;
   (iv) forecasting new uses for existing products;
   (v)   test marketing;
   (vi) research into the development of a product line (range).

(c) *Price research* includes:

   (i)   analysis of elasticities of demand;
   (ii) analysis of costs and contribution or profit margins;
   (iii) the effect of changes in credit policy on demand;
   (iv) customer perceptions of price (and quality).

(d) *Sales promotion research* includes:

   (i)   motivation research for advertising and sales promotion effectiveness;
   (ii) analysing the effectiveness of advertising on sales demand;
   (iii) analysing the effectiveness of individual aspects of advertising such as copy and media used;

(iv) establishing sales territories;
(v)   analysing the effectiveness of salesmen;
(vi) analysing the effectiveness of other sales promotion methods.

(e) *Distribution research* includes:

(i)   the location and design of distribution centres;
(ii)   the analysis of packaging for transportation and shelving;
(iii) dealer supply requirements;
(iv)   dealer advertising requirements;
(v)   the cost of different methods of transportation and warehousing.

The most important of these are product and market research, which we will now examine in more detail.

Product research

2.2 This aspect of marketing research attempts to make product research and development customer-oriented. Product research is concerned with the product itself, whether new, improved or already on the market, and customer reactions to it.

2.3 New product ideas may come from anywhere – from research and development personnel, marketing and sales personnel, competitors, customers, outside scientific or technological discoveries, individual employees or executives. Research and development is carried out by company scientists, engineers or designers; much wasted effort can be saved for them, however, if new ideas are first tested in the market; that is, if product research is carried out.

2.4 New ideas are first screened by a range of specialists (market researchers, designers, research and development staff etc) and are rejected if they:

(a) have a low profit potential or insufficient market potential;
(b) have a high cost and involve high risk;
(c) do not conform to company objectives;
(d) cannot be produced and distributed with the available resources.

Ideas which survive the screening process should be product tested and possibly test marketed. Test marketing in a selected area will give a better indication of how well the product will sell if produced for a wider market, but it also gives competitors an early warning of what is happening.

2.5 Typical considerations in product research for a new product are:

(a) the combination of quality, price, value and associated image, together with the shape, colour and size of product, which will appeal most successfully to customers;

(b) the extent to which a new product will encroach on the market for existing lines;

(c) whether the new product extends or improves the existing product range of the company;

(d) the extent to which action by a competitor forces a firm to develop a new product.

2.6 Typical considerations for improving an existing product are:

(a) customer (or dealer) reaction to the existing product and the possibility that this could be improved by changing the product itself, its size, colour or packaging and so on;

(b) customer reaction to after-sales service and the possibility that this could be improved.

2.7 Product research also includes the need to keep the product range of a company's goods under review for the following reasons.

(a) *Variety reduction* may be desirable to reduce production costs, or when there are insufficient sales of certain items in the product range to justify continued production. In practice, there is often strong resistance, both from within a company and from customers, to the elimination of products from the market.

(b) *Product diversification* increases a product range by introducing new items, and a wide range of products can often improve a company's market image.

(c) *Segmentation* is a policy which aims at securing a new class of customers (a new market segment) for an existing range of products, perhaps by making some adjustments to the products to appeal to the new segments. It is examined further in Chapter 9.

2.8 Product research also involves finding *new uses* for existing products, and this could be considered a means of extending a product range. The uses for plastics and nylon, for example, have been extended rapidly in the past as a result of effective research.

2.9 As in all aspects of marketing research, it is important to be aware of the activities of competitors in product research because:

(a) it is necessary to know what new or improved products they are making and what their product range is;

(b) a company must also be aware of the advantages and disadvantages, both real and imaginary, of a competitor's products, and attempt to maintain the advantages and reduce the disadvantages of its own products in relation to these.

Market research

2.10 The information for market research can be collected directly (for example, from sample market results or questionnaires filled in by customers) or from secondary sources (such as analyses of past sales, or external information such as *Nielsen index*, which gives summary information on sales by products and geographical areas).

2.11 The information should reduce the risk involved in marketing decisions and thus increase the chances of making the right choice. But the quantity and quality of information provided by market research has an associated cost and the trade-off between cost and accuracy is important, particularly because risk cannot be eliminated. There is no such thing as perfect information when dealing with decisionmaking in an uncertain world. Market research can provide information which should help to reduce the risk in decisionmaking but, usually, the more accurate the information, the higher the cost. Market research should always be cost effective.

2.12 We will now look at some specific market research techniques:

    (a)   market forecasts;
    (b)   sales forecasts;
    (c)   research into potential sales;
    (d)   information on concentration ratios;
    (e)   market signals.

2.13 *Market forecast*
This is a forecast for the market as a whole. It is mainly involved in the assessment of environmental factors, outside the organisation's control, which will affect the demand for its products/services. Often it consists of three components.

    (a)   An *economic review* (national economy, government policy, covering forecasts on investment, population, gross national product, and inflation).

    (b)   *Specific market research* (to obtain data about specific markets and forecasts concerning total market demand).

    (c)   Evaluation of *total market demand* for the firm's and similar products - including such factors as profitability and market potential.

2.14 *Sales forecasts*
These are estimates of sales of a product in a future period:

    (a)   at a given price;
    (b)   using a stated method of sales promotion which will cost a given amount of money.

Unlike the market forecast, a sales forecast concerns the firm's activity directly. It takes into account such aspects as sales to certain categories of customer, sales promotion activities, the extent of competition, product life cycle, performance of major products.

Sales forecasts are expressed in volume, value and profit, and in the case of national and international organisations regional forecasts are usual, by product.

Research into potential sales

2.15 Sales potential is an estimate of the part of the market which is within the possible reach of a product. The potential will vary according to the price of the product and the amount of money spent on sales promotion, and market research should attempt to quantify these variations. Sales potential also depends on:

    (a)   how essential the product is to consumers;
    (b)   whether it is a durable commodity whose purchase is postponable;
    (c)   the overall size of the possible market;
    (d)   competition.

Whether sales potential is worth exploiting will depend on the cost of sales promotion and selling which must be incurred to realise the potential.

2: MARKETING RESEARCH

Example: research into sales potential

2.16 Market research has led a company to the opinion that the sales potential of product X is:

	Sales value	Contribution* earned before selling costs deducted	Cost of selling
either	£100,000	£40,000	£10,000
or	£110,000	£44,000	£15,000

*Contribution is an accountancy term which means sales revenue less direct costs. The contribution is made towards covering fixed costs (those not affected by the level of production).

In this example, it would not be worth spending an extra £5,000 (£15,000 - £10,000) on selling in order to realise an extra sales potential of £10,000 (£110,000 - £100,000), because contribution only rises by £4,000 and so the net effect would be a loss of £(5,000 - 4,000) = £1,000.

2.17 Sales potential will influence the decisions by a company on how much of each product to make: its *production mix*. The market is dynamic, and market research should reveal any significant changes. A company might decide, for example, that maximum profits will be earned by concentrating all its production and sales promotion efforts on one segment of a market. Action by competitors might then adversely affect sales and market research might reveal that another market segment has become relatively more profitable. The company might therefore decide to divert some production capacity and sales promotion spending to the new segment in order to revive its profits.

2.18 Estimates of sales potential are required in deciding whether to invest money in the development of a new or improved product.

2.19 Market research, to be comprehensive, must show an awareness of the economic, fiscal, political and social influences which may affect supply and demand for a product. Changes within this framework should wherever possible be anticipated.

2.20 Other aspects of market research include investigation of:

(a) the expansion or decline of demand within a particular market segment;
(b) the expansion or decline of demand within a particular geographical area;
(c) the timing of demand - is there a cyclical or seasonal pattern of demand?

Information on concentration ratios

2.21 To develop a market share strategy, an organisation might want to obtain information about the concentration ratios in the market, that is, what proportion of firms hold most of the market.

2.22 One way of expressing concentration ratios is to assess the percentage of the market that is held by the top five firms, say, and the top ten firms.

2: MARKETING RESEARCH

2.23 A more detailed concentration ratio analysis can be charted on a Lorenz curve.

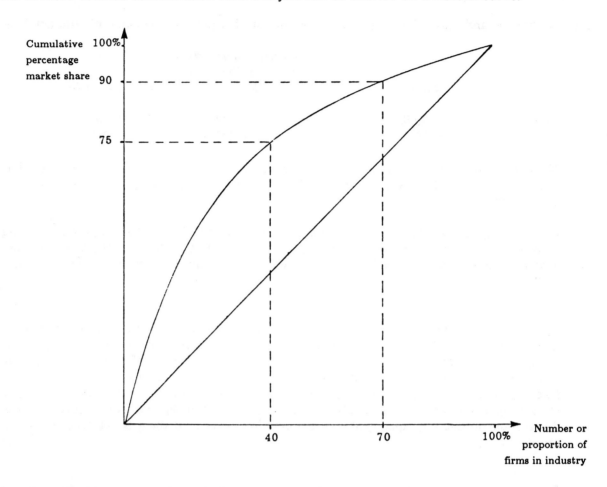

2.24 In this example, for instance, the top 40% of the firms in the industry have 75% of the total market, and the top 70% have 90% of the market. The greater the bend on the curve away from the straight line (which would indicate equal market shares for every firm) the greater is the concentration of the firm in the hands of the market leaders.

Market signals

2.25 Market signals are information that comes to light about competitors' actions in the market. They may be 'honest' or they may be 'bluffs'; nevertheless, they are significant for making decisions about market strategy.

2.26 Market signals can take any of the following forms.

    (a)   A competitor makes an announcement of what he intends to do, but before he has done it. Prior announcements are publicity measures intended:

        (i)   to warn off competitors from trying to do the same, because the organisation making the announcements intends to get in first;

        (ii)   to test competitors' reactions;

      (iii) to win support for the move from the investing public, on which it will rely for financial support;

      (iv) as a threat of retaliatory action against something another competitor has already done.

  (b) A competitor makes an announcement of what he has done, after the event; such as signing a major contract with a supplier or customer, or making a takeover bid for another company.

  (c) Competitors adopt a particular course of action when they would have been expected to do something else. What does their unexpected action signal?

  (d) An aggressive marketing action by a competitor. When a firm's competitor takes an aggressive marketing action directed specifically against the firm, it might be a signal that the competitor thinks the firm is gaining too much market share, and the aggressive action might be the first stage in an intensification of competition.

3. MARKETING RESEARCH PROCEDURE: SECONDARY DATA

3.1 Marketing research involves the following five stages of work.

  (a) *Definition of the problem.* An individual market research project cannot be undertaken successfully until the marketing problem which management wishes to resolve has been properly defined.

  (b) *Design of the research.* Once the research team knows what problem it must help to resolve, it will establish the type of data (secondary or primary - see below), the collection method to be used (postal questionnaire, personal interview), the selection of a research agency (if appropriate) and if a sample is to be taken, the design of the sample. Any questions put to respondents must be carefully designed.

  (c) *Collection of the data.*

  (d) *Analysis of the data.*

  (e) *Presentation of a report* which should then lead to a management marketing decision.

3.2 The sources of marketing research information are secondary data and primary data. Primary data will be discussed in the next section. First we will look briefly at secondary data.

3.3 Secondary data is 'data neither collected directly by the user nor specifically for the user, often under conditions that are not well known to the user' (American Marketing Association). The collection of secondary data for marketing research is sometimes known as *desk research.*

3.4 Desk research involves collecting data from internal and external sources.

  (a) Records inside the firm, gathered by another department or section for its own purposes may be useful for the research task in hand. Internal data would include:

      (i)   production data about quantities produced, materials and labour resources used etc;
      (ii) data about inventory;

      (iii)   data about sales volumes, analysed by sales area, salesman, quantity, price, profitability, distribution outlet, customer etc;

      (iv)   data about marketing itself, such as promotion and brand data;

      (v)   all cost and management accounting data;

      (vi)   financial management data relating to the capital structure of the firm, capital tied up in stocks and debtors and so on.

  (b) Published information from external sources includes:

      (i)   publications of market research agencies, such as the Nielsen Index;

      (ii)   government statistics;

      (iii)   publications of trade associations;

      (iv)   professional journals.

3.5 Sources of secondary data for marketing vary according to the needs of the organisation.

3.6 The *government* is a major source of economic information and information about industry and population trends. Examples of UK government publications are:

  (a) the Annual Abstract of Statistics and its monthly equivalent, the Monthly Digest of Statistics, containing data about manufacturing output, housing, population etc;

  (b) the Digest of UK Energy Statistics (published annually);

  (c) Housing and Construction statistics (published quarterly);

  (d) Financial Statistics (monthly);

  (e) Economic Trends (monthly);

  (f) Census of Population;

  (g) Census of Production (annual), which has been described as 'one of the most important sources of desk research for industrial marketers and provides data about production by firms in each industry in the UK;

  (h) Department of Employment Gazette (monthly) giving details of employment in the UK;

  (i) British Business, published weekly by the Department of Trade and Industry, giving data on industrial and commercial trends at home and overseas;

  (j) Business Monitors, giving detailed information about various industries.

3.7 *Non-government* sources of information include:

  (a) the national press (Financial Times etc) and financial and professional magazines and journals;

  (b) companies and other organisations specialising in the provision of economic and financial data (eg the Financial Times Business Information Service, the Data Research Institute, Reuters and the Extel Group) and research organisations who analyse certain markets and publish and sell the results (eg Mintel, Euromonitor);

(c) directories and yearbooks;

(d) professional institutions (eg Chartered Institute of Marketing, Industrial Marketing Research Association, British Institute of Management, Institute of Practitioners in Advertising);

(e) specialist libraries, such as the City Business Library in London, which collects published information from a wide variety of sources;

(f) trade sources: many industries have an industry body which provides useful market research data. The Association of British Insurers (ABI) provides market share data on the life insurance industry; the Society of Motor Manufacturers and Trades (SMMT) provides detailed data on the registration of new vehicles by brand on a regular basis. In addition trade press is often a valuable source of information about competitors; computing firms for instance will scour Computing, PC News, The Economist and The Financial Times for news on their competitors.

4. MARKETING RESEARCH PROCEDURE: PRIMARY DATA

4.1 The collection of primary data is sometimes known as *field research*.

4.2 Field research may be carried out in a number of areas, notably customer research, advertising research, product research, packaging research and distribution research. There are several techniques involved in the collection and analysis of primary data and we shall consider in detail:

(a) experimentation;
(b) observation;
(c) sampling;
(d) interviewing;
(e) questionnaires;

(f) consumer panels;
(g) trade audits, such as retail audits;
(h) pre-tests;
(i) post-tests;
(j) attitude scales and methods of analysis.

Experimentation

4.3 In a *controlled experiment* a controlled research environment is established and selected stimuli are then introduced. To the extent that 'outside' factors can be eliminated from the environment (and therefore depending on the degree to which a controlled environment is established) the observed effects can be measured and related to each stimulus. Controlled experiments have been used to find the best advertising campaign, the best price level, the best incentive machine and the best sales training method.

Observation

4.4 Observation can be used as a means of obtaining sample data where quantitative data is required. For example, if data is needed about the volume of traffic passing along a road at a certain time of day, observers (either people or recording equipment) can be placed so as to count the traffic as it passes by.

4.5 Observation can also be used to study consumer behaviour, although this is usually within a controlled experiment.

(a) Direct observation involves the examination by an observer of how people behave in particular situations. This is important in retail trade research (such as watching how customers react to product displays and promotions).

(b) Recording devices can be used to monitor the responses of individuals:

    (i) an *eye camera* records eye reactions and is sometimes used to test response to advertisements;

    (ii) a *psychogalvanometer* measures perspiration (which is in turn a measure of involuntary physical response) and is also used in advertising testing;

    (iii) a *tachitoscope* exposes material for a brief moment, and measures the visual impact of an advertisement or its legibility when exposed for this short time.

Sampling

4.6 In marketing research for consumer goods, it will be impossible to obtain data from every consumer in the market, because not only would this take too much time and cost too much money, but it would also be impracticable in any case. (In a small market, however, such as an industrial market or government market, a 100%, or *census* survey might be practicable and preferable to a sample survey.) To obtain data, it is therefore usually necessary to obtain a sample to provide an estimate of the characteristics of the entire 'population' and the accuracy of the sample will depend on:

(a) how the sample is taken;
(b) the amount of variability in the population;
(c) the size of the sample.

4.7 The larger the sample, the greater the likelihood that the sample will provide an accurate reflection of the population as a whole.

4.8 To make a truly random sample we need a *sampling frame*. This is a list of every member of the target 'population'. If we wished to obtain a sample of opinions among people eligible to vote in an election, a sampling frame would be provided by the Electoral Register. If a sampling frame is prepared which excludes any 'members' or items, a sample chosen by reference to the sampling frame cannot be truly random.

4.9 A complete sampling frame is difficult to obtain in practice because:

(a) comprehensive lists of a population (eg a list of the members of a professional accountancy body) get out of date as soon as they are published, since new members join and existing members leave, retire or die;

(b) a comprehensive sampling frame would not be justified if the benefits from greater confidence in the accuracy of sample estimates are less than the cost of obtaining or maintaining the sampling frame. For example, if a company manufacturing snack foods wished to obtain data about the reaction of potential customers to a new product, a comprehensive sampling frame would need to consist of every potential customer in the entire market. This would not be justified on grounds of cost (as well as on grounds of practicality).

4.10 For these reasons, various techniques of sampling (methods of sample design) have been developed so that samples which are 'nearly' random ('quasi-random') can be obtained. You must have some understanding of these techniques and which of them might be used in certain circumstances, because an examination question may ask you to suggest what sort of samples you would recommend in a particular situation in order to obtain some marketing research data.

Random sampling

4.11 A *random sample* is one selected in such a way that every item in the population has an equal chance of being included. To obtain a random sample, we need a sampling frame, which has already been described. A random sample can be selected from the sampling frame by two main methods:

(a)   the 'lottery method' (picking numbers out of a hat);

(b)   the use of random number tables, which is to be preferred as it provides a high guarantee against bias.

4.12 You should note the following points.

(a)   It is first necessary to number all the items in the sampling frame in sequential order.

(b)   The sample can now be found by selecting groups of random numbers with the same number of digits as the total population size. For example:

Total population size	Number of digits in random numbers
0 - 9	1
10 - 99	2
100 - 999	3
1000 - 9999	4

The items selected for the sample are those corresponding to the random numbers selected.

(c)   When a large sample is required it is more convenient to use a computer to select the items at random.

Example: use of random number tables

4.13 Set out below is part of a typical random number table:

93716	16984	98953	73231
32886	58790	09958	18065
92052	06831	19640	99413
39510	35905	84244	34159
27699	06494	93152	19121
92962	61773	22109	78508
10274	12202	94205	50380
75867	20717	82037	10268
85783	47619	87481	37220

An investigator wishes to select a random sample from a population of 800 people. As there are three digits in 800 the random numbers will be selected in groups of three. Working along the first line of the table given above, the first few groups are:

937   161   698   498   953   732

Numbers over 800 are discarded. The first four people in the sample will therefore be the 161st, 689th, 498th and 732nd.

Non-random sampling

4.14 In many situation it is either not possible or else undesirable to use a random sample. The main methods of *non-random sampling* are as follows:

(a)   systematic sampling;
(b)   stratified sampling;
(c)   multistage sampling;
(d)   quota sampling;
(e)   cluster sampling.

Some of these methods try to approximate the random sampling technique, and are 'quasi-random' sampling methods.

4.15 *Systematic sampling* may provide a good approximation to random sampling. Select every nth item after a random start. For example, if it was decided to select a sample of 20 from a population of 800, then every 40th (800 ÷ 20) item after a random start in the first 40 should be selected. The starting point could be found using the lottery method or random number tables. If (say) 23 was chosen, then the sample would include the following items:

23rd, 63rd, 103rd, 143rd 783rd

The gap of 40 is known as the *sampling interval*.

4.16 The investigator must ensure that there is no regular pattern to the population which if it coincided with the sampling interval, might lead to a biased sample. In practice, this problem is often overcome by choosing multiple starting points and using varying sampling intervals whose size is selected at random.

4.17 A typical example of systematic sampling might be quality control checking where every nth item produced is selected for a control inspection.

4.18 In many situations *stratified sampling* is the best method of choosing a sample. It is another 'quasi-random' sampling method. The population must be capable of being divided into strata, which may conform to a consumer characteristics or a market segment.

For example, a manufacturer of machine equipment may know that 40% of its sales come from one industry A, 30% from another industry B, 10% from industry C and so on. A stratified sample would aim to obtain 40% of its respondents from industry A, 30% from group B, and 10% from C. If all potential customers in each industry are known, the sample within each group could then be selected by random sampling methods using a sampling frame.

4.19 *Multistage sampling* is normally used to cut down the number of investigations and the costs of travelling etc. Again an example will serve to illustrate the principles.

A national survey of cheese consumption is to be carried out. The country is divided into a number of areas and a small sample of these is selected at random. Each of the areas selected is subdivided into smaller units and again, a small number of these is selected at random. This process is repeated as many times as necessary and finally, a random sample of the relevant people living in each of the smallest units is made. A fair approximation to a random sample can be obtained.

Thus we might choose a random sample of 8 areas and from each of these areas, select a random sample of 5 towns. From each town, a random sample of 200 people might be selected so that the total sample size is $8 \times 5 \times 200 = 8,000$ people.

4.20 Using *quota sampling*, investigators are told to interview all the people they meet up to a certain quota. However, a large degree of bias can be introduced. For example, an interviewer may fill up his quota by only meeting housewives out shopping. In practice, this problem is partially overcome by subdividing the quota into different types of people, eg on the basis of age, sex and social class. For example, an interviewer might be expected to take a sample of 100 people, but told that the total must be made up of 50 men and 50 women, and that each sub-total of 50 should contain, say, 5 people from socio-economic group A, 10 from each of B, C1, C2 and D, and 5 from group E. It should be clear that one major advantage of quota sampling is that, although a fairly detailed knowledge of the characteristics of a population are required, it is not necessary to establish a sampling frame.

4.21 Using *cluster sampling*, the field under examination is cut down in much the same way as for a multistage sample. The investigators are then told to examine every item in the small areas which fit the required definition. The purpose of multistage sampling is to cut down costs but the purpose of cluster sampling is to find a sample. Like quota sampling, it will normally only be used when no sampling frame is available. Cluster sampling has the advantage of low costs in the same way as multistage sampling.

4.22 A cluster sample might be gathered as follows: by use of map references, a geographical area might be broken down into smaller areas. Some of these smaller areas will then be selected by random sampling. The 'sampling unit' is *every* person or household within the selected small area (in most samples, the 'sampling unit' selected is an individual or household).

4.23 A possible problem with cluster sampling is that if the individuals in the selected small areas show a similarity to one another, the findings of the sample (perhaps because they live in the same block of flats) may not be representative of the population as a whole.

4.24 Instead of interviewing every individual in the small area, the sample may select one in every 'n' individuals - say 1 in 5. This would be a type of two-stage sampling.

Exercise

A large retailing group wishes to evaluate the effect upon store sales of using window space for advertising purposes. Given the following data, show how a 20% sample of its stores should be drawn.

Type	No. of stores	Range of window sizes	Average window size
A	150	4m² - 10m²	8m²
B	80	11m² - 17m²	15m²
C	50	18m² - 25m²	20m²
D	20	More than 25m²	30m²
	300		

Solution

A stratified sample should be obtained. If the effect of using window space for advertising is the object of the research, the sample should relate to the total window size of the population.

Workings

Type	No. of stores	Average window size m²	Total window size m²	% of total
A	150	8	1,200	30
B	80	15	1,200	30
C	50	20	1,000	25
D	20	30	600	15
			4,000	100

The sample should consist of 30% of store type A, 30% of B, 25% C and 15% D. Since the total sample will be 20% of the number of stores (ie 20% of 300 = 60 stores) then the sample should consist of 18 stores of type A, 18 of type B, 15 of C and 9 of D.

Workings

Type	Total number	Number in sample	% of total in sample	% of window size
A	150	18		30%
B	80	18		30%
C	50	15		25%
D	20	9		15%
	300	60	20%	100%

The stores in the sample should be randomly selected - eg the stores of type A should be randomly selected from the total of 150 type A stores.

Potential faults in a sampling exercise

4.25 There are several faults or weaknesses which might occur in the design or collection of sample data.

(a)   *Bias:* in choosing a sample, unless the method used to select the sample is the random sampling method, or a quasi-random sampling method, there will be a likelihood that some 'units' (individuals or households) will have a poor, or even zero chance of being selected for the sample. Where this occurs, samples are said to be biased.

A biased sample may occur when:

(i)   the sampling frame is out of date, and excludes a number of individuals or 'units' new to the population; or
(ii)   some individuals selected for the sample decline to respond. If a questionnaire is sent to 1,000 households, but only 600 reply, the failure of the other 400 to reply will make the sample of 600 replies inevitably biased; or
(iii) a questionnaire contains leading questions, or a personal interviewer tries to get respondents to answer questions in a particular way.

(b)   *Insufficient data:* the sample may be too small to be reliable as a source of information about an entire population.

(c)   *Unrepresentative data:* data collected might be unrepresentative of normal conditions. For example, if an employee is asked to teach a trainee how to do a particular job, data concerning the employee's output and productivity during the time he is acting as trainer will not be representative of his normal output and productivity.

(d)   *Omission of an important factor:* data might be incomplete because an important item has been omitted in the design of the 'questions'.

(e)   *Carelessness:* data might be provided without any due care and attention. An investigator might also be careless in the way he gathers data.

(f)   *Confusion of cause and effect (or association):* it may be tempting to assume that if two variables appear to be related, one variable is the cause of the other. Variables may be associated but it is not necessarily true that one causes the other. For example, in a period of hot weather both sales of swimwear and ice creams are likely to rise. However, one is not causing the other; they are both caused by the hot weather.

(g)   Where questions call for something more than simple 'one word' replies, there may be difficulty in interpreting the results correctly. This is especially true of 'depth interviews' which try to determine the reasons for human behaviour (*motivation research*).

4.26 One method of checking the accuracy of replies is to insert *control questions* in the questionnaire, so that the reply to one question should be compatible with the reply to another. If they are not, the value of the interviewee's responses are dubious, and may be ignored.

Questionnaires

4.27 Questionnaires may be administered by personal interview, telephone or post. By their nature postal questionnaires tend to be highly structured in contrast to questionnaires that are used to support an interview by acting as an aide memoire that can be relatively open ended. In common with all other forms of marketing research it is important to attempt to survey a relatively large representative sample. It would be a mistake to assume that the need to obtain a large sample for statistically significant results necessarily favours the use of a postal survey.

4.28 Postal surveys have the additional problem in that whilst the mail out may be to a representative group the subsequent response is likely to be biased towards those who responded because they found the topic of particular interest. Postal surveys tend to attract a relatively low response rate, with unsolicited questionnaires often obtaining only a 2% or 3% return. Under these circumstances great care should be taken when extrapolating from such results.

4.29 Measures can be taken to improve the response rate from postal surveys. These include sending to named individuals and taking care that information such as job titles is up to date. This can be difficult if the sample is being drawn from a trade directory. It takes up to one year to update such directories, and the current year's edition will be on average six months old when reference is made. The reference can therefore easily be some eighteen months of out date. It also helps to send a covering letter and to stress confidentiality and anonymity for the respondent. Finally, the inclusion of a stamped and addressed envelope for the reply helps, particularly if a stamp rather than a prepaid envelope is used. Some evidence of moral pressure here!

4.30 It can be seen that it is a mistake to assume that using a postal survey will always be the most cost efficient means of conducting a survey.

Questionnaire design

4.31 There are two main considerations in designing questionnaires:

(a) Questions should generate valid and reliable information on the matter being surveyed. Respondents must therefore find the questions comprehensible. Questions that are likely to produce biased answers should also be avoided.

(b) The questionnaire should be designed to facilitate the subsequent data analysis.

4.32 The following guidelines should therefore be adopted.

(a) Leading questions should be avoided.

(b) Questions should be short and unambiguous.

(c) No calculations should be required.

(d) Questions should fall in a logical sequence.

(e) The working language of the target group should be used.

(f) *Filter questions* should be used to avoid wasting time. For example: do you own a car? YES/NO. A no response then enables questions on garages to be missed.

(g) *Funnelling,* a technique of moving from general to restricted questions more directly related to the research objectives, can be applied. This technique is sometimes reversed to check limited responses.

(h) Personal questions on sex, politics, religion and personal habits should only be asked in exceptional circumstances. Before attempting such questions interviewers need to have established goodwill.

Pilot testing

4.33 One can never be certain as to the actual response of individuals to a questionnaire. However carefully the questionnaire design has been conducted, it is still necessary to pilot the questionnaire, by surveying a limited number of respondents in some depth, before going to the cost of launching a survey that might product some meaningless results. As an example, a question that appeared obvious to the design team might be found in practice to be highly confusing or misleading.

Classification of respondents

4.34 It is often important, especially when identifying potential market segments, to classify individuals, often by socio-economic grouping or age. Questions to establish these grouping should be treated with care as they can subsequently colour the individual's response to other questions. Socio-economic groupings are still determined by the occupation of the 'head of the household', the man in the case of a couple. This is a remarkably archaic notion now that so many women work full or part-time. However, if asked at the outset of the interview what her husband's occupation is, a woman may spend the rest of the interview trying to portray her household as belonging to a higher socio-economic grouping than it actually does. No, she rarely buys baked beans, and yes, she usually purchases sirloin in preference to cheaper cuts of meat. If questions on occupation and the like are to be asked they should be left to the end of the interview. Often it is safer even then to allow a trained market researcher to infer such classifications using their subjective appraisal.

4.35 Questionnaires can be used in a variety of ways.

(a) *Telephone interviews* have the advantage of speedy response and can cover a wide geographical area fairly cheaply. The drawback is that interviews must be fairly short and cannot use 'showcards' or pictures.

(b) *Personal interviews*.

(c) *Replies by mail*. Questionnaires can be returned by post (and delivered by post, by hand etc) after the respondent has completed it in his/her own time. This is fairly cheap, and avoids interviewer interference; however, there is no control over the completion of the questionnaire and (unless backed by legal authority, such as income tax returns) is unlikely to produce a large response. Low response (say 10 - 30%) might make the sample data unrepresentative.

(d) *Self-completion*, perhaps at the place of purchase. For example, a theatre or cinema owner might ask members of the audience to complete a questionnaire on their theatregoing or cinemagoing habits and preferences. The disadvantage of this form of survey is that respondents may not understand questions properly (as with mail surveys) and the questionnaire will also need to be short in order to persuade people to fill it in.

Consumer panels

4.36 Some research firms have created consumer panels consisting of a cross-section of consumers who have agreed to give information about their attitudes or buying habits (through personal visits or mail questionnaires) at regular intervals of time. Consumer panels with personal visits are called *home audit panels* and panels which send data by post are called *diary panels*. Panels might be established for either the long term or the short term.

4.37 Consumer panels provide a useful illustration of the difficulties which exist in obtaining reliable market research findings. The advantages of consumer panels are that they provide continuous information over time from willing guinea pigs. The problems, however, are as follows.

(a) It is difficult to select a panel which is a representative sample. The panel must be representative of:

    (i)   all the customers in the target market;

    (ii)   the decision making units who will make the purchase decision (husbands as well as wives, for example).

(b) Panel members tend to become sophisticated in interviewing techniques and responses.

(c) It is difficult to maintain a stable personnel; turnover of members may be high and this will affect results as new members are enlisted.

Trade audits or retail audits

4.38 Trade audits are carried out among panels of wholesalers and retailers, and the term 'retail audits' refers to panels of retailers only. A research firm sends auditors to selected outlets at regular intervals to count stock and deliveries, thus enabling an estimate of throughput to be made.

4.39 The audits provide details of:

(a) retail sales for selected products and brands, sales by different type of retail outlet, market shares and brand shares;

(b) retail stocks of products and brands (enabling a firm subscribing to the audit to compare stocks of its own goods with those of competitors);

(c) selling prices in retail outlets, including information about discounts.

4.40 Retail audits, because they provide continuous monitoring of retail activity, may be of value to a manufacturing firm because:

(a) problems in retail sales provide an early warning of problems the manufacturer may soon have to expect in ex-factory sales;

(b) they indicate long-term trends in the market place, thus providing helpful information for strategic marketing planning;

(c) in the shorter term, they may indicate the need for changes in pricing policy, sales promotion or advertising, distribution policy, package design or product design.

4.41 A well-known example of a retail audit is the *Inventory Audit of Retail Sales*, also called the *Nielsen Index* (after its originator) which has operated since 1939. This monitors sales and stock levels for three product groups: food, drugs and pharmaceuticals. The Nielsen Food Index audits about 800 grocers bi-monthly and reports on each brand, size, flavour etc specified by the client, together with an 'all other' category, showing:

(a) consumer sales in units and £;

(b) retailer purchases in units;

(c) the source of delivery (co-operatives, multiple stores depot, independent wholesalers);

(d) retailers' stocks and stock cover (in days/weeks);

(e) prices;

(f) details of out of stock items;

(g) press, magazine and TV expenditure.

The report is subdivided into shop types (all grocers, cooperatives, multiples, major multiples and independents) and television regions.

Pre-testing and post-testing

4.42 Marketing research may be carried out before, during and after marketing decisions are implemented. Such research is often directed at attempting to measure the effectiveness of advertising campaigns. However, whereas the effects of sales promotions (coupons, three for the price of two and the like) are directly measurable in terms of sales, the effectiveness of advertising often needs to be inferred.

4.43 The reason for these difficulties is that the advertising effect might be swamped by other more powerful influences in the market place, such as price cuts and sales promotions by competitors. The impact of these and other marketing activities can then mask the true effect of the company's advertising campaign. Much research therefore focuses on the effectiveness of the campaign in communicating with its target audience, the logic being that any beneficial changes in awareness and attitudes will later be reflected in increased sales.

It therefore follows that measurement of the *communication effect* is more reliable than attempts to measure the *sales effect* attributable to a particular advertising campaign.

Pre-testing

4.44 (a) Before the advertisement copy is finalised, *motivational research* may be carried out on a sample of potential customers. Members of the public might be invited to watch a film show which includes new TV advertising, and a measure of the shift in their brand awareness would be taken after the show. *Copy research* might involve showing members of the public a number of press advertisements and then asking questions about them (in order to measure the impact of different slogans or headlines).

(b) *Laboratory tests* have been carried out to measure the physiological reactions of people watching advertisements (eg heart beat, blood pressure, dilation of the pupil of the eye, perspiration). Such tests measure the arousal power or attention-drawing power of an advertisement, but cannot measure its effectiveness in communicating the message.

(c) *Ratings tests* involve asking a panel of target consumers to look at alternative advertisements and to give them ratings (marks out of ten) for attention-drawing power, clarity, emotional appeal and stimulus to buy.

4.45 In 1979, when Ford launched the Fiesta their advertising agency, Ogilvy, Benson, Mather, abandoned their first creative idea after motivational research. The proposed copy for the advertisement focused on the theme of Ford's 'new baby'. An expectant father was seen pacing up and down outside his garage. Suddenly, from inside the garage came the sounds of a new born baby crying. The garage door was opened to reveal a proud wife with the new Fiesta. Women reacted very unfavourably to the advertisement which was shown in its pre-production animatic form (drawings with soundtrack). They expressed uncomfortable feelings and anxiety at the thought of a baby being locked up in a garage. Wisely the advertisement was reformulated to a high technology theme.

4.46 The purpose of test marketing is to obtain information about how consumers react to the product - will they buy it, and if so, will they buy it again? Will they adopt the product as a regular feature of their buying habits, and if so, how frequently will they buy it? With this information an estimate of the total market demand for the product can be made.

4.47 A test market involves testing a new consumer product in selected areas which are thought to be 'representative' of the total market. This avoids a blind commitment to the costs of a full-scale launch while permitting the collection of market data. In the selected areas, the firm will attempt to distribute the product through the same types of sales outlets it plans to use in the full market launch, and also to use the advertising and promotion plans it intends to use in the full market. A test marketing exercise can be expensive, but it enables the company to 'test the water' before launching the product nationally. Not only does it help to make sales forecasts, it can also be used to identify flaws in the product or promotional plans which can then be dealt with before the product is launched nationally.

4.48 Other forms of product testing include the following.

(a) *Simulated store technique* (or laboratory test markets). In these tests, a group of shoppers are invited to watch a selection of advertisements for a number of products, including an advertisement for the new product. They are then given some money and invited to spend it in a supermarket or shopping area. Their purchases are recorded and they are asked to explain their purchase decisions (and non-purchase decisions). Some weeks later they are contacted again and asked about their product attitudes and repurchase intentions. These tests help to assess advertising effectiveness as well as to forecast sales volumes; in addition the results are made available relatively quickly.

(b) *Controlled test marketing*. In these tests, a research firm pays a panel of stores to carry the new product for a given length of time. The research firm can decide on shelf locations, point-of-sale displays and pricing etc; the sales results are then monitored. This test (also known as 'minimarket testing') helps to provide an assessment of 'in-store' factors in achieving sales as well as to forecast sales volumes for the new product.

4.49 There are several drawbacks to test marketing.

(a) The marketing staff may become so involved in the testing that they develop an 'emotional' commitment to the product's success and seek every reason to justify a full market launch.

(b) The test markets may be unrepresentative of the total market, so that predictions of market sales will be biased an inaccurate. 'Despite the various claims of media owners, it is clear that no perfect microcosm exists and that test marketing is of dubious value if undertaken for predictive purposes alone' (Baker).

(c) Test marketing invites the attention of competitors who are given advance warning of the new product and can then develop aggressive counter-tactics in order to prevent a successful launch of the new product (eg expensive advertising or price reductions may be planned). If the counter-tactics are introduced during the test marketing phase, the test will then fail to obtain reliable predictions of future sales volumes, due to the abnormal trading conditions during the test. If the test market is for an entirely new product, it will give competitors time to study it and develop their own substitutes.

For these reasons, test marketing is only used occasionally in Britain. Many firms rely on marketing mix tests, and then proceed to a full market launch without test marketing.

Post-testing

4.50 During an advertisement campaign attempts can be made to measure the resulting changes in sales. However, as noted above with the exception of responses to mail order advertisements, such direct effects might not be easy to assess. Post-testing will therefore concentrate on the following measures of the communication effect of advertisements.

(a) *recall tests* ask the interviewee to remember, unaided, advertisements which have been seen before the interview;

(b) *recognition tests* involve giving the interviewee some reminder of an advertisement, and testing his/her recognition of it.

EPOS

4.51 The recording and use of *electronic point of sales* (EPOS) data is still in its infancy with the exception of advanced retailing systems in companies such as Sainsbury's and Next. Information from smart tills will provide a real opportunity in the near future to directly measure the effect of, say, local radio advertising on the immediate sales of a brand in the media's catchment area. The use of such disaggregated tactical data will overcome the problems of external effects distorting aggregated sales figures.

EPOS will therefore enable major retailers, such as the supermarkets, to measure directly the performance of competitive brands. Hitherto, this information has had to be inferred from the use of consumer purchasing audits conducted by organisations like Audits of Great Britain (AGB).

Recording data about attitudes

4.52 When a survey collects data about customer attitudes, it is necessary to use some method of recording differing attitudes for analysis and evaluation. (Note: it has been suggested earlier that favourable consumer attitudes to a product do not necessarily cause the consumer to buy the product; nevertheless, the causal link possibly exists, and attitude surveys are fairly common in marketing research.)

4.53 Attitudes are measured by means of attitude scales, and there are three common types used in marketing research.

(a) *Thurstone scales*. A Thurstone scale contains 7, 9 or 11 statements which appear to cover a range of attitudes in equal intervals. Respondents are then asked to select the statement which most closely reflects their attitude.

(b) *Likert scales*. A respondent is asked to indicate his measure of agreement or disagreement with a series of statements put to him, such as 'strongly agree, agree, uncertain, disagree, strongly disagree'.

(c) *Semantic differential scales* are based on extreme objectives (strong-weak, good-bad, always-never) with perhaps intermediate attitudes as well (eg. extremely good, very good, fairly good, neither good nor bad, fairly bad, very bad, extremely bad).

Evaluating data

4.54 The evaluation of data collected in a survey will be carried out using statistical techniques. Some forms of analysis are:

(a) *multiple regression analysis:* this might be used, for example, to analyse the effect on sales of changes in a variety of other variables such as price and advertising;

(b) *discriminant analysis:* this might be used when the researcher wants to know what consumer traits (eg. socio-economic groupings, lifestyle, age and sex) are associated with frequent, or infrequent purchase of a particular product or brand;

(c) *tests of statistical significance,* eg. chi-squared tests and calculation of standard errors.

The reliability of sample data

4.55 The results of a sample are intended to indicate the attitudes or behaviour of a population as a whole. This is usually done by making statistical tests of significance. For example:

(a) A sample survey might show that 35% of people in Britain prefer coffee to tea. From the sample data, it might then be possible to predict with a certain degree of confidence (typically, a 95% level of confidence is used by researchers) that the percentage of the total population who prefer coffee to tea is, say, 35% plus or minus $1\frac{1}{2}$%.

(b) Suppose that young people are seen as a market segment with its own different characteristics. A subsequent sample might show that, say, 45% of young people in Britain prefer coffee to tea. In comparison with the results of the sample in (a), this would indicate that there is a significant statistical difference between the preferences of young people and the preferences of the community as a whole.

4.56 Sampling can be used to identify consumer attitudes and behaviour, but also to identify potential market segments. To be reliable, however, sample data must be random or quasi-random, and it is important to avoid the potential faults in a sampling exercise listed above.

Example: statistical significance

4.57 A manufacturer of frozen foods decided to plan a national TV advertising campaign for a particular product and to assess the results in terms of sales achieved. A sample survey undertaken before the campaign over a period of four weeks revealed the following:

Channel	Product A	Sales (units) Product B	Total
Multiple stores	160,250	71,300	231,550
Independent stores	40,500	18,160	58,660
Total	200,750	89,460	290,210

The advertising campaign (for Product B) lasted for four weeks, and, immediately thereafter, a further sample survey over a period of four weeks showed the following changes:

Channel	Product A	Sales (units) Product B	Total
Multiple stores	176,275	89,125	265,400
Independent stores	42,525	20,430	62,955
Total	218,800	109,555	328,355

(a) What conclusion can be drawn from these results?

(b) What other information would you require before making any positive statements on the effect of the campaign?

Solution

4.58 *Workings*

Method 1

Channel	Increase in sales of A Units	%	Increase in sales of B Units	%	Increase in total sales Units	%
Multiple stores	16,025	10	17,825	25	33,850	14.6
Independent stores	2,025	5	2,270	12.5	4,295	7.3
Total	18,050	9	20,095	22.5	38,145	13.1

Method 2

	Product A Period 1	Period 2	Product B Period 1	Period 2
% of total sales in multiple stores	69.2	66.4	30.8	33.6
% of total sales in independent stores	69.0	67.5	31.0	32.5
% of total sales	69.2	66.6	30.8	33.4

Discussion

4.59 Sales of both products increased between one period and the next, but sales of B increased by a greater percentage amount. B accounts for about 22% more of total sales in period 2 than in period 1. Without statistical analysis it is impossible to state whether there is any statistical significance in the difference between the periods.

A superficial assessment, even so, might lead us to predict that the difference is significant.

However, we have no evidence to link the greater increase in B sales with the advertising campaign.

4.60 Before we can make any positive statements about the connection between the higher growth in B sales and the advertising campaign, we need the following information.

(a) What was the aim of the campaign? The purpose of the campaign might have been to maintain B's existing share of the market, rather than to increase unit sales.

(b) Are there any seasonal factors or other factors which might explain the higher growth in B sales? The campaign was a national campaign: in practice, many firms select a control area such as a TV region in which to launch a campaign, and then to compare sales results in the region with the rest of the country. If sales are better in the TV region, the advertising campaign might then be judged successful, and extended to a national coverage.

(c) A market research team might carry out a post-testing exercise to measure consumer response to the campaign.

(d) Is the sample reliable and unbiased?

(e) Since we are dealing here with consumer products, the sample shows sales by stores to their customers. The manufacturer's customers are the stores. An advertising campaign would only be judged successful if higher consumer sales resulted in higher purchases of goods by stores from the manufacturer. No data is provided in the question about this.

(f) An advertising campaign's effects are likely to be greatest in the short term. However, the effect of the campaign should be measured over a period of longer than just four weeks.

(g) Are there any other elements in the marketing mix which might explain the higher sales of B? For example, the price of B might have been cut, or a sales promotion offer might have been made (such as money off next order coupons).

(h) Might the growth in sales of B have had an adverse effect on sales of A? For example, if B is frozen beans and A is frozen peas, higher sales of beans might result in lower sales of peas.

Marketing research in non-consumer products industries

4.61 There are particular aspects of marketing research that apply in industries other than those for consumer products.

(a) *Service industries.* Research on behalf of financial institutions such as banks or insurance companies requires data which may be considered personal and confidential. For example, it may be necessary to know details of the respondents' income. Given that respondents may be wary about the improper use of confidential information, great care and tact are required to conduct a survey.

(b) *Industrial marketing research.* The researcher must have some understanding of the industry or industries in order to design a research survey. In addition, it may be possible to carry out a census instead of a sample. It may be difficult to identify the person (or persons) in a customer firm who makes the buying decisions, therefore care must be taken to ensure that the researcher goes to the 'real' buyer.

(c) *Non-profit making organisations.* A considerable amount of market research is carried out on behalf of the national or local government. Social problems concerning the old, disabled, unemployed etc may call for information about their opinions and circumstances so that marketing research can help government officials to make policy decisions.

4.62 The possible disadvantage of marketing research for smaller non-profit making bodies such as universities or charities is the cost of conducting a research project. There might be a temptation for an organisation to use its own inexperienced staff to do research, with the result that findings might be incomplete, or biased and misleading.

The value of research information

4.63 Information is only worth having if the benefits derived from it exceed the costs of its collection. The greater the accuracy of information provided, the more it will cost. At high levels of accuracy the marginal costs of collection will probably exceed the marginal benefits of the extra accuracy obtained.

It is also worth noting that it is only worth paying for market research that provides additional information. Marketing research that merely confirms information that is already widely known has little real value.

Interpretation of results

4.64 Interpretation of results takes great care. There is some controversy as to how much interpretation market researchers should offer clients. One school of thought suggests presentation of the facts only, leaving the client to draw conclusions. A contrasting approach is for the researcher to interpret results and suggest conclusions or interpretations based on evidence in the findings. The guiding principle should be the brief given to the researcher at the outset of the project.

5. MARKETING INFORMATION SYSTEMS

5.1 Marketing information systems (MIS, or sometimes MKIS) represent a systematic attempt to supply continuous, useful, usable marketing information within an organisation to decision makers, often in the form of a database. Individual market research projects can be seen as an integral part of the MIS.

5.2 The design of an MIS should start with the information needs of decision-makers rather than with technical considerations of the database. It has three components which need to be planned.

    (a) *System inputs*

        The sources of information which can form an input to an MIS are, in principle, the same as those discussed aboveYthat is, internal and external sources and primary research. The starting point is very likely to be existing customer account records. These sources can be used to identify the types of service which each type of customer is buying along with trend data. These records can be amended as necessary over time and can be augmented by specific market research projects so as to provide a complete picture.

    (b) *Data manipulation*

        Once collected, the data needs to be manipulated into a suitable form for use by decision-makers. Again, the principles of this manipulation are those noted in the earlier part of this Section in that the mass of information needs to be summarised so that trends and major features can be identified.

    (c) *System outputs*

        Once manipulated into a form in which the information can be used by decision makers, outputs from the system can be determined. Information can be applied to the whole range of marketing decisions.

6. CONCLUSION

6.1 Marketing research has been a growing source of organisation expenditure in recent years. Very few organisations believe that they can shoulder the cost of a large full-time staff of marketing research workers, especially a 'field force' of researchers spread around the country. It is quite probable, therefore, that:

    (a) the organisation will have a small full-time marketing research department, and

    (b) use the services of external marketing research consultants for specific projects. In addition to market research agencies, there are market research departments in many of the large UK advertising agencies.

6.2 An external agency would bring *expertise* in marketing research which an organisation might not be able to supply in-house, although it would need to liaise with the organisation through its marketing research department.

6.3 A further advantage of marketing research agencies is that they may bring together their general knowledge of a particular market and supply this information to all clients or subscribers. An example of such information provision is the Television Consumer Audit.

6.4 Marketing research enables companies to gain information on the market and marketing mix variables and therefore to make decisions in the light of this information. The tools of marketing are often termed as the Four P's, that is product, price, place and promotion. It is to these we now turn our attention, firstly with 'place' aspects or as often termed 'distribution'.

TEST YOUR KNOWLEDGE

Numbers in brackets refer to paragraphs of this chapter

1 Differentiate between market research and marketing research. (1.4)

2 What is involved in (i) price research and (ii) distribution research? (2.1)

3 What is a market forecast? (2.13)

4 What is a concentration ratio? (2.21)

5 Give examples of market signals. (2.26)

6 Secondary data is collected directly by the user. True or false? (3.3)

7 What is field research? (4.1)

8 Why is a sampling frame necessary to make a truly random sample? (4.8)

9 Explain how systematic sampling is used. (4.15)

10 What are the major advantage and disadvantage of quota sampling? (4.20)

11 List the potential faults which may occur in sampling. (4.25)

12 What is a diary panel? (4.36)

13 What details are provided by trade and retail panels? (4.39)

14 List the drawbacks to test marketing. (4.49)

15 How can EPOS data be used in market research? (4.51)

Now try questions 3 to 5 at the end of the text

Chapter 3

DISTRIBUTION

This chapter covers the following topics.

1. What are distribution channels?
2. Types of distribution channel
3. Channel dynamics
4. International channels
5. Logistics management

---

1. WHAT ARE DISTRIBUTION CHANNELS?

1.1 The fourth 'P' in the marketing mix is place and this component is essentially concerned with the processes by which the product is made available to the consumer. Other more commonly used terms for 'place' include distribution, delivery systems and marketing channels. The terms are often used interchangeably since they all concern themselves with making products available to the market. Although place is normally the last element in the list of marketing mix variables, its importance should not be underestimated, especially in provision of services. After all, a considerable amount of marketing effort will be wasted if the product is not actually in the right place at the right time to enable a purchase to be made. Furthermore, it is beneficial to any organisation to give thorough consideration to the place component of the marketing mix since effective and efficient distribution can be an important source of competitive advantage.

1.2 Distribution is often seen as the Cinderella of the marketing mix. In companies where distribution involves the physical transport of goods and stores, the marketing executive may have insufficient control over the distribution function, resulting in a lack of real co-ordination within the marketing mix. However, the choice of a particular distribution policy, such as whether or not to use wholesalers, may result in the company delegating to intermediaries much of its marketing function, such as selling to the end user.

1.3 It is important to recognise that independently owned and operated distributors have their own objectives, strategies and plans which, in their decision making processes, are likely to take precedence over those of the manufacturer or supplier with whom they are dealing. This fact can lead to conflict and in some cases suppliers solve the problem by buying their own distribution route or by distributing direct to their customers. Direct distribution is common for many industrial and/or customised systems suppliers. In some consumer markets direct distribution is also in evidence, for instance for insurance ('the man from the Pru'), double glazing and Avon cosmetics.

1.4 However a product is distributed a number of basic distributive functions usually need to be fulfilled.

(a) *Transport*

This function can be provided by the supplier or by the distributor or indeed can be sub-contracted to a specialist. For some products, such as perishable goods, transport planning is vital. The 'rent or buy' decision on transport is important and has both financial and operational consequences.

(b) *Stock holding and storage*

For production planning purposes a smooth flow of production is often essential, so stocks of raw materials and components accumulate and need to be stored. Significant costs and risks can be involved in holding stock.

For consumer goods, the costs of holding stock at the point of sale is very expensive; the cost of city centre retail locations is prohibitive and a good stock control system must be used, designed to avoid stockouts whilst keeping stockholding costs low.

(c) *Local knowledge*

As production has tended to become centralised to obtain maximum economies of scale, the need to understand local markets has grown. This point applies particularly when international marketing takes place. To understand the intricacies and idiosyncrasies of local markets is a key marketing input. Whilst it is possible to buy specialist market research help, the local distributor with day to day customer contact has a vital role.

(d) *Promotion*

Whilst major promotional campaigns for national products are likely to be carried out by the supplier, the translation of the campaign to local level is usually the responsibility of the local distributor, often as a joint venture. Hence the advertising agency of the supplier will produce local advertising material which leaves space for the local distributor's name to be added. National press campaigns can feature lists of local stockists.

(e) *Display*

Presentation of the product at the local level is often a function of the local distributor. Again, specialist help from merchandisers can be bought in but decisions on layout and display need to be taken by local distributors, often following patterns produced centrally.

Points in the chain of distribution

1.5 *Retailers:* independent traders operating outlets selling directly to households.

Wholesalers: an intermediary who sells a range of products from competing manufacturers to sell to other business organisations such as retailers.

Agents and brokers: intermediaries acting on behalf of the manufacturer and earning commissions on sales.

Distributors: similar function to a wholesaler but usually offering a narrower product range. Can be an exclusive distributor. In addition to selling on the manufacturer's product, distributors often promote the product and provide after sales service.

Specialist service organisations: manufacturers may need to use other market intermediaries with special expertise or facilities, such as commodity exchanges, freight carriers, credit agencies, finance companies, advertising and market research agencies.

2.   TYPES OF DISTRIBUTION CHANNEL

2.1   The choice of distribution channels is an important one for any organisation, not least because once a set of channels has been established, subsequent changes can be costly and are likely to be slow to implement. In very broad terms we can consider distribution channels as falling into one of two categories: *direct* and *indirect channels*. The distinction is fairly crude, but nevertheless useful.

2.2   *Direct distribution* concerns itself with ways in which the product can be supplied directly from producer to consumer without the use of a specific intermediary. These methods are often described as active since they typically involve the supplier making the first approach to a potential customer. Direct distribution methods generally fall into two categories: those using *media* such as the press, leaflets and telephones to invite reponse and purchase by the consumer and those using a *sales force* to contact consumers face to face.

2.3   The alternative type of distribution system is *indirect distribution* which typically refers to systems of distribution, common among manufactured goods, which make use of an intermediary; usually a wholesaler, retailer or both. In contrast to direct distribution, these methods are often thought of as being passive in the sense that they rely on consumers to make the first approach by entering the relevant retail outlet.

Channel design decisions

2.4   In setting up a channel of distribution, the supplier has to take into account a number of factors and influences: customers, product characteristics, distribution characteristics, the channel chosen by competitors and the supplier's own characteristics.

Customers

2.5   The number of potential customers, their buying habits and their geographical locations are key influences. The use of mail order for those with limited mobility (rural location, illness) is an example of the influence of customers on channel design. Marketing industrial components to the car industry needs to take account of location of the car industry in the UK. Selling to supermarket chains in the UK is now very difficult as the concentration of grocery retailing into a few large chains has increased the power of the buyers: specialist centralised buyers can extract highly favourable terms from suppliers. Unless the supplier is successful in selling to the big chains, the product will only be available to small numbers of shoppers each week.

3: DISTRIBUTION

Product characteristics

2.6 Some product characteristics have an important effect on design of the channel of distribution:

(a) *Perishability*
Fresh fruit and newspapers are examples of perishable products which must be distributed very quickly or they become worthless. Speed is therefore a key factor in the design of the distribution system.

(b) *Customisation*
Customised products tend to be distributed direct. Where a wide range of options are available, such as fitted kitchens, sales are made from demonstration units with customised delivery to follow.

(c) *After sales service/technical advice*
When these are to be offered, the extent and cost must be considered, training given and quality control systems set up. Training programmes are often provided for distributors by suppliers. Exclusive area franchises can be allocated to ensure distributor co-operation; the disadvantage of this is that a poor distributor may cost a supplier dearly in a particular area.

(d) *Franchising*
Franchising has become a popular means of growth both for suppliers like Body Shop and for franchisees who carry the set-up costs and licence fees and are clearly controlled by the supplier. The supplier gains more outlets more quickly and exerts more control than is usual in distribution.

Distributor characteristics

2.7 The capability of the distributor to take on the distributive functions already discussed above is obviously an important choice influence for the supplier.

Competitors' channel choice

2.8 For many consumer goods, a supplier's brand will sit side by side with its competitors' products and there is little the supplier can do about it. For other products it is common for distributors to stock one name brand only (for example, in car distribution) and in return to be given an exclusive area. In this case new suppliers can face difficulties in breaking into a market if all the best distribution outlets have been taken up.

Supplier characteristics

2.9 A strong financial base offers the supplier the option of buying and operating a distribution channel: Boots the Chemist is a prime example. The market position of the supplier is also important: distributors are keen to be associated with the market leader but the third, fourth or fifth brand in a market is likely to find more distribution problems.

3: DISTRIBUTION

Making the channel decision

2.10 The above considerations can be translated into a number of decision options.

(a) What types of distributor are to be used (wholesalers, retailers, agents)?

(b) How many of each type will be used? The answer to this depends on what degree of market exposure will be sought:

    (i) intensive - blanket coverage;
    (ii) exclusive - appointed agents for exclusive areas;
    (iii) selective - some but not all in each area;

(c) Who will carry out specific marketing tasks such as:

    (i) credit provision;
    (ii) delivery;
    (iii) after sales service;
    (iv) training (sales and product);
    (v) display?

(d) How will performance of distributors be evaluated?

    (i) In terms of cost?
    (ii) In terms of sales levels?
    (iii) According to the degree of control achieved?
    (iv) By the amount of conflict that arises?

2.11 To sum up, to develop an integrated system of distribution, the supplier must consider all the factors influencing distribution combined with a knowledge of the relative merits of the different types of channel available.

Factors favouring the use of direct selling

2.12 (a) There may be a need for an expert sales force to demonstrate products, explain product characteristics and provide after sales service. Publishers, for example, use sales reps to keep booksellers up to date with new titles, to arrange for the return of unsold books and so on.

(b) Intermediaries may be unwilling or unable to sell the product. For example, the ill fated Sinclair C5 eventually had to be sold by direct mail.

(c) Existing channels may be tied to other producers or reluctant to carry new product lines.

(d) The intermediaries willing to sell the product may be too expensive. After all, they make their profits from selling goods for more than they pay for them. Alternatively, they may not be maximising potential sales. This is the problem which caused Nissan to terminate its contract with its sole UK distributor in 1991: Nissan believed that the distributor's pricing strategy was inappropriate.

(e) If specialised transport requirements are required intermediaries may not be able to deliver goods to the final customer.

    (f)   Where potential buyers are geographically concentrated it is easy for the supplier's own sales force to reach them (typically an industrial market). One example is the financial services market centred on the City of London.

Factors favouring the use of intermediaries

2.13 These are as follows.

    (a)   There may be insufficient financial resources to finance the extra overhead of a large sales force.

    (b)   It may be a policy decision to invest in increased productive capacity rather than extra marketing effort.

    (c)   The supplier may not have sufficient in-house marketing 'knowhow' in selling to retail stores, such as lack of shelf-space allocation skills.

    (d)   The assortment of products may be insufficient for a sales force to carry. A wholesaler can complement a limited range and make more efficient use of his sales force.

    (e)   Intermediaries can market small lots as part of a range of goods. The supplier would incur a heavy sales overhead if its own sales force took 'small' individual orders.

    (f)   There may be large numbers of potential buyers over a wide geographical spread (typically consumer markets).

Multi-channel decisions

2.14 A producer serving both industrial and consumer markets may decide to use intermediaries for his consumer division and direct selling for his industrial division. For example, a detergent manufacturer might employ salesmen to sell to wholesalers and large retail groups in their consumer division. It would not be efficient for the sales force to approach small retailers directly.

The distribution channels appropriate for industrial markets may not be suitable for consumer markets. The common channels for each sector will now be outlined.

Industrial and consumer distribution channels

2.15 *Industrial markets* may be characterised by having fewer, larger customers often purchasing expensive products that may be custom built. It is due to these characteristics that industrial distribution channels tend to be more direct and shorter than for consumer markets. It has to be remembered, however, that the most appropriate distribution channels will depend specifically on the objectives of the company regarding market exposure. There are specialist distributors in the industrial sector, which may be used as well as, or instead of, selling directly to the companies within this sector.

2.16 There are fewer direct distribution channels, from the manufacturer to the consumer in the *consumer market*. Examples can be found in small 'cottage' industries or mail order companies. It is more usual for companies in consumer markets to use wholesalers and retailers to move their product to the final consumer.

3: DISTRIBUTION

(a) *Wholesalers* break down the bulk from manufacturers and pass products on to retailers. In doing so they take on some of the supplier's risks by funding stock. Recently in the UK there has been a reduction in importance of this type of intermediary.

(b) *Retailers* sell to the final consumers. In so doing they may give consumers added satisfaction by providing services such as credit, delivery and a wide variety of goods. In the UK, retailers have increased in power whilst wholesalers have decreased. Retailing has also become more concentrated with increased dominance of large multiples.

Distribution strategy

2.17 There are three main strategies.

(a) Intensive distribution involves concentrating marketing effort on a segment of the total market, such as choosing limited geographical distribution rather than national distribution.

(b) Using *selective distribution*, the producer selects a group of retail outlets from amongst all retail outlets. The choice may be on grounds of the brand image ('quality' outlets), or the choice may be related to the retailers' capacity to provide after sales service. Rolls Royce's image is safe in the hands of H R Owen but would be damaged if sold by an 'Arthur Daley'.

(c) *Exclusive distribution* is an extension of selective distribution. Particular outlets are granted exclusive handling rights within a prescribed geographical area. Sometimes exclusive distribution or franchise rights are coupled with making special financial arrangements for land, buildings or equipment, such as petrol station agreements.

2.18 *Selective* and *exclusive distribution* have been criticised by the European Commission as being restraints on competition (Articles 65 and 66 Treaty of Rome). Grundigs, who had earlier refused to sell through the Comet electrical discount stores, could have run foul of this ruling. In the UK the Monopolies and Mergers Commission has criticised the brewers' 'tied house' system, a form of exclusive distribution.

3. CHANNEL DYNAMICS

3.1 Channels are subject to conflicts between members. This conflict need not be destructive as long as it is manageable. Manufacturers may have little influence on how their product is presented to the public by way of displays or maybe even final pricing. Conflicts are usually resolved by arbitration rather than judicial means.

(a) A distribution system with a central core organising marketing throughout the channel is termed a *vertical marketing system*. Vertical marketing systems provide channel role specification and co-ordination between members.

(b) In *corporate marketing systems* the stages in production and distribution are owned by one corporation. Because of this common ownership close integration becomes possible and therefore the corporation has control over activities along the distribution chain. An example on a small scale would be a farm shop, selling products produced on the farm. On a larger scale, Laura Ashley shops sell goods produced in Laura Ashley factories.

(c) *Contractual marketing systems* involve the agreement of aspects of distribution marketing. One example of a contractual marketing system that has become popular over the last decade is franchising.

(d) If a plan is drawn up between channel members to help reduce conflict this is often termed an *administered marketing system.*

3.2 Channel leadership by a member of the channel means that power lies with that member. We considered earlier in this section the changing power relationship between manufacturers and retailers in consumer goods markets. In industrial markets where channel lengths are generally shorter (more direct) then power often lies with manufacturers of products rather than 'middlemen'.

4. INTERNATIONAL CHANNELS

4.1 As more markets become open to international trade, then channel decisions become more complex. A company can export using host country middlemen or domestic middlemen. These may or may not take title of the goods. Implications of channel management in the case of exporters include, a loss of control over the product (price, image, packaging, service etc). A producer may undertake a joint venture or licensing agreement or even manufacture abroad. All will have implications for the power structure and control over the product.

5. LOGISTICS MANAGEMENT

5.1 Logistics management includes physical distribution and materials management. It therefore encompasses the inflow of raw materials and goods together with the outflow of finished products. Logistics management has developed because of an increased awareness of:

(a) customer benefits that can be incorporated into the overall product offering because of efficient logistics management;

(b) the cost savings that can be made when a logistics approach is undertaken;

(c) trends in industrial purchasing that necessarily mean closer links between buyers and sellers, for example Just in Time purchasing and computerised purchasing.

5.2 Logistics managers organise inventories, warehouses, purchasing and packaging to produce an efficient and effective overall system. There are benefits to consumers of products that are produced by companies with good logistic management. There is less likelihood of goods being out of stock, delivery should be efficient and overall service quality should be higher.

Example: the logistics industry

5.3 Contracted-out distribution services require enormous trust, especially in the food business. Sensitive information must be exchanged between the retailer or manufacturer and the distribution company and responsibility for food safety and hygiene must be shared. However, contracting out offers great benefits in terms of flexibility and the elimination of the need for costly capital investment: hence the success of specialist distribution companies such as

NFC, Christian Salvesen and Hays. Hays, for example, runs a distribution centre which delivers short-life food products to 97 Waitrose supermarkets. It receives goods from 200 suppliers and handles 2,500 chilled product lines and 440,000 cases of products a week.

Example: the paper industry and Just In Time purchasing

5.4 Distribution is now a critical factor in Europe's paper industry. Logistics is seen as a means of reducing costs and increasing efficiency, to counteract declining demand and 'dumping' of cut-price products from overseas. The *buyer* dominates the market and manufacturers therefore expect their distribution specialists to develop supply systems that result in zero damage and allow customers to minimise stockholding costs. One of the leading UK producers of paper for packaging has customers in the Benelux countries and northern France who expect orders to be delivered within 24 hours. The supplier is therefore having to set up warehouses to hold stock closer to the customers and speed up the delivery reaction time.

Exercise

Consider the following extract from a recent article in the *Financial Times* (September 1992).

'British Steel is aware of the stiff competition it faces in its planned assault on European mainland markets. Physical distribution is an important plank in its campaign and the costs and efficiency of the service will help determine the success or failure of the venture.

High on the agenda for discussion is the setting up of regional distribution centres closer to customers and the development of world class information technology (IT) links between production plants, distribution operators and customers.

Meanwhile, the company spends some £375m a year on shipping products to mainland Europe and tends to deal direct with transport operators and suppliers rather than go through forwarding agents.

Its sales in Europe represent about 2.5 per cent of the total European market and the objective is to achieve significant increases.

Its main European destinations are Italy, Germany and Spain, followed by France, Greece and the Netherlands.'

If you were the marketing manager of a *small* business contemplating the opportunities of the Single European Market would you be encouraged or discouraged by this article?

Solution

Initially you might be discouraged. It is more difficult to identify target markets in a foreign culture and there are language barriers, and problems of control to be overcome. The cost of overseas representation (people/offices or both) may be prohibitive.

On the other hand most of these barriers are pyschological rather than real. A relationship with an agent could be established. Costly investment in high tech systems may be unnecessary for the smaller business, especially if products are specialised, high value items. The potential for obtaining a share of the *total* European market as opposed to restricting operations to the domestic market must be a temptation.

---

6. CONCLUSION

6.1 Distribution is then a very important aspect of the marketing mix. Without an efficient system goods are less able to be delivered to the target customers. The options open to companies are vast, complicated if the company decides to export goods. Each way in which goods are distributed has advantages and disadvantages, although often this comes down to 'control' aspects. The longer the length of the distribution chain, usually the greater the loss of control over how the product is delivered. It is to the actual product we now turn our attention.

TEST YOUR KNOWLEDGE
Numbers in brackets refer to paragraphs of this chapter

1   Give examples of direct distribution in consumer markets. (1.3)

2   What effect do product characteristics have on channel design? (2.6)

3   Why use direct selling? (2.12)

4   List the factors favouring the use of intermediaries. (2.13)

5   Distinguish between intensive, selective and exclusive distribution. (2.17)

6   What is a vertical marketing system? (3.1)

7   To which type of marketing system does franchising belong? (3.1)

8   Why has logistics management developed? (5.1)

Now try questions 6 to 8 at the end of the text

Chapter 4

PRODUCT

```
This chapter covers the following topics.

1.  Product/market decisions
2.  Market segmentation
3.  The product life cycle
4.  Product portfolio planning
5.  Innovation management
6.  Services
7.  Brands and packaging
```

1. PRODUCT/MARKET DECISIONS

1.1 In order to grow, an organisation can decide to use particular combinations of product and market decisions. Ansoff expressed these options in terms of a diagram.

	Existing Products	*New Products*
Existing Markets	Market Penetration	Product Development
New Markets	Market Development	Diversification

1.2 *Market penetration* involves trying to increase the market share for existing products in existing markets. This aim could be achieved by better *market segmentation* (see below), that is by tailoring products more closely to the needs of target groups of customers within the existing market. The danger to be borne in mind with this strategy is of putting all the organisation's eggs in one basket.

1.3 *Product development* involves developing new products for the existing market. Using existing knowledge of customers and the existing distribution network it may be possible to extend the product range and increase sales. A danger is *cannibalisation:* that is, sales of new products may be achieved at the expense of existing products. Nevertheless, such a strategy may work if the new products make a greater contribution per unit to profit or if there is a danger that, without the new product, customers would switch from the existing product anyway, but to competitors' products.

1.4 *Market development* involves marketing existing products into new markets. Clearly, there is a need for market research to ensure a thorough understanding of the needs of the new market.

1.5 *Diversification*. The highest risk strategy is to enter new markets with new products. Not only is there a need to understand the new market but also intensive product development work is likely to be necessary.

2. MARKET SEGMENTATION

What is market segmentation?

2.1 It is obvious that not all of an organisation's customers are the same. Market segmentation is an attempt to take different customer characteristics into account. It is thus the subdivision of a market into subsets of customers. Within each subset, customers have similar needs which differ in some definable way from those in other subsets.

2.2 The major reason for segmenting markets is that, by using different marketing approaches to each segment, it should be possible to increase profit contribution when compared with using an undifferentiated marketing approach for the whole market. The marketing approach used for each segment should reflect the particular needs of customers and potential customers in that segment. It is akin to using a rifle (to aim at specific targets) rather than a shotgun (to aim at all targets at the same time).

Requirements for effective market segmentation

2.3 Clearly there are many possible characteristics of buyers which could be used as a basis for segmenting markets and there are criteria to be used to identify the most effective characteristics for use in market segmentation decisions.

(a) *Measurability*
The degree to which information exists or is obtainable cost effectively in respect of the particular buyer characteristic. Whilst a bookshop may be able to obtain information on sales relatively easily, it is more difficult for shops to obtain information about the personality traits of buyers.

(b) *Accessibility*
The degree to which the organisation can focus effectively on the chosen segments using marketing methods. Thus whilst educational establishments in a bookshop's catchment area can be identified easily and approached using direct mail or telemarketing, individuals with income over £30,000 per annum in the catchment area might be more difficult to isolate effectively.

(c) *Substantiality*
The degree to which the segments are large enough to be worth considering for separate marketing cultivation. Devising different marketing approaches is expensive, and so a minimum size of segment can be set and measured, perhaps by potential profitability. Thus, whilst a large number of people in social group DE aged over 65 could be identified, their potential profitability to a bookshop is likely to be less in the long term than a smaller number of 17-18 year old students. This latter group might be worth cultivating using a specially devised marketing approach whereas the former might not be.

4: PRODUCT

Benefits of market segmentation

2.4 Besides the overall aim of improved contribution to profits, a number of other benefits may result from successful market segmentation.

(a) The organisation will be in a better position to spot new marketing opportunities. This benefit should flow from a better understanding of customer needs in each segment.

(b) Specialists can be used for each of the organisation's major segments. Thus, small business counsellors can be employed by banks to deal effectively with this market segment, and a computer consultancy can have specialist sales staff for, say, shops, manufacturers, service industries and local authorities.

(c) The total marketing budget can be allocated to take into account the needs of each segment and the likely return from each segment.

(d) The organisation can make fine adjustments to the product and service offerings and to the marketing appeals used for each segment.

(e) The organisation can try to dominate particular segments, thus gaining competitive advantage.

(f) The product range can more closely reflect differences in customer needs.

Bases for market segmentation

2.5 A number of different bases for segmenting a market will now be considered which could be (either alone or in combination) suitable for use by many organisations.

2.6 *Geographic segmentation*
Here, the basis for segmentation is location. Consider the example of a national chain of supermarkets: geographic segmentation interacts closely with the chain's outlet strategy. Each branch or group of retail outlets could be given mutually exclusive areas to service and so the method enables the supermarket chain to make more effective use of target marketing. The obvious advantage to customers is convenience of access, which is a primary motivation to retailers when considering ways of segmenting the grocery shopping market. Of course this customer benefit needs to be considered against the cost of provision of retail branches, but research has shown that one of the major reasons why customers choose particular stores in which to shop is convenience of access.

2.7 *Demographic segmentation*
Here the market is divided on the basis of age, gender, socio-economic group, housing, family characteristics or family life cycle stage, or by some combination of these factors.

2.8 A good example of *age segmentation* in target marketing is the attempt by the High Street banks to attract 18 year olds as customers, especially new students in the higher education sector. Working on the premise that customers are unlikely to switch accounts between competing suppliers, banks expect long-term relationships (and profit) to result from success in this target marketing effort. It is a highly competitive market segment.

2.9 Many products are targeted by *gender*. Cosmetics, clothing, alcohol, cars and even financial services are all products in which the market can be perceived to be segmented by gender.

2.10 The UK market research industry uses standardised social groupings which are based entirely on occupation.

Socio-economic groups in the UK

Social grade	Description of occupations	Example
A	Higher managerial and professional	Company director
B	Lower managerial and supervisory	Middle manager
C1	Non-manual	Bank clerk
C2	Skilled manual	Electrician
D	Semi-skilled and unskilled manual	Labourer
E	Those receiving no income from employment/casual workers	Unemployed

2.11 This classification is very commonly used in marketing and market research in the UK, yet it is simplistic. For example, in terms of disposable income (the take-home pay of workers) C2 members often have more money than do C1, which obviously affects buying capability. Also there is class mobility in that individuals and their families can move between groups, although their underlying influences may remain as they were or change only slowly.

2.12 However, socio-economic groups are a useful and usable way of segmenting markets for the following reasons:

(a) they provide a generally reliable picture of the relationship between occupation and income;

(b) they indicate differences in purchase and consumption patterns even where the total disposable income between two groups may be similar;

(c) the categories are stable and enduring;

(d) each group carries identifiable attitude patterns. For instance, ABCI groups tend to be more 'future orientated' than do C2DE groups which are more 'present orientated'. Such attitudes are clearly highly significant for the marketing of endowment policies or private education, for example.

2.13 Because of criticisms of the A-E classification, more sophisticated measures of socio-economic and group membership have been devised. Housing type and ownership are particularly important methods of segmentation for many types of good. The use of this method is made much easier by the major categorisation scheme for all housing types in the UK, known as ACORN (A Categorisation Of Residential Neighbourhoods), which enables precise target marketing based on housing type to be conducted by suppliers.

4: PRODUCT

2.14 This system introduces house type into the classification and every UK household has been classified in ACORN groups. Other work has cross-referenced ACORN with postcodes for every address in the UK making specific identification of customer types more flexible.

1985 ACORN profile of Great Britain

ACORN Groups		1985 Population	%
A	Agricultural areas	1,837,585	3.4
B	Modern family housing, Higher incomes	9,056,851	16.8
C	Older housing of intermediate status	9,519,639	17.7
D	Older terraced housing	2,309,097	4.3
E	Council estates - category I	7,015,875	13.0
F	Council estates - category II	4,892,746	9.1
G	Council estates - category III	3,935,124	7.3
H	Mixed inner metropolitan areas	2,088,892	3.9
I	High status non-family areas	2,265,371	4.2
J	Affluent suburban housing	8,531,179	15.9
K	Better-off retirement areas	2,048,658	3.8

ACORN Types		1985 Population	%
A1	Agricultural villages	1,404,704	2.6
A2	Areas of farms and smallholdings	432,881	0.8
B3	Post-war functional private housing	2,276,963	4.2
B4	Modern private housing, young families	1,805,955	3.4
B5	Established private family housing	3,173,195	5.9
B6	New detached houses, young families	1,475,680	2.7
B7	Military bases	325,058	0.6
C8	Mixed owner-occupied and council estates	1,877,008	3.5
C9	Small town centres and flats above shops	2,185,911	4.1
C10	Villages with non-farm employment	2,523,830	4.7
C11	Older private housing, skilled workers	2,932,890	5.5
D12	Unmodernised terraces, older people	1,349,349	2.5
D13	Older terraces, lower income families	752,530	1.4
D14	Tenement flats lacking amenities	207,218	0.4
E15	Council estates, well-off older workers	1,879,887	3.5
E16	Recent council estates	1,460,237	2.7

4: PRODUCT

ACORN Types		1985 Population	%
E17	Better council estates, younger workers	2,642,427	4.9
E18	Small council houses, often Scottish	1,033,324	1.9
F19	Low rise estates in industrial towns	2,498,587	4.6
F20	Inter-war council estates, older people	1,607,711	3.0
F21	Council housing, elderly people	786,448	1.5
G22	New council estates in inner cities	1,075,117	2.0
G23	Overspill estates, higher unemployment	1,678,631	3.1
G24	Council estate with some overcrowding	839,998	1.6
G25	Council estates with greatest hardship	341,378	0.6
H26	Multi-occupied older housing	204,279	0.4
H27	Cosmopolitan owner-occupied terraces	577,592	1.1
H28	Multi-let housing in cosmoplitan areas	388,292	0.7
H29	Better -off cosmopolitan areas	918,729	1.7
I30	High status non-family areas	1,132,770	2.1
I31	Multi-let big old houses and flats	833,500	1.5
I32	Furnished flats, mostly single people	299,101	0.6
J33	Inter-war semis, white collar workers	3,056,752	5.7
J34	Spacious inter-war semis, big gardens	2,671,266	5.0
J35	Villages with wealthy older commuters	1,560,179	2.9
J36	Detached houses, exclusive suburbs	1,242,982	2.3
K37	Private houses, well-off older residents	1,204,778	2.2
K38	Private flats, older single people	843,880	1.6
U39	Unclassified	294,080	0.5
Area Total		53,795,097	100.0

4: PRODUCT

2.15 Another method of segmentation is based on the family type: the size and constitution of the family unit. There have been changes in the characteristics of the family unit in the last few decades; this is shown in the table below.

Households by type

	1961		1971		1981	
	Million	% of total	Million	% of total	Million	% of total
One person, under retirement age	0.7	4	1.1	6	1.5	8
One person, over retirement age	1.2	7	2.2	12	2.8	14
Two or more persons (non-family)	0.8	5	0.7	4	0.9	5
Married couple alone	4.1	26	4.9	27	5.0	26
Married couple + dependent child(ren)	6.1	38	6.3	34	6.0	31
Married couple + independent child(ren)	1.7	10	1.6	8	1.6	8
Lone parent + dependent child(ren)	0.4	2	0.5	3	0.9	5
Lone parent + independent child(ren)	0.7	4	0.7	4	0.7	4
Two or more families	0.4	3	0.3	1	0.2	1
Total	16.2		18.3		19.5	

Percentages may not add up due to rounding. *Source:* Social Trends 15.

2.16 An increase in the divorce rate is one of the factors which has led to an increase in single parent families and a decline in the 'traditional' family of working husband, housewife and dependent children. The increase in unemployment in the early 1980s was weighted towards males in traditional industries and the subsequent increase in employment in the late 1980s was weighted towards females in service-orientated industries, often involving part-time rather than full-time work. Thus one would now expect to find more households in which the sole or main breadwinner is female rather than male.

2.17 These household structural changes have been accompanied by other important social trends:

(a) later marriage and delayed childbearing;

(b) house price rises have meant that newly formed households contain partners who both work;

(c) the 'enterprise economy' has encouraged a greater interest in career development;

(d) greater financial independence for women caused by recent economic and social changes;

(e) products aimed at the increased number of 'single person of pensionable age' households are also likely to increase.

2.18 The implication for marketing is that new niche markets are likely to grow whilst traditional markets may be declining. The use of customer databases to direct more specific target marketing may be one solution, as may product proliferation.

2.19 The *family life cycle (FLC)* is a summary demographic variable; that is, it combines the effects of age, marital status, career status (income) and the presence or absence of children. Herein lies its appeal, for it is able to identify the various stages through which households progress. The table below shows features of the family at various stages of its life cycle. It is clear that particular products and services can be target-marketed at specific stages in the life cycle of families.

Table 4.3: The family life cycle

	I	II	III	IV	V	VI	VII	VIII	IX
Stage	Bachelor Stage: young single people not living at home	Newly married couples; young, no children	Full nest I: youngest child under six	Full nest II: youngest child six or over	Full nest III: older married couples with dependent children	Empty nest I: older married couples, no children living with them, head of family still in labour force	Empty nest II: older married couples, no children living at home, head of family retired	Solitary survivor in labour force	Solitary survivor(s) retired
Features	Few financial burdens. Fashion/ opinion leader led. Recreation orientated. Buy: Basic kitchen equipment, basic furniture, cars, equipment for the mating game holidays. Experiment with patterns of personal financial management and control.	Better off financially than they will be in the near future. High levels of purchase of homes and consumer durable goods. Buy: Cars, fridges, cookers, life assurance, durable furniture, holidays. Establish patterns of personal financial management and control.	Home purchasing at peak. Liquid assets/savings low. Dissatisfied with financial position and amount of money saved. Reliance on credit finance, credit cards, overdrafts etc. Child dominated household. Buy necessities: washers, dryers, baby food and clothes, vitamins, toys, books etc.	Financial position better. Some wives return to work. Child dominated household. Buy necessities: foods, cleaning material, clothes, bicycles, sports gear, music lessons, pianos, holidays etc.	Financial position still better. More wives work. School and examination dominated household. Some children get first jobs; others in further/higher education. Expenditure to support children's further/higher education. Buy: New, more tasteful furniture, non-necessary appliances, boats etc: holidays.	Home ownership at peak. More satisfied with financial position and money saved. Interested in travel, recreation, self-education. Make financial gifts and contributions. Children gain qualifications; move to Stage I. Buy luxuries, home improvements eg. fitted kitchens etc.	Significant cut in income. Keep home. Buy: medical appliances or medical care, products which aid health, sleep and digestion. Assist children. Concern with level of savings and pension. Some expenditure on hobbies and pastimes.	Income still adequate but likely to sell family home and purchase smaller accommodation. Concern with level of savings and pension. Some expenditure on hobbies and pastimes. Worries about security and dependence.	Significant cut in income. Additional medical requirements. Special need for attention, affection and security. May seek sheltered accommodation. Possible dependence on others for personal financial management and control.

2.20 Demographic segmentation methods are powerful tools to specify target market segments. This conclusion is particularly true when each of the bases is used in combination with other methods, since it is clear that the bases for demographic segmentation are not independent but are interdependent. Age and family life cycle stage are linked, as are housing and socio-economic groups. By using bases in combination it is possible to be highly specific in selecting targets for marketing campaigns.

Psychographic segmentation

2.21 Psychographics or *lifestyle segmentation* is a method which seeks to classify people according to their values, opinions, personality characteristics and interests; by its inherent nature it should be very dynamic. In today's competitive world where innovation is the key to improved organisational performance a system which is able to introduce new perspectives is worthy of investigation. Lifestyle segmentation fits this criterion because it deals with the person as opposed to the product and attempts to discover the particular unique lifestyle patterns of customers, which will give a richer insight into their preferences for various products and services. Lifestyle refers to 'distinctive ways of living adopted by particular communities or subsections of society.' Lifestyle is a manifestation of a number of behavioural factors, such as motivation, personality and culture. Its use in marketing depends on accurate description, and the numbers of people following a particular lifestyle must be quantified. Then marketers can assign and target products and promotion at particular target lifestyle groups. Lifestyle is a controversial issue, and a full analysis of the arguments is beyond the scope of this text. Its implications for marketing, and the problems of definition involved, can perhaps best be illustrated by some examples.

2.22 One simple example generalises lifestyle in terms of four categories, as follows.

(a) *Upwardly mobile, ambitious:* seeking a better and more affluent lifestyle, principally through better paid and more interesting work, and a higher material standard of living. A customer with such a lifestyle will be prepared to try new products.

(b) *Traditional and sociable:* compliance and conformity to group norms bring social approval and reassurance to the individual. Purchasing patterns will therefore be 'conformist'.

(c) *Security and status seeking:* stressing 'safety' and 'ego-defensive' needs. This lifestyle links status, income and security. It encourages the purchase of strong and well known products and brands, and emphasises those products and services which confer status and make life as secure and predictable as possible. These would include insurance, membership of the AA or RAC etc. Products that are well established and familiar inspire more confidence than new products, which will be resisted.

(d) *Hedonistic preference:* placing emphasis on 'enjoying life now' and the immediate satisfaction of wants and needs. Little thought is given to the future.

2.23 Two more complex lifestyle analyses are shown in the table below. These sets of analysis are based on empirical attitude research, and the agencies that have constructed them use them to advise their clients on how best to design and position existing and new products at target segments made up of people who have similar lifestyle patterns.

Life-style categories

McCann-Erikson Men

Avant Guardians. Concerned with change and well-being of others, rather than possessions. Well educated, prone to self righteousness.

Pontificators. Strongly held, traditional opinions. Very British, and concerned about keeping others on the right path.

Chameleons. Want to be contemporary to win approval. Act like barometers of social change, but copiers not leaders.

Self-admirers. At the young end of the spectrum. Intolerant of others and strongly motivated by success. Concerned about self-image.

Self-exploiters. The 'doers' and 'self-starters', competitive but always under pressure and often pessimistic. Possessions are important.

Token triers. Always willing to try new things to 'improve their luck', but apparently on a permanent try-and-fail cycle. Includes an above average proportion of unemployed.

Sleepwalkers. Contented under-achievers. Do not care about most things, and actively opt out. Traditional macho views.

Passive endurers. Biased towards the elderly, they are often economically and socially disfranchised. Expect little of life, and give little.

McCann-Erikson Women

Avant Guardians. 'Liberal left' opinions, trendy attitudes. But out-going, active, sociable.

Lady Righteous. Traditional, 'right-minded' opinions. Happy, complacent, with strong family orientation.

Hopeful seekers. Need to be liked, want to do 'right'. Like new things, want to be trendy.

Lively ladies. Younger than above, sensual, materialistic, ambitious and competitive.

New unromantics. Generally young and single, adopting a hard-headed and unsentimental approach to life. Independent, self-centred.

Lack-a-daisy. Unassertive and easy-going. Try to cope but often fail. Not very interested in the new.

Blinkered. Negative, do not want to be disturbed. Uninterested in conventional success - in fact, few interests except TV and radio.

Down-trodden. This group is shy, introverted, but put upon. Would like to do better. Often unhappy and pressurised in personal relationships.

Taylor Nelson

Self-explorers. Motivated by self-expression and self-realisation. Less materialistic than other groups, and showing high tolerance levels.

Social resisters. The caring group, concerned with fairness and social values, but often appearing intolerant and moralistic.

Experimentalists. Highly individualistic, motivated by fast-moving enjoyment. They are materialistic, pro-technology but anti-traditional authority.

Conspicuous consumers. They are materialistic and pushy, motivated by acquisition, competition, and getting ahead. Pro-authority, law and order.

Belongers. What they seek is a quiet, undisturbed family life. They are conservative, con-ventional rule followers.

Survivors. Strongly class-conscious, and community spirited, their motivation is to 'get by'.

Aimless. Comprises two groups, (a) the young unemployed, who are often anti-authority, and (b) the old, whose motivation is day-to-day existence.

2.24 It is possible to gain further insights into lifestyle behaviour by cross-referring demographic variables to observed behaviour which indicates lifestyle types. The table below gives one example relating to leisure, social and travel facilities.

Profiles by sex, age and social grade, of users of various leisure, social and travel facilities.

	all adults	travel by air (in past 3 years)	use London underground	visit cinemas	visit pubs	visit licensed clubs	visit rest-aurants (day)	visit rest-aurants (evenings)	used Yellow Pages in last 4 weeks	listen to Radio Luxembourg
Population (in 000's)	44,150 %	15,333 %	13,397 %	15,749 %	30,300 %	16,411 %	17,590 %	22,881 %	16,990 %	4,417 %
All adults	100.0	100.0	100.0	100.0	100.0	100.0	100.0	100.0	100.0	100.0
Men	47.9	49.1	52.9	50.2	52.6	54.1	43.3	49.6	51.7	53.6
Women	52.1	50.9	47.1	49.8	47.4	45.9	56.7	50.4	48.3	46.4
15–24	20.0	20.8	22.2	35.6	24.5	28.7	16.0	22.2	21.0	42.7
25–34	17.0	19.1	18.6	23.6	21.6	19.4	15.8	22.4	21.6	20.8
35–44	16.3	16.5	18.6	19.2	19.0	17.0	17.9	20.2	19.6	12.9
45–54	13.8	15.2	15.2	10.9	13.7	13.0	15.0	15.7	14.3	8.2
55–64	14.5	14.9	13.3	7.0	11.4	11.8	15.5	11.5	12.1	6.7
65 or over	18.4	13.5	12.1	3.8	9.8	10.0	19.7	8.0	11.4	8.7
AB	16.7	26.5	28.9	23.9	18.3	13.1	24.1	23.6	23.1	10.9
C1	22.1	27.6	27.9	26.3	24.6	23.0	26.8	26.6	24.9	20.8
C2	28.8	26.7	24.8	28.4	30.1	33.1	25.5	29.6	29.0	33.7
D	18.1	12.3	11.4	14.2	17.1	19.6	13.4	13.6	14.4	20.1
E	14.3	7.0	7.1	7.3	10.0	11.2	10.2	6.6	8.5	14.4

Geo-demographic segmentation

2.25 Geo-demographics is a segmentation technique which was introduced in the early 1980s, but came into its own in the late 1980s and early 1990s. Basically, it is an approach which classifies people by where they live. It is rooted in the belief that households within a particular neighbourhood exhibit similar purchasing behaviour, outlook and so on: 'birds of a feather flock together'.

2.26 The central themes of geo-demographics was outlined by one leading market research expert as:

'... that two people who live in the same neighbourhood, such as a Census Enumeration District, are more likely to have similar characteristics than are two people chosen at random. The second is that neighbourhoods can be categorised in terms of the characteristics of the population which they contain, and that two neighbourhoods can be placed in the same category, that is they can contain similar types of people, even though they are widely separated'.

2.27 Geo-demographics is thus able to target customers in particular areas who exhibit similar behaviour patterns. The implication for organisations is very significant, as this system allows them to profile the users or potential users of a product or service and then proceed to target customers who match these profiles. This of course should increase the profitability and take-up of the offered product/service.

Customer database

2.28 It should be clear from the above discussion of segmentation methods that for large scale usage of the more sophisticated methods to be used effectively, computerised systems have to be adopted. These systems can often be used by organisations which actually hold detailed data on customers, such as banks, building societies and insurance companies. The systems are based on the array of data held about each customer in a relational database. In other words, a sub-sample of customers could be formed by the use of any one specifying variable (or combination of variables). Thus all customers aged 18-24 could be identified, for the development of long-term relations, as discussed above, as could all customers aged 25-34 with incomes over £20,000 pa and who live in ACORN type B6 housing.

Direct mailing

2.29 Such customer database systems allow highly specific target marketing. The most obvious marketing use is by direct mail methods, the particular advantage of which is the capability for exact monitoring of results using the computer system. The costs of each mailshot can be related to the increase in business which results and the types of customers who do buy can be used to refine the target marketing further.

Exercise 1

C2 met C1 and fell in love. They moved to FLCII and lived in a C11. He was a belonger and she was lady righteous: it would not be long before they reached stage III of the FLC!

What are we talking about?

---

3. THE PRODUCT LIFE CYCLE

3.1 This is a concept that is frequently found in the marketing literature. However, it is not without its critics and there is little good empirical evidence supporting its existence. The concept has an almost 'biological' basis. Products are born (or introduced), grow to reach maturity and then enter old age and decline.

3.2 Nevertheless, the product life cycle has proved to be a useful control device for monitoring the progress of new products after introduction. As Professor Robin Wensley of Warwick University puts it: 'The value of the product life cycle depends on its use, ie it has greater value as one goes down the scale from a predictive or forecasting tool, through a planning tool to a control tool.'

3.3 The profitability and sales position of a product can be expected to change over time. The 'product life cycle' is an attempt to recognise distinct stages in a product's sales history.

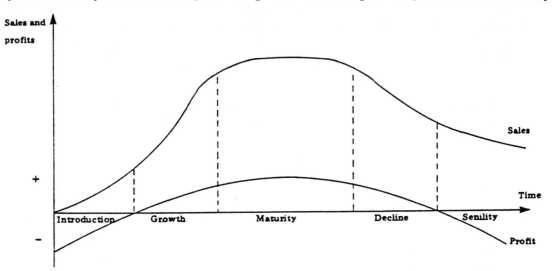

The classic representation of the product life cycle

(a) *Introduction:* a new product takes time to find acceptance by would be purchasers and there is a slow growth in sales. Only a few firms sell the product; unit costs are high because of low output; there may be early teething troubles with production technology and prices may be high to cover production costs and sales promotion expenditure as much as possible. For example, pocket calculators, video cassette recorders and mobile telephones were all very expensive when launched. The product for the time being is a loss maker.

(b) *Growth:* if the new product gains market acceptance, sales will eventually rise more sharply and the product will start to make profits. New customers buy the product and as production rises, unit costs fall. Since demand is strong, prices tend to remain fairly static for a time. However, the prospect of cheap mass production and a strong market will attract competitors so that the number of producers is increasing. With the increase of competition, manufacturers must spend a lot of money on product improvement, sales promotion and distribution to obtain a dominant or strong position in the market.

(c) *Maturity:* the rate of sales growth slows down and the product reaches a period of maturity which is probably the longest period of a successful product's life. Most products on the market will be at the mature stage of their life. Eventually sales will begin to decline so that there is overcapacity of production in the industry. Severe competition occurs, profits fall and some producers leave the market. The remaining producers seek means of prolonging the product life by modifying it and searching for new market segments.

(d) *Decline:* most products reach a stage of decline which may be slow or fast. Many producers are reluctant to leave the market, although some inevitably do because of falling profits. If a product remains on the market too long, it will become unprofitable and the decline stage in its life cycle then gives way to a 'senility' stage.

Buying participants through PLC stages

3.4 The introductory stage represents the highest risk in terms of purchasing a new, as yet untested product. Buyers reflect this: they typically consist of the relatively wealthy, to whom the risk of a loss is relatively small, and the young, who are more likely to make risky purchases.

3.5 In the growth and mature stages the mass market needs to be attracted. By the time decline sets in the product is well tested with all its faults 'ironed' out. At this stage enter the most risk averse buyers, termed *laggards*. These are the mirror image of those who participated in the introductory stage, being the poorer and older sections of the community.

Comparing products at different PLC stages

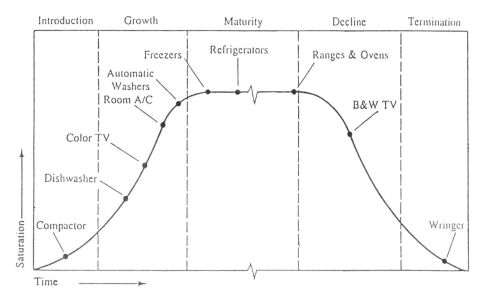

3.6 The above display of products at various stages through the PLC represents the USA in the late 1960s and early 1970s. Studies were conducted to establish whether or not there were significant differences in the purchasers of refrigerators in the mature stage and compacters (waste disposal units) in the introductory stage.

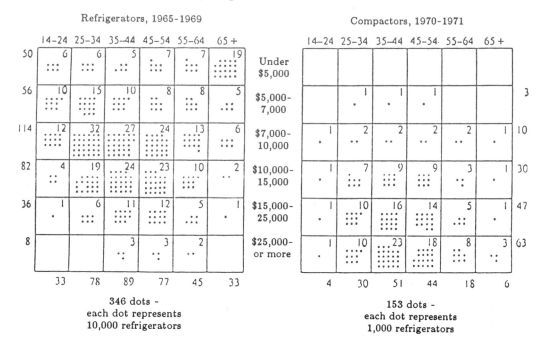

3.7 The above matrices show income on the vertical axis and age on the horizontal axis. It can be noted that the high income group with a family income of $10,000 or more make up some 90% of those purchasing compacters. There is also a noticeable lack of 65+ year olds. In contrast, the mature refrigerator market appears to reflect the complete population range.

4: PRODUCT

How are life cycles assessed?

3.8 It is perhaps easy enough to accept that products have a life cycle, but it is not so easy to sort out how far through its life a product is, and what its expected future life might be.

(a) There ought to be a regular review of existing products, as a part of marketing management responsibilities.

(b) Information should be obtained about the likely future of each product and sources of such information might be:

   (i)   an analysis of past trends;
   (ii)   the history of other products;
   (iii) market research;
   (iv)   if possible, an analysis of competitors.

The future of each product should be estimated in terms of both sales revenue and profits.

(c) Estimates of future life and profitability should be discussed with any experts available to give advice - for example R & D staff about product life, management accountants about costs and marketing staff about prices and demand.

3.9 Once the assessments have been made, decisions must be taken about what to do with each product. The choices are:

(a) to continue selling the product, with no foreseeable intention of stopping production;

(b) to initiate action to prolong a product's life, perhaps by advertising more, by trying to cut costs or raise prices, by improving distribution, or packaging or sales promotion methods, or by putting in more direct selling effort etc;

(c) to plan to stop producing the product and either to replace it with new ones in the same line or to diversify into new product-market areas.

3.10 Costs might be cut by improving productivity of the workforce, or by redesigning the product slightly, perhaps as a result of a value analysis study.

Exercise 2

Where do you consider the following products or services to be in their product life cycle?

(a) Mobile telephones
(b) Baked beans
(c) Satellite television
(d) Cigarettes
(e) Carbon paper
(f) Mortgages
(g) Writing implements
(h) Car alarms
(i) Organically grown fruit and vegetables

4: PRODUCT

Solution

You could perhaps pin down some of these items, but most are open to discussion, especially if you take an international perspective. For many you may consider that the PLC is not valid, and you will not be alone: see the following paragraphs.

Criticisms of the product life cycle

3.11 There have been contradictory papers directed at establishing or refuting the validity of the product life cycle by empirical tests. Polli and Cook tested 140 categories of non-durable consumer products. They tested whether the sequence that a product has passed through conformed to a PLC pattern. For instance, if a product was judged to be in a mature phase, they tested whether this was preceded by growth or maturity and followed by maturity or decline. If this test were positive then any sequence of these either/ors would be consistent with the PLC concept.

May be preceded by:	Period	May be followed by:
Introduction, growth	Growth	Growth, maturity, decline
Growth, maturity	Maturity	Maturity, decline
Growth, maturity, decline	Decline	Decline

(*Note.* The model was further subdivided into 'sustained maturity', 'maturity' and 'decaying maturity'.)

The results

Non-durable product class	Number of product categories	% sequences significantly different from chance at: 5% confidence	% sequences significantly different from chance at: 1% confidence
Health and personal care	51	60.8	31.3
Food	56	19.6	7.1
Cigarettes	33	60.6	51.5
ALL PRODUCTS	140	44.0	34.0

Source: *The validity of the Product Life Cycle* Polli & Cook, Journal of Business, October 1969.

3.12 Polli and Cook tested whether the results were significantly different from random events. They concluded that 44% of the total of all products were significantly different from chance at the 95% level of significance and 34% at the 99% level. Within the sample there was a considerable range of results when classified into non-durable product groups. 61% of 'cigarettes' and 'health and personal care' product groups were significantly different from chance at the 95% confidence level. This contrasts with only 20% of 'food'.

81

3.13 Polli and Cook concluded that the PLC was most likely to be relevant for products where consumer demand is high. From these results Polli and Cook concluded that 'for given categories of goods the product life cycle can be a useful model for marketing planning.'

3.14 A contradictory paper by Dhalla and Yuspeh attempts to expose what they term the myth of the PLC. They point out that 'in the absence of the technological breakthroughs many product classes appear to be almost impervious to normal life cycle pressures, provided they satisfy some basic need, be it transportation, entertainment, health, nourishment or the desire to be attractive'.

3.15 Whilst accepting the possibility of the existence of a *product* life cycle, the paper denies the existence of *brand* life cycles. They consider that any underlying PLC is a dependent variable which is determined by marketing actions; it is not the independent variable to which companies should adapt. In other words, if a brand appears to be in decline, this is not happening by Act of God, but as a result of market changes: either reduced or inappropriate marketing by the producer, or better marketing by competitors.

3.16 Dhalla and Yuspeh consider that treatment of the PLC as a binding constraint has led to many marketing errors. They sight the example of Ipana, an American toothpaste, that was marketed by a leading packaged goods company until 1968 when it was abandoned after entering a 'decline'. Two Minnesota businessmen then acquired the brand name and with hardly any promotion generated 250,000 dollars sales in the first seven months of operations. They point to how intelligent marketing has kept such brands as Budweiser Beer, Colgate toothpaste and Maxwell House around for a long time after competitive brands have been allowed to extinguish.

3.17 They cite conclusions reached by the Marketing Science Institute who examined over 100 product categories using Polli and Cook's test. 'After completing the initial test of the life cycle expressed as a verifiable model of sales behaviour, we must register strong reservations about its general validity, even stated in its weakest, most flexible form. In our tests of the model against real sales data, it has not performed equally well at different levels of product sales aggregation .... Our results suggest strongly that the life cycle concept, when used without careful formulation and testing as an explicit model, is more likely to be misleading than useful.'

3.18 Dhalla and Yuspeh come to the general conclusion that managers adhering to the sequences of marketing strategies recommended for succeeding stages of the cycle are likely to do more harm than good. In particular they cite the potential neglect of existing brands and wasteful expenditures on replacement 'me-too' products.

3.19 There are some legitimate criticisms of the product life cycle concept as a practical tool in strategic planning.

   (a) How can marketing managers, or other managers, recognise just where a product stands in its life cycle? An extrapolation of past sales into the future together with experience of other product life cycles in the past might be an insufficient basis for forecasting a current product's future life with any reliable accuracy.

(b) The traditional S-shaped curve of a product life cycle

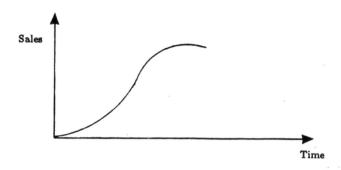

does not always occur in practice. Some products have no maturity phase, and go straight from growth to decline. Others have a second growth period after an initial decline. Some have virtually no introductory period and go straight into a rapid growth phase.

(c) Strategic decisions can change a product's life cycle: for example, by repositioning a product in the market, its life can be extended. If strategic planners 'decide' what a product's life is going to be, opportunities to extend the life cycle might be ignored.

(d) Competition varies in different industries, and the strategic implications of the product life cycle will vary according to the nature of the competition. The 'traditional' life cycle presupposes increasing competition and falling prices during the growth phase of the market and also the gradual elimination of competitors in the decline phase. Strategic planning would be based on these presuppositions. But in practice, this pattern of events is not always found. The financial markets are an example of markets where there is a tendency for competitors to follow-my-leader very quickly, so that competition has built up well ahead of demand. The rapid development of various banking services is an example of this: for example, with bank cash dispenser cards, when one bank developed the product all the other major banks followed immediately.

The strategic implications of the product life cycle

3.20 Having made these reservations about product life cycle planning, the strategic implications of the product life cycle might be as follows.

	Phase			
	Introduction	*Growth*	*Maturity*	*Decline*
Product	Initially, poor quality	Competitor's products have marked quality differences and technical differences	Products become more standardised and differences between competing products less distinct	Products even less different-iated. Quality becomes more variable
	Product design and development are a key to success			

4: PRODUCT

Phase

	Introduction	*Growth*	*Maturity*	*Decline*
Product (continued)	No standard product and frequent design changes (eg microcomputers in the early 1980)	Quality improves Product reliability may be important		
Customers	Initial customers willing to pay high prics Customers need to be convinced about buying	Customers increase in number	Mass market Market saturation Repeat-buying of products becomes significant. Brand image also important	Customers are 'sophisticated buyers of a product they understand well
Marketing	High advertising and sales promotion costs High prices possible	High advertising costs still, but as a % of sales, costs are falling Prices falling	Markets become segmented Segmentation and extending the maturity phase of the life cycle can be key strategies	Less money spent on advertising and sales promotion
Competition	Few or no competitors	More competitors enter the market Barriers to entry can be important	Competition at its keenest: on prices, branding servicing customers, packaging etc	Competitors gradually exit from the market Exit barriers can be important
Profit margins	High prices but losses due to high fixed costs	High prices. High contribution margins, and increasing profit margins High P/E ratios for quoted companies in the growth market	Falling prices but good profit margins due to high sales volume High prices in some market segments	Still low prices but falling profits as sales volume falls, since total contribution falls towards the level of fixed costs Some increases in prices may occur in the late decline stage

4: PRODUCT

Phase

	Introduction	*Growth*	*Maturity*	*Decline*
Manufacturing and distribution	Overcapacity	Undercapacity	Optimum capacity	Overcapacity because mass production techniques still used
	High production costs	Move towards mass production and less reliance on skilled labour	Low labour skills	
	Few distribution channels		Distribution channels fully developed, but less successful channels might be cut	Distribution channels dwindling
	High labour skill content in manufacture	Distribution channels flourish and getting adequate distribution is a key to marketing success		

4.   PRODUCT PORTFOLIO PLANNING

4.1

Product mix	*Characteristics of company's product line*
Width	Number of product lines
Depth	Average number of items per product line
Consistency	Closeness of relationships in product range eg end users, production, distribution

4.2   A company's product mix (or product assortment or portfolio) is all the product lines and items that the company offers for sale.

   (a)   *Width* is the number of product lines that the company carries.

   (b)   *Depth* is calculated by dividing the total number of items carried by the number of product lines.

   (c)   *Consistency* is the closeness of items in the range in terms of marketing or production characteristics.

4.3 The product mix can be extended in a number of ways:

   (a)   by introducing variations in models or style;
   (b)   by changing the quality of products offered at different price levels;
   (c)   by developing associated items, eg a paint manufacturer introducing paint brushes;
   (d)   by developing new products that have little technical or marketing relationships to the existing range.

4.4 *Managing the product portfolio* goes beyond the simple extension or reduction of a company's product range. It also raises broad issues such as what role should a product play, how should resources be allocated between products and what should be expected from each product. Of particular importance is the notion of maintaining some balance between well established and new products, between cash generative and cash using products and between growing and declining products. This process of managing the product portfolio is thus a key component of marketing. If products are not suitable for the market or not profitable, then attempts to achieve corporate objectives will be jeopardised and the marketing function will be failing to fulfil its stated goals. Equally, if potentially profitable products are ignored or not given sufficient support then crucial marketing opportunities may be lost.

4.5 Given the importance of this process, there are some benefits to be gained from using a *systematic approach* to the management of the product range. Unfortunately, marketing is not an exact science and there is no definitive approach or technique which will determine which products should remain, which should be pruned and how resources should be shared between the current product range. There are, however, a number of techniques which can act as an aid to decision making. While ultimately the burden of the decision is a management responsibility and will require managerial judgement, techniques such as product-market matrices and the product life cycle can guide the decision process and provide a useful framework within which the product range can be evaluated.

Product-market matrices

4.6 The product-market matrix refers to a simple technique which can be used to classify a product or even a business according to the features of the market and the features of the product. Such a technique is often used at the level of corporate strategy to determine the relative positions of businesses and identify strategies for resource allocation between them. Thus, for example, a bank might apply such a technique to evaluate the relative position and profitability of its corporate division vis a vis that of its personal division, its international division, its merchant banking division etc. However, the same techniques are equally valuable when considering products and the management of the product portfolio. The two most widely used approaches are the *Boston Consulting Group (BCG) growth-share matrix* and the *General Electric (GE) Business Screen*.

The BCG Matrix

4.7 The BCG matrix, which is illustrated below, works by classifying products (or businesses) on the basis of their market share relative to that of their competitors and according to the rate of growth in the market as a whole. The split on the horizontal axis is based on a market share identical to that of the firm's nearest competitor, while the precise location of the split on the vertical axis will depend on the rate of growth in the market. Products are positioned in the matrix as circles with a diameter proportional to their sales revenue. The underlying assumption in the growth-share matrix is that a larger market share will enable the business to benefit from economies of scale, lower per unit costs and thus higher margins.

The Boston Consulting Group Growth/Share Matrix

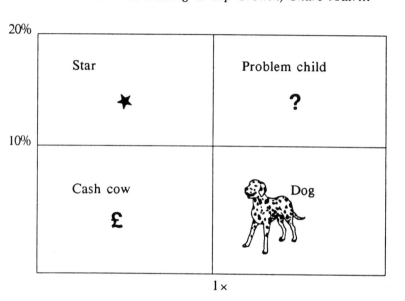

4.8 Each product can then fall into one of four broad categories.

(a) *Problem Child* (or question mark): a small market share but in a high growth industry. The generic product is clearly popular, but customer support for the specific company version is limited. A small market share implies that competitors are apparently in a strong position and that if the product is to be successful it will require a substantial injection of funds, particularly on the marketing side. If the market looks good and the product is viable, then the company should consider a *'build'* strategy to increase market share. This would essentially involve increasing the resources available for that product to permit more active marketing. If the future looks less promising then the company should consider the possibility of withdrawing the product. At this stage it is important to take decisive action to ensure that the product moves to a less ambiguous situation.

(b) *The Star:* this is a product with a high market share in a high growth industry. By implication, the star has potential for generating significant earnings currently and in the future. However, at this stage it may still require substantial marketing expenditures to 'maintain' this position, but would be regarded as a good investment for the future.

(c) *The Cash Cow:* a high market share but in a comparatively mature and slower growing market. Typically, a well established product with a high degree of consumer loyalty. Product development costs are typically low and the marketing campaign is well established. The cash cow will normally make a substantial contribution to overall profitability. The appropriate strategy will vary according to the precise position of the cash cow. If market growth is reasonably strong then a 'holding' strategy will be appropriate, but if growth and/or share are weakening, then a *harvesting* strategy may be more sensible - cut back on marketing expenditure and maximise short term cash flow.

(d) *The Dog:* a product characterised by low market share and low growth - again, typically a well established product, but one which is apparently losing consumer support and may have cost disadvantages. The usual strategy would be to consider *divestment* unless cash flow position is strong, in which case the product would be harvested in the short term prior to deletion from the product range.

4.9 We should note that implicit in the matrix is the notion that markets are dynamic. The typical new product is likely to appear in the 'problem child' category to begin with; if it looks promising and with effective marketing it might be expected to become a 'star', then, as markets mature, a 'cash cow' and finally a 'dog'. The suggestion that most products will move through these stages does not weaken the role played by marketing - on the contrary, it strengthens it, since poor marketing may mean that a product moves from being a problem child to a dog without making any substantial contribution to the profitability. Equally, of course, good marketing may enable the firm to prolong the 'star' and 'cash cow' phases, thus maximising cash flow from the product.

4.10 The framework provided by the matrix can offer guidance in terms of developing appropriate strategies for products and in maintaining a balanced product portfolio - ensuring that there are enough cash generating products to match the cash using products.

4.11 However, there are a number of criticisms.

(a) The BCG matrix oversimplifies product analysis. It concentrates only on two dimensions of product markets, size and market share, and therefore may encourage marketing management to pay too little attention to other market features.

(b) It is not always clear what is meant by the terms 'relative market share' and 'rate of market growth'. Not all companies and not all products will be designed for market leadership, in which case describing performance in terms of relative market share may be of limited relevance. Many firms undertaking this approach have found that all their products were technically 'dogs' and yet were still very profitable, so saw no need to divest. Firms following market nicheing strategy will commonly find this occurring since they are looking to appeal only to a limited segment of the market.

(c) The validity of the matrix depends on the notion of a relationship between profitability and market share. There is empirical evidence for this in many industries, but it may not always be the case, particularly in situations were there is demand for more customised products.

(d) The basic approach may oversimplify the nature of products in large diversified firms with many divisions. In these cases, each division may contain products which fit into several of the categories. Despite these criticisms, the BCG matrix can offer guidance in achieving a balanced portfolio. However, given the difficulty of generalising such an approach to deal with all product and market situations, its recommendations should be interpreted with care.

The General Electric Business Screen

4.12 The basic approach of the GE business screen is similar to that of the BCG matrix. The key difference is that it attempts to avoid the criticism of using a highly restrictive classification system and instead attempts to include a broader range of company and market factors in assessing the position of a particular product or product group. A typical example of the GE matrix is given below. This matrix classifies products (or businesses) according to industry attractiveness and company strengths. Obviously, there is no single number which can be used to measure industry attractiveness or company (product) strength; rather, the approach is to consider a variety of factors which will contribute to both these variables and sectionalise the matrix based on simple ordinal measures - namely high, medium and low. Typical examples of the factors which determine industry attractiveness and company strength are the following.

(a) *Industry attractiveness:* market size, market growth, competitive climate, stability of demand, ease of market entry, industry capacity, levels of investment, nature of regulation, profitability.

(b) *Company strengths:* relative market share, company image, production capacity, production costs, financial strengths, product quality, distribution systems, control over prices/margins, benefits of patent protection.

4.13 Although a broader range of factors are used in the classification of products, the manager should be aware that this is a much more subjective assessment. Products are positioned on the grid with circles representing market size and segments representing market shares. The strategy for an individual product is then determined according to that position. The possible options are shown below and it is interesting to note the apparent similarity in recommendations between the BCG matrix and the GE matrix; the basic difference arises simply from the method of classification.

The General Electric Business Screen

High ◄——————— Market Attractiveness ———————► Low

	High		Low
High	Invest for growth	Invest selectively for growth	Develop for income
Business Strength	Invest selectively and build	Develop selectively for income	Harvest or divest
Low	Develop selectively Build on strengths	Harvest	Divest

4.14 The GE matrix, because of its broader approach, places emphasis on the notion of trying to match distinctive competences within the company to conditions within the market place. However, the difficulties associated with measurement and classification mean that again the results of such an exercise should be interpreted with care and not seen as an immediate prescription for expanding or divesting particular products.

5. INNOVATION MANAGEMENT

5.1 Innovation is the life blood of a successful organisation and the management of innovation is central to this success. New products can be developed following a major technical breakthrough in the field, or changes in society; or simply to copy existing products. Within the organisation itself management can adopt a proactive response to product development. Organisations can set up research and development departments to look into new product development. Ideas for new products do not have to come through this formal departmentalised system. Management, sales people, customers and competitors can all generate new product ideas. It is the task of marketing management to 'tap' these ideas and select some for further development. Later in this section new product development will be discussed in more detail.

5.2 *What is a new product?*

(a) One that opens up an entirely new market.
(b) One that replaces an existing product.
(c) One that broadens significantly the market for an existing product.

An old product can be new if:

(a) it is introduced to a new market;
(b) it is packaged in a different way (qualified);
(c) a different marketing approach is used (qualified).

Any new product must be perceived in terms of customer needs and wants.

Exercise 3

Can you think of examples of new products and 'new' old products to fit into each of the above categories?

Solution

You should try to think of your own examples, but these suggestions may help.

New product	
Entirely new market	Fax machine
Replacing an existing product	Spin dryer
Broadening the market	Amstrad PCW 8256

'New' old product	
In a new market	Cider (Red Rock, for example)
New packaging	Anything
New marketing	Brylcreem, 7●up

5.3 There are several degrees of newness.

   (a) *The unquestionably new product*, such as the electronic pocket calculator. Marks of such a new product: high price – performance problems – patchy distribution.

   (b) *The partially new product*, such as the cassette tape recorder. Marks of such a product: it performs better than the old ones did.

   (c) *Major product change*, such as the Mini car. Marks of such a product: radical technological change altering the accepted concept of the order of things.

   (d) *Minor product change*, such as styling changes. Marks of such a product: extras which give a boost to a product.

5.4 There are several sources of new products, including the following.

   (a) Licensing: Formica, Monopoly.
   (b) Acquisition: buy the organisation making it.
   (c) Internal product development: your own Research and Development team.
   (d) Customers: listen to and observe them, analyse and research.
   (e) External inventors: both Kodak and IBM rejected Xerox.
   (f) Competition: for example Kodak instant cameras, following the Polaroid concept.
   (g) Patent agents.
   (h) Academic institutions: for example the pharmaceutical industry.

Screening new product ideas

5.5 The mortality rate of new products is very high.

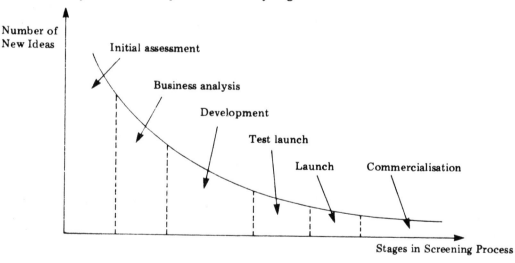

5.6 To reduce the risk of failure new product ideas should be screened. There is some evidence that the product screening process is becoming more effective. A study by Booz, Allen and Hamilton in 1968 concluded that it took fifty-eight ideas to yield one successful product that achieved commercial success. A repeat study by Booz, Allen and Hamilton in 1981 showed a dramatic improvement. This study of 700 companies in the USA found that on average only seven ideas were needed for every successful product. An eightfold increase in success rate!

4: PRODUCT

New product development plan

5.7 New products should only be taken to an advanced development stage if they fit the criteria of:

    (a) adequate demand;
    (b) compatibility with existing marketing ability;
    (c) compatibility with existing production ability.

Initial concept testing

5.8 Before investing money in making prototypes the concept for the new product could be tested on potential customers to obtain their reactions. It is common to use the company staff as guinea pigs for a new product idea although their reaction is unlikely to be typical. But it is difficult to get sensible reactions from customers. For example:

    (a) New designs for wallpaper. When innovative new designs are tested on potential customers it is often found that they are conditioned by traditional designs and are dismissive of new design ideas.

    (b) New ideas for chocolate confectionery have the opposite problem. Potential customers typically say they like the new concept (because everyone likes chocolate bars) but when the new product is launched it is not successful because people continue to buy old favourites.

Product testing

5.9 Here, money is invested to produce a working prototype of the product which can be tried by customers. This stage is also very useful to ensure that the product could be produced in sufficient quantities at the right price if it were to be launched. The form which the product test takes will depend very much on the type of product concerned. The best advice seems to be that to get realistic responses the test should replicate reality as clearly as possible. Thus, for example:

    (a) if the product is used in the home, a sample of respondents should be given the product to use at home;

    (b) if the product is chosen from amongst competitors in a retail outlet (as with chocolate bars) then the product test needs to rate response against competitive products;

    (c) if inherent product quality is an important attribute of the product then a 'blind' test could be used in which customers are not told who is producing the new product;

    (d) an industrial product could be used for a trial period by a customer in a realistic setting.

Quality policy

5.10 This is an important policy consideration. Customers do not necessarily want the best quality of goods, and there may be a market potential for a lower quality as well as a higher quality article. When a market is dominated by established brand names, a means of getting into a market might be to tap the potential demand for a lower quality (cheaper, or fashion) item.

5.11 Customers do not always know properly what they are buying, and tend to judge the quality of an article by its price. One aspect of quality policy may therefore be to decide a price and then manufacture a product to the best quality standard that can be achieved for the price, rather than making a product of a certain quality and then deciding what its price should be.

5.12 Quality should also be determined by the expected physical, technological and social life of the product because:

(a) there is no value in making one part of a product good enough to have a physical life of five years, when the rest of the product will wear out and be irreplaceable within two years (unless the part with the longer life has an emotional or irrational appeal to customers, so that, for example, a leather covering may be preferred to plastic);

(b) if technological advances will make a product obsolescent within a certain number of years, there is little value in producing an article which will last for a longer time;

(c) if social tastes determine the life of a product, the quality required need only be sufficient to cover the period of demand; the quality of fashion clothes, for example, is usually governed by their fashion life.

5.13 Quality policy must be carefully integrated with sales promotion, which will have poor success if a product is branded and advertised as having a certain quality which customers then find is not actually true. The quality of a product (involving its design, production standards, quality control and after-sales service) must be properly established and maintained before a sales promotion campaign can use it as a selling feature.

Test marketing

5.14 The purpose of test marketing is to obtain information about how consumers react to the product - will they buy it, and if so, will they buy it again? Will they adopt the product as a regular feature of their buying habits, and if so, how frequently will they buy it? With this information an estimate of the total market demand for the product can be made.

5.15 A test market involves testing a new consumer product in selected areas which are thought to be 'representative' of the total market. This avoids a blind commitment to the costs of a full-scale launch while permitting the collection of market data. In the selected areas, the firm will attempt to distribute the product through the same types of sales outlets it plans to use in the full market launch, and also to use the advertising and promotion plans it intends to use in the full market. A test marketing exercise can be expensive, but it enables the company to 'test the water' before launching the product nationally. Not only does it help to make sales forecasts, it can also be used to identify flaws in the product or promotional plans which can then be dealt with before the product is launched nationally.

4: PRODUCT

5.16 In short, then, the stages of new product development are as follows.

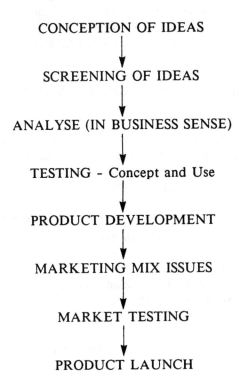

CONCEPTION OF IDEAS

↓

SCREENING OF IDEAS

↓

ANALYSE (IN BUSINESS SENSE)

↓

TESTING - Concept and Use

↓

PRODUCT DEVELOPMENT

↓

MARKETING MIX ISSUES

↓

MARKET TESTING

↓

PRODUCT LAUNCH

The diffusion of innovation

5.17 The diffusion of the new product is the spread of information about the product in the market place. Adoption is the process by which consumers adopt the product. The diffusion process usually is assumed to follow a similar shape to the PLC curve. Adoption is thought to usually follow a 'normal' bell shaped curve. The classification of adopters is shown below.

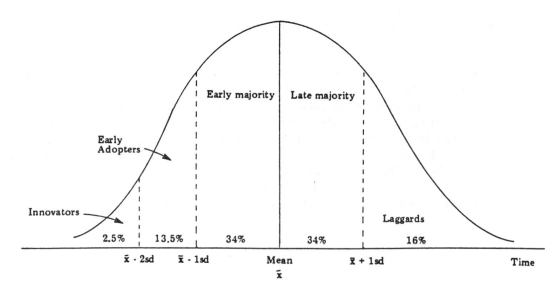

5.18 Early adopters and innovators are often considered to be 'opinion leaders' and are therefore targeted by companies to promote their product to their friends by word of mouth means.

5.19 The main problem with using this model is that the categories appear to add up to 100% of the social system - the target market. This is not a reflection of marketers' experience, since some potential consumers do not adopt/purchase at all. It has been suggested that an additional category should be added: *nonadopters*, or nonconsumers.

5.20 Some researchers prefer a two or three category scheme, comparing innovators/early triers with later triers and/or non-triers. This enables then to generalise the characteristics of the important innovator/early trier segments, which has practical significance for marketing.

6. SERVICES

6.1 'Products' is a generic term including 'services'. It is worth spending some time looking at specific aspects of service marketing. Services are characterised by four aspects.

   (a) *Intangibility:* services cannot be seen, touched, felt or tasted until after puchase.
   (b) *Inseparability:* services are sold then produced.
   (c) *Variability:* the standard of service varies from day to day.
   (d) *Perishability:* services cannot be stored.

   There are very few pure products or services. Most products have some service attributes and many services are in some way attached to products.

6.2 The major determinants of service quality can be seen to fit into a number of dimensions, some of which are more easily measured than others.

   (a) *Tangibles:* the physical evidence: the quality of fixtures and fittings of the service area, for example.

   (b) *Reliability:* getting it right first time.

   (c) *Responsiveness:* the apparent (to the customer) willingness to deal with the customer's queries.

   (d) *Communication:* explaining to customers in non-technical language which they can understand rather than trying to confound customers with technical language.

   (e) *Credibility:* perceived honesty and trustworthiness, seen as acting in the best interests of customers and not trying to make as much commission as possible, for example.

   (f) *Security:* the customer needs to feel that conversations with service staff are private and confidential. This factor needs to influence design of the service area.

   (g) *Competence:* all the service staff need to appear competent in understanding the product range and relating these to needs of the customers. In part this dimension can be resolved through training programmes.

(h) *Courtesy:* customers (even rude ones) should perceive service staff as polite, respectful and friendly. This basic requirement is often difficult to achieve in practice although training programmes can help.

(i) *Understanding the customer's needs:* the use of computer-based customer databases can be very impressive in this context. The service personnel can call up the customer's records and use this data in the service process, thus personalising it. Service staff need to meet customer needs rather than to try to sell products. This is a subtle but important difference.

(j) *Access:* minimising queues, having a fair queuing system and speedy but accurate service are all factors which can avoid irritation building up in customers. A pleasant relaxing environment is a useful design factor in this context.

Achieving improvements in service quality

6.3 The features of service quality and their determinants identified above lead to the need for a focus on customers in terms of:

(a) customer satisfaction;
(b) putting the customer first;
(c) anticipating customer needs or problems;
(d) tailoring products to customer needs;
(e) establishing lasting customer relationships.

6.4 To achieve this customer focus, there is a need to ensure that service staff are trained in product knowledge so that the organisation is providing:

(a) a high quality of service;
(b) a personal service - applying the right product to the specific customer situation;
(c) a friendly, caring and polite service;
(d) personalised advice and problem solving;
(e) quick, efficient and accurate service;

and is getting the service right first time while maintaining (high) standards.

6.5 These factors identify the need to appreciate fully the important role in the organisation of the service encounter - the organisation-customer interface. This recognition needs to come from the top, perhaps by means of a mission statement. Strategically, there is a need to create an internal environment which supports customer consciousness amongst the personnel. Training can be used in part to achieve these aims but only within a corporate culture which recognises and fully supports the importance of the customer. Recruitment and selection policies also have a part to play; the characteristics of good service personnel should be stressed in recruitment. Working conditions and fringe benefits should also make service personnel feel an important and integral part of the organisation. A happy workplace is likely to transfer these feelings through the service encounter to the customer.

6.6 In summary, it is easy for the management of an organisation to pay lip service to the need for better customer care. In reality, higher service quality can only be achieved by careful planning and implementation of operating systems which can be monitored to ensure that they meet set performance standards. Cultural change is much easier to write about than it is to achieve. In practice, it involves the following actions.

(a) Breaking down barriers. An essential element in large, stable organisations particularly can be to change the typically traditional, autocratic, paternalistic and hierarchical culture and structure. Examples of how to achieve this aim include:

(i)   mixing staff from widely different levels of the hierarchy at training sessions;
(ii)   promoting the use of first names between management and staff;
(iii) sharing facilities, including single status restaurants and meeting rooms;
(iv) reducing the number of tiers of management.

(b) Improving internal communication. Adequately informing staff about their role in the organisation is very important; both vertical and horizontal communications often need to be improved.

(c) Overcoming inflexible attitudes and behaviour by some staff who do not accept the need for change. Such staff resist change and often do not want to accept new concepts of development of responsibility and authority. Apathy and open resistance to change can be very difficult to overcome.

7. BRANDS AND PACKAGING

7.1 A manufacturer might produce goods under his own brand name and at the same time (or perhaps exclusively) supply large retailers with goods under their own brand name, 'own label' brands or dealer brands. The major examples are the own brands of supermarkets and major chain stores (eg Tesco, Sainsburys, St Michael for Marks & Spencer and Winfield for Woolworths). The advantages of dealer brands to a manufacturer are:

(a) a high level of sales may be necessary to cover fixed costs of production and supplying dealer branded goods to a large retail organisation may be a necessary way of achieving a profitable sales level;

(b) large retailers with a high sales turnover and considerable control over the retail trade may insist on having their own brand, and supplying dealer branded goods may be essential to retain their business;

(c) it may be a well established and common practice in the industry;

(d) a manufacturer may wish to concentrate on production only, leaving the problem of design, quality and distribution to a multiple retailer.

7.2 The attraction of dealer brands to dealers are:

(a) the use of a brand helps to create customer loyalty to the store;

(b) the buying in price is lower and cost of sales promotion (if any) negligible; therefore the price of dealer branded goods to customers can be lower. Price consciousness is a notable feature of dealer brands.

4: PRODUCT

Packaging

7.3 Packaging has five functions:

   (a) protection of the contents of the package;

   (b) distribution - ie helping to transfer products from the manufacturer to the customer;

   (c) selling - ie the design of the package and the words printed on it should help to attract buyers to the product;

   (d) user convenience, as an aid to selling, such as aerosol cans and handy packs;

   (e) to conform to government regulations (eg by printing the contents of the package, as required by law).

   Remember that goods are usually packaged in more than one layer. Consumer goods might be packaged for sale to individual customers, but delivered to resellers in cartons or some similar bulk package.

The qualities required of a pack

7.4 The qualities required of a pack are as follows.

   (a) It should be reduced to a small range of size and variety in order to keep down purchasing, production and distribution costs, but the range should be sufficiently wide to improve sales with different, distinctive packs.

   (b) In industries where distribution is a large part of total costs, packaging should be an important consideration:

      (i) packs should be designed so that they convey the product to its destination in the desired condition;

      (ii) they should assist in the maximum utilisation of space in the transport vehicles;

      (iii) they should help the mechanisation of distribution where mechanical handling is cheaper than labour;

      (iv) they should make optimum use of space in warehouses and retail stores, and lend themselves to display;

      (v) they should be informative so that assistants in self-service stores are not asked about the product by customers;

      (vi) they should keep the product in good condition throughout its shelf life in a retail store.

   (c) Packaging is an important aid to selling. Where a product cannot be differentiated by design techniques, the pack takes over the design selling function. This is crucial where there are no real product differences between rival brands, or in the case of commodities such as flour.

(i) a pack should help to promote the advertising/brand image; eg the brand should be clearly identifiable on the package, in order to take advantage of customer brand loyalty to a range of products;

(ii) it should be the correct shape, colour and size to exploit customer motivation;

(iii) it should be the correct size for the expected user of the product (eg family size packets of food);

(iv) it should be designed so as to exploit impulse buying;

(v) where labour-saving convenience is important, it should be a convenience pack (eg tubes, aerosols);

(vi) it should maintain the product at its expected quality standard;

(vii) in self-service stores, it should attract the eye of potential customers.

7.5 It should be apparent that packaging must appeal not only to consumers, but also to resellers who must stock the product. A reseller wants a package design that will help to sell the product, but also one which minimises the likelihood of broken packs and wasted goods, or which adds to the product's shelf life, or which makes more economic use of shelf space.

7.6 The packaging of industrial goods is primarily a matter of conveyance in good condition to the point of use and this in itself is a selling aid in future dealings with the customer. The packaging of large pieces of equipment is only as good as the weakest point.

Example: packaging as a selling point

7.7 Here is an example of packaging as a *unique selling point* in advertising. In the mid-1960s, Heinz held a 95% share of the baby foods market in the UK, selling their food in tins. Gerber then entered the market and secured a wide distribution network, but needed a unique selling point for consumers. The USP they decided upon was glass jars instead of tins, in the belief that mothers would consider them to be more hygenic. This campaign was successful and won Gerber a 10% share of the baby foods market (in spite of counter-measures by Heinz who produced their own range of foods in glass jars).

8. CONCLUSION

8.1 We have outlined the main aspects of product policy and new product development. In the next section we will be looking at how marketers can set the price for the goods they have produced.

TEST YOUR KNOWLEDGE

Numbers in brackets refer to paragraphs of this chapter

1. What is Ansoff's product/market matrix? (1.1)

2. Cannibalisation is a danger in adopting a market penetration strategy. True or false? (1.2, 1.3)

3. What are the requirements for effective market segmentation? (2.3)

4. What are the advantages and disadvantages of using socio-economic groups as a basis for market segmentation? (2.11, 2.12)

5. Outline the changing social trends in UK households of which marketers should be aware. (2.15-2.17)

6. Describe the stages in the product life cycle. (3.3)

7. Describe and explain the major criticisms of the PLC. (3.11-3.19)

8. A cash cow is a product with a high market share in a growth market. True or false? (4.8)

9. Using the GE Business Screen, what should be done with a strong product in an unattractive market? (2.8)

10. List sources of new products. (5.4)

11. Why might one aspect of quality policy in NPD be to fix a price before fixing a quality standard? (5.11)

12. How can an organisation promote cultural change within itself? (6.6)

13. Why should a manufacturer produce a dealer brand? (7.1)

14. What qualities are required of a pack? (7.4)

Now try questions 9 and 10 at the end of the text

Chapter 5

PRICE

This chapter covers the following topics.

1. The objectives of pricing
2. Methods of price determination
3. Pricing policy
4. Price setting strategies

---

1. THE OBJECTIVES OF PRICING

1.1 All profit organisations and many non-profit organisations face the task of setting a price on their products or services. Price can go by many names: fares, tuitions, rent, assessments etc. Historically price was the single most important decision made by the sales department. Over time, the importance of the interrelated elements of the marketing mix has been realised. To the modern marketing executive, price, whilst important, is not necessarily the predominant factor. As an example, marketing managers may now seek to interpret and satisfy consumer wants and needs by modifying existing products or introducing new products to the range. This contrasts with earlier production oriented times when the typical reaction was to cut prices in order to sell the firm's product.

1.2 In fact, it is often suggested that one of the functions performed by marketing is to make price relatively unimportant to the consumers' decision making process. There is certainly some truth in this view, in that the other elements of the marketing mix are ultimately concerned with adding value to the product and tailoring it to the consumers' needs, to ensure that the choice between two products is not simply based on their different prices. However, this devalues the role of pricing as an element of the marketing mix. Price can be defined as a measure of the value exchanged by the buyer for the value offered by the seller. As such it might be expected that the price should reflect the costs to the seller of producing the product and the benefit to the buyer of consuming it.

1.3 Unlike the other marketing mix elements, pricing decisions affect profits through their impact on revenues rather than costs. Pricing is the only element of the mix which generates revenue rather than creating costs. In addition, it also has an important role to play as a competitive tool which can be used to differentiate a product and an organisation and thus exploit market opportunities. It is also important that pricing is consistent with other elements of the marketing mix since it contributes to the overall image created for the product. No organisation can hope successfully to offer an exclusive high quality product to the market with a low price - the price must be consistent with the overall product offer.

5: PRICE

1.4 Pricing can be thought of as fulfilling a number of roles within a marketing context. However, in overall terms a price must produce the desired level of sales in order to meet the objectives of the overall business strategy. Pricing must be systematic and it must take into full consideration the internal needs and the external constraints of the organisation.

1.5 Ultimately, the objective of pricing, as with other elements of the marketing mix, is to ensure that the required level of sales is generated to enable the organisation to achieve its specified objectives. Two broad categories of objectives may be specified for pricing decisions; they may not be mutually exclusive, but they are different.

   (a) *Maximising profits*
   This approach to pricing will be one that concerns itself with maximising the returns on assets or investments. This may be realised with a comparatively small market share depending on the patterns of cost and demand.

   (b) *Maintaining or increasing market share*
   The alternative approach which is concerned with increasing or maintaining the customer base may require a different and possibly more competitive approach to pricing, and the company with the largest market share may not necessarily be the company which earns the best profits.

1.6 Either of these approaches may be used in specifying pricing objectives, and as was mentioned earlier, they may appear in some combination based on a specified rate of return and a specified market share. It is important that the stated objectives are consistent with overall corporate objectives and corporate strategies.

2. METHODS OF PRICE DETERMINATION

Price setting in theory

2.1 In classical economic theory, price is the major determinant of demand and brings together supply and demand to form an equilibrium market price. More recently, emphasis has been placed, especially in marketing, on the importance of non-profit factors in demand. Thus the roles of product quality, promotion, personal selling and distribution and, in overall terms, brands, have grown. Whilst it can be relatively easy for a competitor to copy a price cut, at least in the short term, it is much more difficult to copy a successful brand image based on a *unique selling proposition*. Successful branding can even imply premium pricing.

2.2 Economic theory can only determine the optimal price structure under the two extreme market conditions.

   (a) *Perfect competition:* many buyers, many sellers all dealing in an identical product. Neither producer nor user has any market power and both must accept the prevailing market price.

   (b) *Monopoly:* one seller who dominates many buyers. The monopolist can use his market power to set a profit maximising price.

2.3 However, in practice most of British industry can be described as an *oligopoly:* where relatively few competitive companies dominate the market. Whilst each large firm has the ability to influence market prices the unpredictable reaction from the other giants makes the final industry price indeterminate. Economists in the field of oligopoly pricing think that price competition is dangerous, given that there are no clear market forces to support a given price level.

Example: air fares

2.4 When Sir Freddie Laker introduced his cut price Skytrain service on the transatlantic air routes he challenged the legally protected cartel of IATA (the International Air Traffic Association). IATA fixed air fares on many international routes. The fares were typically priced at a relatively high level that allowed the least efficient, marginal carrier to remain in business. IATA has international blessing as its rules allow every small (and therefore high cost) national airline carrier to remain in business. As having an airline is a mark of national prestige this approach is much favoured in the United Nations.

2.5 Initially, British Airways, TWA and Pan Am ignored Laker. But when the service started picking up significant market share, the major airlines reacted by introducing their own cut-price transatlantic fares. The result was that every major carrier recorded losses on its transatlantic business. These losses were only alleviated when Laker himself went out of business.

2.6 It is also difficult in economic theory terms to identify precisely what is market power. Many small producers enjoy some market power because they are producing distinctly different products and have a degree of local monopoly.

2.7 The agricultural sector comes closest to perfect competition with farmers having to accept market prices that they cannot directly influence.

2.8 To summarise, economic theory, whilst giving an insight into price decisions, may be of little practical help.

2.9 However, the concept of *price elasticity* is important. You may already know from your economics studies that price elasticity is measured as

$$\frac{\% \text{ change in sales demand}}{\% \text{ change in sales price}}$$

(a) When elasticity is greater than 1 *(elastic),* a change in price will lead to a change in total revenue so that, if the price is:

  (i)   lowered, total sales revenue would rise, because of the large increase in demand;
  (ii) raised, total sales revenue would fall because of the large fall in demand.

(b) When elasticity is less than 1 *(inelastic),* if the price is:

  (i)   lowered, total sales revenue would fall, because the increase in sales volume would be too small to compensate for the price reductions;

  (ii) raised, total sales revenue would go up in spite of the small drop in sales quantities.

2.10 Marketing management needs to be able to estimate the likely effects of price changes on total revenue and profits. 'Price elasticity of demand gives precision to the question of whether the firm's price is too high or too low. From the point of view of maximising revenue, price is too high if demand is elastic and too low if demand is inelastic. Whether this is also true for maximising profits depends on the behaviour of costs'. (Kotler)

Price setting in practice

2.11 There are three main types of influence on price setting in practice: costs, competition and demand.

Costs

2.12 In practice cost is the most important influence on price. Many firms base price on simple cost-plus rules: in other words, costs are estimated and then a profit margin is added in order to set the price. A study by Lanzilotti gave a number of reasons for the predominance of this method:

(a) planning and use of scarce capital resources are easier;
(b) easier assessment of divisional performance;
(c) emulation of successful large companies;
(d) belief by management in a 'fair return' policy;
(e) fear of government action against 'excessive' profits;
(f) tradition of production orientation rather than marketing orientation in many organisations;
(g) tacit collusion in industry to avoid competition;
(h) adequate profits for shareholders are already made, giving no incentive to maximise profits;
(i) easier administration of cost-based pricing strategies based on internal data;
(j) stability of pricing, production and employment produced by cost-based pricing over time;
(k) social equability.

Cost based pricing is in the main an accountants' method.

2.13 There are two types of cost-based pricing: full cost pricing and cost-plus pricing.

2.14 *Full cost pricing* takes account of the full average cost of production of a brand, including an allocation for overheads. A conventional profit margin is then added to determine the selling price. This method is often used for non-routine jobs which are difficult to cost in advance, such as the work of solicitors and accountants where the price is often determined after the work has been performed.

2.15 Although full cost pricing method is basically straightforward in principle, the allocation or apportionment of overheads between brands in a multibrand company can be difficult, especially when joint or by-products are involved.

2.16 Superficially, it would appear that demand factors are ignored in this analysis; in practice, however, especially in the longer term, demand can be reflected through the level of the profit margin which is added (the margin is not going to be high if demand is being squeezed). The profit margin is also likely to reflect the level of actual or potential competition from firms already in the industry or capable of entering it.

2.17 Using *cost-plus pricing* only the more easily measurable direct cost components such as labour and raw material inputs are calculated in the unit cost, whilst an additional margin incorporates an overhead charge and a residual profit element. This method is used where overhead allocation to unit costs is too complex or too time consuming to be worthwhile.

2.18 A common example occurs with the use of mark up pricing by retailers in which a fixed margin is added to the buying in price of goods for resale. This fixed margin tends to be conventional within product classes. In the UK, for example, fast moving items such as cigarettes carry a low 5-8% margin (also because of tax factors), fast moving but perishable items such as newspapers carry a 25% margin, while slow moving items which involve retailers in high stockholding costs such as furniture or books carry 33%, 50% or even higher mark up margins.

2.19 The percentage margin may vary to reflect changes in demand or competition, while the cost basis for calculations may be actual costs, expected costs or standard costs. If all the firms in the industry use the same pricing basis then prices will reflect efficiency, the lowest price firm being the most efficient.

2.20 The problems with cost-plus pricing arise out of difficulties in defining direct costs and allocating overheads, and with over- or underestimation of attainable production levels (particularly where standard costs are used). Also price adjustments may cause high administrative costs because of the cost-based price-setting process used.

2.21 Because the cost-plus approach leads to price stability, with price changing only to reflect cost changes, it can lead to a marketing strategy which is *reactive* rather then *proactive*.

2.22 There is very limited consideration of *demand* in cost-based pricing strategies. From a marketing perspective, cost-based pricing can reflect missed opportunities as little or no account is taken, particularly in the short run, of the price consumers are willing to pay for the brand, which may prove to be higher than the cost-based price.

2.23 But the approach does provide a practical and popular solution to the pricing problem, whereas the traditional imperfect competition model in economic theory is of limited practical value for a number of reasons:

(a) it assumes that the demand curve can be identified with certainty;
(b) it ignores the market research costs associated with acquiring knowledge of demand;
(c) it assumes the firm has no productive constraint which could mean that the equilibrium point between supply and demand cannot be reached;
(d) it is a static analysis (concerned with only one point in time).

5: PRICE

2.24 The use of cost-based pricing for a new brand can cause particular problems as initial low production levels in the introduction stage could lead to a very high average unit cost and hence a high price. It may thus be necessary to take a longer term view which accepts short-term losses until full production levels are attained. Finally, if the firm is using a product line promotion strategy then there is likely to be added complexity in the pricing process.

Competition

2.25 Prices may be set on the basis of what competitors are charging rather than on the basis of cost or demand. A theoretical justification of the phenomenon was presented by Sweezy as the kinked demand curve theory. This is shown below.

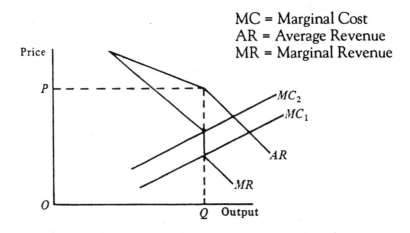

2.26 It is argued that price remains at OP even if marginal costs increase from MC1 to MC2. The justification is that firms assume that competitors will all follow a price decrease but that none will follow a price increase. Thus they assume that demand is elastic for a price rise, but is inelastic for a price fall. In each case a price change would reduce sales revenue. But note that this approach does not explain how the price is arrived at in the first place!

2.27 In practice the kinked demand curve theory would lead to *going rate pricing* in which some form of average level of price becomes the norm, perhaps, in the case of a high level of branding in the market, including standard price differentials between brands.

2.28 In certain market structures price competition may be avoided by tacit agreement leading to concentration on non-price competition; the markets for cigarettes and petrol are examples of this. In such cases price-setting is influenced by a need to avoid retaliatory responses by competitors which would lead to a breakdown in the tacit agreement and so to price competition. Often price changes based on real cost changes are led by a 'representative' firm in the industry and followed by other firms. From time to time tacit agreements break down leading to a period of price competition which may then be followed by a resumption of the tacit agreement. Often such actions are the result of external factors affecting the industry. Industry level agreements do not necessarily preclude short-term price competition for specific brands, especially where sales promotion devices, such as special offers, are used (these are discussed later in this text).

2.29 A special case of competition-based pricing is *competitive bidding*. Many supply contracts, especially concerning local and national government purchases, involve would be suppliers submitting a *sealed bid tender*. In such circumstances, the firm's submitted price needs to take account of expected competitor bid prices. Frequently the firms involved will not even know the identity of their rivals for the bid. However, often past successful bids are published by purchasers and, if this is the case, it is possible to use this data to formulate a current bid price.

2.30 If the firm has the particular problem of bidding for a number of contracts before the result of any one bid is known, the production (or supply) capacity may be important. The firm may need to win some contracts only: not too few nor too many.

2.31 If past bid data is not published then there is very little objective basis for bid price setting. The firm may have to rely on trade gossip, on conjecture or on an estimate of likely competitors' cost and profit requirements in price-setting.

2.32 If the contract is not awarded purely on price (that is, if the lowest bid is not automatically accepted) the problem is exacerbated. In the case of the supply of branded goods, the relative value of each brand must be considered on a value for money basis by the purchaser. The bidder may have to rely on subjective 'feel of the market' analysis in determining bid prices. There are, of course, numerous instances where cases of actual and attempted bribery of officials have been uncovered in attempts by firms to use underhand means of winning contracts.

Demand

2.33 Rather than use cost or competition as the prime determinants of price a firm can base pricing strategy for a product or service on the intensity of demand, although, of course, cost and competition factors remain influences or constraints on its freedom to set price.

2.34 A strong intensity of demand may lead to a high price, and a weak intensity to a low price: much depends on the ability of the firm to segment the market price by elasticity.

2.35 The diagram below shows a simple downward sloping demand curve in which there is one price (Po) and the total quantity demanded is Qo. The shaded area A represents *consumer surplus*, that is an area of extra benefit to the consumer. For example, a consumer may be willing to pay P1 but only pays Po, the market price, gaining a consumer surplus of P1 - Po. If the firm can increase prices to those willing to pay more then it could reduce this area of consumer surplus without necessarily causing the consumer not to buy.

5: PRICE

Consumer surplus and price setting

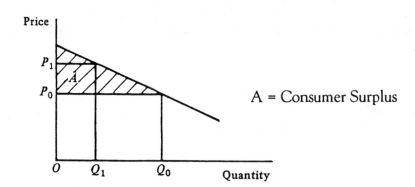

2.36 Identifying a consumer surplus and addressing it is difficult in practice as customers are unlikely to admit to a willingness to pay a higher price! However, where a firm can successfully identify consumer surpluses and charge higher prices for the same product to people who are willing to pay more there is said to be *price discrimination, or differential pricing.*

2.37 In practice, measurement of price elasticity and hence implementing differential pricing can be very difficult. There are a number of bases on which discriminating prices can be set.

(a) *By market segment*
A cross-channel ferry company would market its services at different prices in England, Belgium and France, for example. Services such as cinemas and hairdressers are often available at lower prices to old age pensioners and/or juveniles.

(b) *By product version*
Many car models have 'add on' extras which enable one brand to appeal to a wider cross-section of customers. The final price need not reflect the cost price of the add on extras directly: usually the top of the range model would carry a price much in excess of the cost of provision of the extras, as a prestige appeal.

(c) *By place*
Theatre seats are usually sold according to their location so that patrons pay different prices for the same performance according to the seat type they occupy.

(d) *By time*
Perhaps the most popular type of price discrimination. Off-peak travel bargains, hotel prices, telephone and electricity charges are all attempts to increase sales revenue by covering variable but not necessarily average cost of provision. British Rail is a successful price discriminator, charging more to rush hour rail commuters whose demand is inelastic at certain times of the day.

2.38 In each of these cases, some customers pay more than others for essentially the same product or service, reflecting different intensities of demand. There is an ethical dimension to this practice and firms need to consider their objectives carefully before using this approach. For instance, by taking advantage of a short-term shortage of a product and increasing price, a firm may harm long-term profit prospects because customers resent what they interpret as exploitation. This is particularly the case as *consumerism* develops, since vociferous groups of consumers can create widespread publicity which can be damaging for the product supplier in the short and/or longer term.

2.39 Price discrimination can only be effective if a number of conditions hold.

(a) The market must be segmentable in price terms, and different sectors must show different intensities of demand. Each of the sectors must be identifiable, distinct and separate from the others, and be accessible to the firm's marketing communications.

(b) There must be little or no chance of a black market developing so that those in the lower priced segment can resell to those in the higher priced segment.

(c) There must be little chance that competitors can and will undercut the firm's prices in the higher priced (and/or most profitable) market segments.

(d) The cost of segmenting and administering the arrangements should not exceed the extra revenue derived from the price discrimination strategy.

2.40 The firm could use a *market test* to estimate the demand effect of a price change. This would involve a change of price in one region and a comparison of demand for the brand with past sales in that region and with sales in similar regions at the old prices. This is a high risk strategy: special circumstances may affect the test area (such as a competitor's advertising campaign) which could affect the results. Also customers may change allegiance from the test brand if a price rise is being considered and become loyal to a competitive brand; they may not switch back even if the price is subsequently lowered again.

2.41 The other alternative is to attempt a *direct attitude survey* with respondents. *Pricing research* is notoriously difficult, especially if respondents try to appear rational to the interviewer or do not wish to offend him or her. Usually there is a lack of realism in such research; the respondent is not in an actual 'choice' situation faced with having to pay out hard earned income and therefore may give a hypothetical answer which is not then translated into actual purchasing behaviour. Nevertheless, pricing research is increasingly common in practice as firms attempt to assess the perceived value customers give to a brand as an input to their pricing decisions.

3. PRICING POLICY

3.1 Price sensitivity will vary amongst purchasers. Those that can pass on the cost of purchases will be the least sensitive and will therefore respond more to other elements of the marketing mix.

(a) The business traveller will be more concerned about the level of service and quality of food in looking for an hotel than price, provided that it fits the corporate budget. In contrast, the family on holiday are likely to be very price sensitive when choosing an overnight stay.

(b) In petrol retailing, the largest take up of trading stamps and other promotional offerings has been from the company representative, looking for perks whilst charging what might be relatively expensive petrol to the company.

(c) In industrial marketing the purchasing manager is likely to be more price sensitive than the engineer who might be the actual user of new equipment that is being sourced. The engineer and purchasing manager are using different criteria in making the choice with the engineer placing product characteristics as the most important element within the marketing mix.

Finding out about price sensitivity

3.2 Research on price sensitivity of customers has shown that:

(a) customers have a good concept of a 'just price' - a feel for what is about the right price to pay for a commodity;

(b) customers search for price information before buying, becoming price aware when wanting to buy but forgetting soon afterwards unless a regular purchase is involved;

(c) customers will buy at what they consider to be a bargain price without full regard for need and actual price;

(d) for consumer durables it is the down payment and instalment price rather than total price which is important;

(e) in times of rising prices the price image tends to lag behind the current price, which indicates a resentment of the price increase. It is thus very important to relate customers' image of price to the actual price as this image will determine reactions to a price change. For instance, Bell Telephones in the US were concerned about the lack of sales of extension telephones. When, as part of a market research survey, customers were asked to name the actual price of an extension telephone, most overestimated it. By keeping the existing price but running an advertising campaign featuring it, Bell were able to increase sales as customers became aware of the lower than anticipated price.

Exercise

You ask a friend to empty his wallet of receipts and lay them on the table. You find receipts from different shops for the following.

(a)	A pint of milk	£0.47
(b)	A man's suit	£149.99
(c)	A bottle of wine	£6.50
(d)	A book of 10 first class stamps	£2.40

In each case the *price* tells you something about one or more of the following:

(a) the product purchased;
(b) the place where it was purchased;
(c) the circumstances in which it was purchased;
(d) the purpose for which it was purchased;
(e) the person making the purchase.

(a) Explain each of the purchases in these terms.
(b) Does your interpretation of the price say anything about you?

Finding out about price perception

3.3 Price perception is an important factor in the ways customers react to prices. The economist's downward sloping demand curve may not in fact hold, at least in the short term. For example, customers may react to a price increase by buying more because:

(a) they expect further price increases to follow (they are 'stocking up');
(b) they assume the quality has increased;
(c) the brand takes on a 'snob appeal' because of the high price.

3.4 Several factors complicate the pricing decisions which an organisation has to make.

Intermediaries' objectives

3.5 If an organisation distributes products or services to the market through independent intermediaries, the objectives of these intermediaries complicate the pricing decision. Such intermediaries are likely to deal with a range of suppliers and their aims concern their own profits rather than those of suppliers. Also, the intermediary will take into account the needs of its customers. Thus conflict over price can arise between suppliers and intermediaries which may be difficult to resolve.

3.6 Many industries have traditional margins for intermediaries and to deviate from these might cause problems for suppliers. In some industries, notably grocery retailing (as we have seen), the power of intermediaries allows them to dictate terms to suppliers. The relationship between intermediaries and suppliers is therefore complex, and price and the price discount structure is an important element.

Competitors' actions and reactions

3.7 An organisation, in setting prices, sends out signals to rivals. These rivals are likely to react to these signals in some way. In some industries (such as petrol retailing) pricing moves in unison; in others, price changes by one supplier may initiate a price war, with each supplier undercutting the others.

Suppliers

3.8 If an organisation's suppliers notice a price rise for the organisation's products, they may seek a rise in the price for their supplies to the organisation on the grounds that it is now more able to pay a higher price. This argument is especially likely to be used by the trade unions in the organisation when negotiating the 'price' for the supply for labour.

5: PRICE

Inflation

3.9 In periods of inflation the organisation may need to change prices to reflect increases in the prices of supplies, labour, rent and so on. Such changes may be needed to keep relative (real) prices unchanged (this is what is meant by saying that prices are adjusted for the rate of inflation).

Quality connotations

3.10 In the absence of other information, customers tend to judge quality by price. Thus a price change may send signals to customers concerning the quality of the product. A price rise may indicate improvements in quality, a price reduction may signal reduced quality, for example through the use of inferior components. Thus any change in price needs to take such factors into account.

New product pricing

3.11 Most pricing decisions for existing products concern price changes for one reason or another: in other words, such changes have a reference point from which to move (the existing price). But when a new product is introduced for the first time there may be no such reference points; pricing decisions are most difficult to make in such circumstances. It may be possible to seek alternative reference points, such as the price in another market where the new product has already been launched, or the price set by a competitor.

Income effects

3.12 In times of rising incomes, price may become a less important marketing variable compared with product quality and convenience of access (distribution). When income levels are falling and/or unemployment levels rising, price will become a much more important marketing variable. This has been particularly noticeable in the recession of the early 1990s. The major grocery multiples such as Tesco, Sainsbury, Safeway and Waitrose steadily moved up market in the 1980s with great success, leaving the 'pile it high, sell it cheap' philosophy behind. However, bargain stores have been a more serious threat during the recession.

Multiple products

3.13 Most organisations market not just one product but a range of products. These products are commonly interrelated, being complements or substitutes for example. The management of the pricing function is likely to focus on the profit from the whole range rather than that on each single product. Take, for example, the use of *loss leaders:* a very low price for one product is intended to make consumers buy other products in the range which carry higher profit margins. Another example is selling razors at very low prices whilst selling the blades for them at a higher profit margin. People will buy many of the high profit items but only one of the low profit items - yet they are 'locked in' to the former by the latter. Loss leaders also attract customers into retail stores where they will usually buy normally priced products as well as the loss leaders.

Sensitivity

3.14 Price decisions are often seen as highly sensitive and as such involve top management more clearly than do other marketing decisions. As already noted, price has a direct relationship with profit. Ethical considerations are a further factor, for example whether or not to exploit short-term shortages through higher prices. The outcry surrounding the series of petrol price rises following the outbreak of the Gulf Crisis in 1990 was a good example of public sensitivity to pricing decisions.

4. PRICE SETTING STRATEGIES

4.1 *Market penetration objective:* here the organisation sets a relatively low price for the product or service in order to stimulate growth of the market and/or to obtain a large share of it. This strategy was used by Japanese motor cycle manufacturers when entering the UK market. It worked famously: UK productive capacity was virtually eliminated and the imported Japanese machines could then be sold at a much higher price and still dominate the market.

4.2 Sales maximising objectives are favoured when:

(a) unit costs fall with output (economies of scale);
(b) the market is price sensitive and relatively low prices will attract additional sales;
(c) low prices will discourage any new competitors.

4.3 *Market skimming objective:* in many ways an opposite objective to market penetration, market skimming involves setting a high initial price for a new product. The intention is to take advantage of those buyers who are ready to pay a much higher price than others for a product because it has a high price value to them. The strategy is initially to command a premium price and then gradually to reduce the price to obtain more price sensitive segments of the market. This strategy is really an example of price discrimination over time.

4.4 This strategy is favoured when:

(a) there is insufficient market capacity and competitors cannot increase capacity;
(b) buyers are relatively insensitive to price increases;
(c) high price perceived as high quality (interaction in marketing mix);
(d) *but* there is the danger of encouraging firms to enter market.

4.5 *Early cash recovery objective:* an alternative pricing objective is to recover the investment in a new product or service as quickly as possible, that is to achieve a minimum payback period. The price is set so as to facilitate this objective. Such an objective would tend to be used in conditions where:

(a) the business is high risk;
(b) rapid changes in fashion or technology are expected;
(c) the innovator is short of cash.

4.6 *Product line promotion objective:* as noted above, management of the pricing function is likely to focus on profit from the range of products which the organisation produces rather than to treat each product as a separate entity. The product line promotion objective will take account of the constitution of the whole range in terms of:

(a) the interaction of the marketing mix;

(b) monitoring returns to ensure that net contribution is worthwhile.

4.7 *Intermediate customers:* some companies set a price to distributors and allow them to set whatever final price they wish. A variation is to publish an inflated *recommended retail price* so that retailers can give large promotional discounts.

4.8 *Cost-plus pricing:* a firm may set its initial price by marking up its unit costs by a certain percentage or fixed amount, as already discussed.

(a) This conforms to internal rules laid down by the company for 'satisfactory' return on investment

(b) This takes no account of risk, riskier product lines should make higher returns

(c) This cannot ultimately avoid market pressures, if 'overpriced' stocks will build up, or if 'underpriced' excess demand will be created that exceeds the firm's capacity and encourages market entrants.

4.9 *Target pricing:* a variant on cost-plus where the company tries to determine the price that gives a specified rate of return for a given output. This is widely used by large USA manufacturers, such as General Motors and Boeing.

4.10 *Price discrimination (or differential pricing):* offering different prices to different classes of buyer. The danger is that price cuts to one buyer may be used as a lever when another buyer is negotiating. To avoid such leverage:

(a) buyers must be in clearly defined segments, such as overseas and home (Rover cars are cheaper in the USA), or students' concessionary fares;

(b) own branding where packaging is changed for supermarkets is a variation on this;

(c) bulk buying discounts and aggregated rebate schemes can favour large buyers.

4.11 *Going rate pricing:* try to keep in line with industry norm for prices. Don't 'rock the boat' if everybody is charging relatively high near-monopolistic prices.

(a) This is typical behaviour of a mature oligopoly, akin to a cartel.

(b) Suppliers engage in less damaging competition than price cutting, such as advertising campaigns and post-sales service.

(c) This is often technically illegal but this does not stop individual firms accepting the role of price leaders in an industry.

4.12 *Quantum price:* in retail selling the concept of a 'quantum point' is often referred to. When the price of an item is increased from, say, £9.65 to £9.95, sales may not be affected because the consumers do not notice the price change. However, if the price is increased from £9.95 to £10.05 a major fall in sales may occur, £10 acting as a *quantum point* which can be approached but not passed if the price is not to deter would be purchasers.

4.13 *Odd number pricing:* as an interesting aside, the odd number pricing syndrome (pricing at £1.99, £2.99 etc rather than £2, £3 etc) is said to have originated not as a marketing concept but in department stores in order to ensure the honesty of sales assistants. The customer has to wait for change from £1.95 when, as is usual, they offer, say, £2 in payment, so the assistant has to use the till. If the price was £2 and the customer need not wait for the change, there was thought to be a greater temptation to shop assistants to pocket the money and not to enter it into the till!

4.14 *One coin purchase:* confectionery firms have used the psychologically based concept of a 'one coin purchase' in pricing tactics. Rather than change price to reflect cost changes, such firms often alter the quantity in the unit of the product and keep the same price. This is a case of 'price-minus' pricing in which the firm determines what the market will bear and works backwards, planning to produce and market a brand which will be profitable to them, selling at the nominated retail price.

4.15 *Gift purchases:* gift purchasing is often based on price where it is taken to reflect quality. Thus if a gift is to be purchased in an unfamiliar product category a price level is often fixed by the buyer and a choice made from the brands available at that price. Cosmetics are often priced at £4.99 and £9.99 to appeal to gift purchasers at the £5 and £10 price level. Importantly, packaging is a major part of the appeal and must reflect a quality brand image, an important part of the psychology of gift choice.

Product line pricing

4.16 When a firm sells a range of related products, or a product line, its theoretical pricing policy should be to set prices for each product which maximise the profitability of the line as a whole. A firm may therefore have a pricing policy for an entire product line.

(a) There may be a *brand name* which the manufacturer wishes to associate with high quality but high price, or reasonable quality and low price etc. All items in the line will be priced accordingly. For example, all major supermarket chains have an 'own brand' label which is used to sell goods at a slightly lower price than the major named brands.

(b) If two or more products in the line are *complementary,* one may be priced as a *loss leader* in order to attract more demand for all of the related products.

(c) If two or more products in the line share joint production costs *(joint products)* the prices of the products must be considered as a single decision. For example, if a common production process makes one unit of joint product A for each one unit of joint product B, a price for A which achieves a demand of, say, 17,000 units, will be inappropriate if associated with a price for product B which would only sell, say, 10,000 units. 7,000 units of B would be unsold and wasted.

5: PRICE

Price changes caused by cost changes in the firm

4.17 In the prolonged period of inflation since the 1970s, price increases caused by increased costs to the manufacturer became a common experience. The effect of inflation on price decisions was very noticeable and different organisations reacted in different ways.

(a) Some firms raised their prices regularly, eg car manufacturers often raised their prices every three or six months.

(b) Other firms gave advance warning of price rises, especially in an industrial market. Customers might then be persuaded to advance their purchases in order to avoid paying the higher price at a later date.

(c) A firm which did not raise its prices was in effect reducing its prices in real terms.

Competitive pricing

4.18 It is in the field of competition that price is the most potent element in the marketing mix. Professor Corey of the Harvard Business School summarised the role of price in competitive game-playing: 'The struggle for market share focuses critically on price. Pricing strategies of competing firms are highly interdependent. The price one competitor sets is a function not only of what the market will pay but also of what other firms charge. Prices set by individual firms respond to those of competitors; they also are intended often to influence competitors' pricing behaviour. Pricing is an art, a game played for high stakes; and for marketing strategists it is the 'moment of truth'. All of marketing comes to focus in the pricing decision.'

Competitive price changes

4.19 A firm may lower its prices to try to increase its market share; on the other hand, a firm may raise its prices in the hope that competitors will quickly do the same (that is, in the expectation of tacit price collusion). The purpose of such competitive initiatives will presumably be to raise profits or the firm's market share; however, in established industries dominated by a few major firms, it is generally accepted that a price initiative by one firm will be countered by a price reaction by competitors. In these circumstances, prices tend to be fairly stable, unless pushed upwards by inflation or strong growth in demand. Thus in industries such as breakfast cereals (dominated in Britain by Kelloggs, Nabisco and Quaker) or canned soups (Heinz, Crosse & Blackwell and Campbells) a certain price stability might be expected without too many competitive price initiatives, except when cost inflation pushes up the price of one firm's products with other firms soon following.

4.20 If a rival cuts its prices in the expectation of increasing its market share, a firm has several options.

(a) It will *maintain its existing prices* if the expectation is that only a small market share would be lost, so that it is more profitable to keep prices at their existing level. Eventually, the rival firm may drop out of the market or be forced to raise its prices.

(b) It may *maintain its prices* but *respond with a non-price counter-attack*. This is a more positive response, because the firm will be securing or justifying its current prices with a product change, advertising, or better back-up services etc.

(c) It may *reduce its prices*. This should protect the firm's market share so that the main beneficiary from the price reduction will be the consumer.

(d) It may *raise its prices* and *respond with a non-price counter-attack*. The extra revenue from the higher prices might be used to finance an advertising campaign or product design changes. A price increase would be based on a campaign to emphasise the quality difference between the firm's own product and the rival's product.

Price leadership

4.21 Given that price competition can have disastrous consequences in conditions of oligopoly, it is not unusual to find that large corporations emerge as price leaders. The operation of such price leadership brings about relative price stability in otherwise unstable price dynamic oligopolies.

4.22 A price leader will have the dominant influence on price levels for a class of products. Price increases or decreases by the price leader provides a direction to market price patterns. The price dominant firm may lead without moving at all. This would be the case if other firms sought to raise prices and the leader did not follow, then the upward move in prices will be halted. The price leader generally has a large, if not necessarily largest, market share. The company will usually be an efficient low-cost producer that has a reputation for technical competence.

4.23 The role of price leader is also earned by a track record of having initiated price moves that have been accepted by both competitors and customers. This is frequently associated with a mature well established management group.

4.24 Any dramatic changes in industry competition, such as a new entrant, or changes in the board room can endanger the price leadership role. In the UK petrol retailing sector Shell is frequently identified as fulfilling the role of price leadership.

5. CONCLUSION

5.1 Pricing decisions are important to the firm as they are the basis of their profits. In the next chapter we will be looking at the promotion that the firm can use to aid awareness and sales of their products.

TEST YOUR KNOWLEDGE

Numbers in brackets refer to paragraphs of this chapter

1 Why do economists believe that price competition in an oligopoly market is dangerous? (2.3)

2 Define price elasticity. (2.9)

3 Why is cost plus pricing popular? (2.12)

4 In determining price by looking at consumer demand, what is a consumer surplus? (2.35)

5 List four bases for price discrimination. (2.37)

6 Why might a price rise lead to a temporary increase in sales? (3.3)

7 When are sales maximising objectives favoured? (4.2)

8 What is a quantum point? (4.12)

9 Why are gift packaged items often sold at £4.99 or £9.99? (4.15)

10 What are the options available to a firm when a competitor cuts its prices? (4.20)

Now try question 11 at the end of the text

Chapter 6

PROMOTION

This chapter covers the following topics.

1. What is promotion?
2. Advertising
3. Planning a promotion campaign
4. Successful advertising
5. Branding
6. Sales promotion
7. Publicity

---

1. WHAT IS PROMOTION?

1.1 'Promotion' is concerned with *communication* between the seller and the buyer and is controlled by the seller who seeks to promote his products. There are different methods of promotion, namely:

(a)   advertising;
(b)   sales promotion activities, also known as *below-the-line* activities;
(c)   publicity or public relations;
(d)   the activities of the sales force (which we will examine in chapter 8).

1.2 Firms will use a combination of these promotion methods and the optimal *communications mix* will depend on the nature of the product, the market and the customer. For example, a manufacturer of industrial goods will rely more heavily on direct selling and sales literature, whereas a consumer goods manufacturer will use more advertising and sales promotion devices.

'Push' and 'pull' effects

1.3 The promotional mix is often described in terms of 'push' and 'pull' effects.

(a)   A 'pull' effect is when customers ask for the brand by name, inducing retailers or distributors to stock up with the company's goods. Thus, an advertisement that persuades customers to go to a retailer to make a purchase has a clear pulling effect in drawing products through the distribution channels.

(b)   A 'push' effect is targeted on getting the company's goods into the distribution network. This could be a special discount on volume to ensure that wholesalers stock up with products that the company is promoting. The analogy is that of pushing the company's products into shops and distributors so that they are available to the end user.

6: PROMOTION

1.4 Note that some promotional activities can have both 'push' and 'pull' effects. For example dealers could be given advance screenings of an advertising campaign that is to run. If the dealers are subsequently convinced that the campaign will generate customer enquiries (the 'pull' effect) they are likely to stock up in advance (the 'push' effect).

Definitions of advertising and sales promotion

1.5 *Advertising* is defined by the American Marketing Association as 'any paid form of non-personal presentation and promotion of ideas, goods or services by an identifiable sponsor'.

1.6 There are three important elements in this definition.

    (a)   Advertising is non-personal communication, and so the seller does not come face to face with potential customers.

    (b)   It is paid for.

    (c)   There is a clear, identifiable sponsor of the advertisements.

This definition clearly distinguishes advertising from personal selling and publicity (which is often not paid for, and if it is, the sponsor does not openly present ideas or products).

1.7 There is a grey area between advertising and publicity which might be called *sponsorship*. This is now a common feature in sporting competitions and events which bear the name of the sponsor.

1.8 *Sales promotions* are 'those marketing activities other than personal selling, advertising and publicity, that stimulate consumer purchasing and dealer effectiveness, such as displays, shows and exhibitions, demonstrations and various non-recurrent selling efforts not in the ordinary routine'. They are also called 'below-the-line' activities, distinguishing them from advertising, personal selling and publicity, which are 'above-the-line' activities.

2. ADVERTISING

2.1 Promotion, especially advertising, can be seen as attempting to move consumers along a continuum stretching from complete unawareness of the product to regular usage (brand loyalty). The AIDA model postulated by Strong in 1925 is a simple example of this approach known as the 'hierarchy of effects' model.

Awareness ⟶ Interest ⟶ Desire ⟶ Action

2.2 Strong's AIDA model has been extended by many writers, notably Engel Blackwell and Kollat in 1978, as follows:

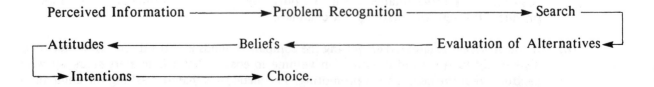

Perceived Information ⟶ Problem Recognition ⟶ Search

Attitudes ◄ Beliefs ◄ Evaluation of Alternatives ◄

Intentions ⟶ Choice.

2.3 Both these models assume that customers formulate a behavioural intention which then leads to actual purchasing behaviour.

The purpose of advertising

2.4 Advertising is 'purposive communication' to a target market. It assists in selling by drawing attention to the characteristics of a product which will appeal to the buying motives (conscious or subconscious) of customers in the target segment of the market. It does not necessarily instruct or inform about all the characteristics of a product; its function is to identify an exploitable characteristic (that is, one which distinguishes it from other products) and to suggest that this characteristic gives it a special value for potential customers. If the product does not have a distinguishing characteristic, uniqueness is promoted by brand image.

2.5 Advertising does not sell a product by itself. 'The purpose of advertising is to enhance potential buyers' responses to the organisation and its offerings. It seeks to do this by providing information, by trying to channelise desires and by supplying reasons for preferring the particular organisation's offerings.' (Kotler).

2.6 Advertising is often classed under one of three headings.

   (a) *Informative advertising:* the advertising is concerned primarily with conveying information and raising consumer awareness of the product or the organisation. This form of advertising is common when a product is in the early stages of its lifecycle, or if it has been modified in some significant way.

   (b) *Persuasive advertising:* this type of advertising is much more concerned with creating a desire for the product and stimulating actual purchase. It will tend to be more common for well established products, often in the growth/maturity stages of the product life cycle. This is probably the most competitive form of advertising.

   (c) *Reminding advertising:* this approach is also often used for well established products and it is concerned with reminding consumers about the product or organisation, reinforcing the knowledge held by potential consumers and reminding existing consumers of the benefits they are receiving from their purchase of a particular good.

Brand vs generic advertising

2.7 All advertising has some generic content as it stimulates demand for all similar products in the market whilst attempting to promote the brand against competitive products.

2.8 It will only be worthwhile for an individual firm to advertise if it can differentiate its products from other competitive products in the eyes of the consumer. In the absence of *product differentiation* all advertising purchased by an individual firm would be generic benefiting all producers equally at the firm's expense.

2.9 It is difficult to differentiate agricultural produce. This led to the evolution of the Milk and Egg Marketing Boards to advertise on behalf of UK farmers. Product differentiation can be strengthened by the creation of a unique brand image using advertising, eg the famous message 'Guinness is Good for You' that made an accumulative impact over some three decades of advertising. Campaigns using this slogan were the major factor in Guinness' growth from being just another stout brewery to the predominant producer of this particular brew. So successful have Guinness been that the term 'stout' has virtually ceased in common usage.

Above-the-line and below-the-line

2.10 Another distinction that you should be aware of is between above-the-line and below-the-line advertising.

(a) Above-the-line advertising refers to adverts in media such as the press, radio, TV and cinema.

(b) Below-the-line advertising media include direct mail, exhibitions, package design, merchandising and so on. This term is sometimes regarded as synonymous with sales promotion, which is discussed in more detail below.

(The 'line' is one in an advertising agency's accounts *above* which are shown earnings on a commission basis and *below* which are shown earnings on a fee basis. You need not worry about this.)

The objectives of advertising

2.11 The objectives of advertising may be any of the following:

(a) to ensure a certain exposure for the advertised product or service;

(b) to create awareness of new products, or developments to existing products;

(c) to improve customer attitudes towards the product or the firm;

(d) to increase sales (although it is difficult to relate advertising to sales volumes) and profits. For a non-profit making organisation, the equivalent purpose will be to increase response to the product or service;

(e) to generate enquiries from potential customers. (Advertisements in magazines might include a coupon or card, to be filled in and returned if the reader would like further information. Similarly, TV advertisements sometimes give a telephone number to call for further information);

(f) to change the attitudes and habits of people at whom the advertisement is directed. Government advertisements often have this objective - eg campaigns against drinking and driving, against smoking, warnings about burglaries and fire hazards and appeals to save energy.

2.12 Unlike sales promotion activities, advertising can have a long-term as well as a short-term effect. For example, 'Fly the Flag' for British Airways or 'This is the age of the train' or 'Clunk-click' for seat belt advertisements have created a lasting impression.

2.13 Advertising is also a means of protecting the longer-term position of a company. A manufacturer of a speciality good, for instance, may advertise the quality image of his product so that if at any time in the future a competitor provides a rival product, the longstanding image of the speciality good might be invaluable in protecting its market.

2.14 The objectives of advertising which were listed above are rather general. The more specific targets of an advertising campaign might be as follows.

(a) To communicate certain information about a product. This is perhaps the most important objective.

(b) To highlight specific features of a product which make it different from the competitors. The concept of the *unique selling proposition* (or USP) is that by emphasising a unique feature which appeals to a customer need, customers will be influenced to buy the product.

(c) To build up a 'brand image' or a 'company image' (*corporate advertising* - for example, oil firms like Esso and BP, the conglomerate Hanson Trust and the industrial giant ICI have all used television advertising in recent years to promote a company image).

(d) To reinforce customer behaviour. It would appear that advertising can reinforce brand loyalty or customer loyalty and 'remind' customers to buy again.

(e) Influencing dealers and resellers to stock the items (on as much shelf-space as possible). Resellers will probably prefer to sell items which are widely advertised.

(f) In the case of government advertising, to achieve a policy objective, such as increasing the takeup of benefits, publicising government unemployment initiatives, increasing recruitment to the teaching and nursing professions and eating more healthily.

The role of advertising in industrial marketing

2.15 Looking specifically at advertising aimed at industrial rather than consumer markets, the following are the principal aims of advertising.

(a) *Awareness building*. If the prospect is not aware of the company or product, he may refuse to see the salesman, or the salesman may have to use up a lot of time in introducing himself and his company.

(b) *Comprehension building*. If the product represents a new concept, some of the burden of explaining it can be effectively carried on by advertising.

(c) *Efficient reminding*. If the prospect knows about the product but is not ready to buy, an advertisement reminding him of the product would be much cheaper than a sales call.

(d) *Lead generation*. Advertisements carrying return coupons are an effective way to generate sales leads for salesmen.

(e) *Legitimisation*. Company salesmen can use tear sheets of the company's advertisements to show prospects in order to demonstrate that their company and products are not fly by night but respectable and sufficiently financially sound to run an advertising campaign.

(f) *Reassurance*. Advertising can remind customers how to use the product and reassure them about their purchase.

6: PROMOTION

The advertising campaign

2.16 Large organisations spend very large sums of money on advertising, and to use the money to the best effect, it is obviously essential to produce an advertising plan. Although organisations usually try to maintain a continual exposure of consumers/customers to their products, there are often periods of intensive advertising, involving perhaps TV advertising in one or more regions. This intensive activity is called an *advertising campaign*.

2.17 An advertising campaign will be planning and executed with reference to the the following factors.

(a) What is the aim of the campaign: to increase awareness and/or increase sales?

(b) The advertising message - what does the organisation want to tell its customers?

(c) Media selection.

(d) The frequency of displaying the message (for example, the number of TV commercial slots).

(e) The style of the message: is it a factual campaign or a humorous campaign?

(f) The budget. How much money will be needed to achieve the desired campaign, or what budget constraints limit what the campaign will do?

(g) Evaluation of the campaign. The organisation and its advertising agency will want to know how effective the advertising might be/has been. Plans should be developed for:

(i) testing reactions to planned advertising during the development of the campaign;

(ii) testing reactions after the campaign has been launched.

2.18 An organisation might hope that sales will increase because of an advertising campaign. This is probably what does happen, but the link between advertising and higher sales has not yet been conclusively or scientifically proved.

3. PLANNING A PROMOTION CAMPAIGN

3.1 A successful promotion campaign must be well planned. There are six distinct steps in planning such a campaign (focusing on advertising as a promotional technique):

Step 1: Identify the target audience
Step 2: Specify the promotional message
Step 3: Select media
Step 4: Schedule media
Step 5: Set the promotional budget
Step 6: Evaluate promotional effectiveness

Step 1: identifying the target audience

3.2 A list of dimensions which could be of use in identifying the target audience, depending on the type of product, is given below.

    (a) Sex
    (b) Age group
    (c) Marital status
    (d) Number and ages of children
    (e) Social group
    (f) ACORN group
    (g) Location
    (h) Income levels
    (i) Social group membership (sports, hobbies, professional)
    (j) Stage in life cycle
    (k) Buying roles within the family (purchaser, user, influencer)
    (l) Ownership of particular consumer durables.

3.3   In addition to these basic factors, personality and attitudinal variables can be added to give a more detailed insight into the lifestyle of the audience. The *psychographics* approach enables campaigns to be planned which emphasise how the brand has relevance for the style of living of the target audience. Creativity is used to emphasise mood, atmosphere and environment for brand usage, usually relying on non-verbal communication such as background setting for an advertisement (indoor/outdoor, relaxed or tense environment, type of music, style of furniture, use of colour schemes, appearance of models etc).

3.4   These factors are particularly relevant when the aim of the campaign involves persuasion of the audience. Various research projects have been conducted which have attempted to identify relevant correlates of persuasibility. On balance the evidence is not conclusive. However, Karlins and Abelson conclude their studies by stating that 'In our society, women are more persuasible than men'. Other studies, summarised by Delozier, have shown that 'in general a person of low self-esteem is more persuasible than someone high in self esteem, especially when social approval is involved' and that 'no consistent relationship exists between general intelligence and persuasibility'.

3.5   For industrial goods the social and sociopsychological variables are still valid but are perhaps not as important as are economic factors in the audience dimension process. Factors affecting behaviour include:

    (a) size of company (turnover, number of employees, profit levels);
    (b) production process;
    (c) type of business activity;
    (d) location;
    (e) centralisation of buying;
    (f) buying process;
    (g) interdepartmental rivalries.

Step 2: specifying the promotional message

3.6   People are very specific about the advertisements to which they pay attention. Most of us have the opportunity to see many hundreds of advertisements in many media each day, and cannot give our attention to each and every one.

3.7 The nature and degree of selectivity reflect the needs, value systems and past experience of the audience. Unless a particular advertisement engages the recipient's attention, it will simply be ignored or forgotten.

3.8 Thinking of a suitable advertising message is not the spectacular creative process it is sometimes made out to be. It is usually a long and painstaking process. Potential messages need to be tested on a representative sample of the target audience. Commonly, this test is carried out using *qualitative market research methods* involving group discussions. In these discussions, the reaction to the proposed message is probed and refinements suggested. Given the competition between advertisements for attention by the target audience the need to maximise the initial impact of the proposed advertisement is vital. Care is also necessary that the correct psychological clues as to nature of the product and of the people to whom it is intended to appeal are incorporated into the advertisement.

3.9 The essence of specifying the promotional message lies in identifying the intended function of the campaign. This function could be:

(a) to convey information;
(b) to alter perceptions;
(c) to stimulate desires;
(d) to produce conviction;
(e) to direct action;
(f) to provide reassurance.

Each function can suggest an appropriate form for, and content of, the message.

Fear appeals

3.10 Much research has been directed at how far the content of the message is likely to be influential in effecting attitude change. In particular, studies have been concerned with the varying effects of persuasive messages, some of which are assumed to have greater influence because they play upon the emotions of an audience, whilst others rely on a rational approach to intelligence and good sense. Both the rational and emotional appeal approaches have strong supporters - people tend to advocate one or the other as being the more potent.

3.11 In many early experiments the findings were quite contradictory. This is understandable if for no other reason than that clear-cut identification of messages and their effects is not easy. What might be regarded as an entirely rational appeal may arouse emotions and, conversely, emotional appeals may make a person think. Other problems were evident also; independent judges could not agree upon which of the two categories the message fell into, and many of the experiments failed to indicate how and why one or other form of appeal was effective.

3.12 A very common type of emotional appeal is the 'fear appeal', often conveyed through the mass media (TV, radio, national papers). Governments try to induce greater efforts on the part of individuals by indicating the likelihood of national bankruptcy if there is a failure to produce and expect more. Medical organisations may emphasise how pain and disease will follow upon disregard for health and hygiene. Insurance companies may display posters of the 'this could happen to you' type when attempting to promote the sales of their varied policies: life, accident, fire, childrens' education and so on. Commercial advertisers play upon our need for acceptance and popularity by showing how these can achieved if we use their toothpaste or deodorants.

3.13 The conclusion from various studies appears to be that a strong appeal induces considerable anxiety but is unlikely to change attitudes. A restrained appeal may well change attitudes (resulting, for example, in purchase of a new brand of toothpaste) and such attitudes are likely to last longer.

Step 3: select media

3.14 'Media advertising' means advertising through the media, which include national newspapers, regional newspapers, magazines and periodicals, trade and technical journals, directories, television, posters and transport advertising, cinema and radio.

Each medium provides access to a certain type of audience, and it is worth looking at some of these media in more detail with a view to recognising audience characteristics.

(a) *National newspapers*. Newspapers have a short life (one day) but a high attention value. If the product advertised has peak periods of demand during the week or month (for example, entertainment at the weekend) newspaper advertising can be timed to coincide with greater customer interest in the product. Some positions in the newspaper are more attention-getting than others but the positioning decisions are made by the newspaper's own advertisement manager. Some firms now rely almost exclusively on newspaper advertisements to sell their products by post.

(b) *Regional newspapers*. Local newspapers reach a concentrated geographical area, and are suitable for advertising to a geographical market segment. Many advertisements in local newspapers are by local firms (for example car dealers, estate agents) but a national firm might also use regional newspaper advertising of its product or service (for example the local electricity or gas showrooms) or to test a proposed national campaign at a local level.

(c) *Magazines and trade press*. The advertiser can select a magazine for advertising according to the content of the magazine which identifies the interests of the audience. Magazines have a longer duration of interest than a newspaper and actual readership is many times in excess of the number of copies sold. Detailed marketing research information about specialist magazines is not usually available, because specialist magazines are not included in the coverage of the National Readership Survey.

(d) *Television*. Television is a mass medium which can be received in most homes in the UK. It is therefore used to advertise mass produced consumer goods. The country is divided into separate independent television regions, however, and a company will not usually advertise at the same time in all regions. The great advantage of television is that the advertising message can be communicated in a mixture of sound, vision and movement (which is unrivalled by any other medium except the cinema). Television reaches every socio-economic group, but the emphasis of the message may generally slant towards the lower groups (the greater numbers). Although television operates seven days a week and for many hours in the day, the prime 'slots' will depend on peak viewing time and the popularity of the programmes shown at any of those times (in comparison with the programmes offered by the rival BBC stations).

(e) *Commercial radio.* The first full year of commercial radio was in 1974. The audience for most stations is local and the target audiences are mainly housewives, younger listeners and commuting motorists. This is a developing field. Classic FM, for example, has been extremely successful in its first year or so of operation.

(f) *Posters and transport advertising.* This medium is often used as a complement to television advertising on the grounds that it can provide a reminder at, or near, the point of sale. As an example, poster advertisements for car seat belts have been positioned on the back of buses so that drivers following the buses could be reminded at the time of driving that they should be wearing their seat belt.

The disadvantage of posters are that the 'copy' needs to be short; there are problems of maintenance (due to damage by weather and vandals) and the prime poster sites are often held by a few industries and firms on long-term contracts.

(g) *Cinema.* The Screen Advertisers Association claim that the cinema is an advertising medium for reaching young adults (single persons with high discretionary spending power, engaged couples or young married couples). Although television is cheaper in terms of cost per 1,000, cinema offers a more specific target market and cinema advertisements (unlike television) have a captive audience.

3.15 The criterion governing the choice of medium for conveying a persuasive message for a potential market is that the medium used should be the one which will contact the optimum number of potential customers most efficiently at the lowest cost. The choice of medium will depend on who the advertiser wishes to reach with the advertising message. If the advertiser wishes to sell to a particular market segment, advertising through a national medium might not be cost effective.

3.16 The choice of medium begins with a study of the target audience's *media habits*. The audience for a particular medium may be analysed and the media which are most used by customers in the potential market will be chosen for advertising.

(a) *Television* is watched by viewers from all social groupings and is an ideal medium for advertising mass consumer goods.

(b) A particular medium may reach audiences with special characteristics; for example:

(i) the cinema is visited mainly by young couples;
(ii) many magazines and local newspapers are read predominantly by women;
(iii) there are magazines for qualified accountants, magazines for student accountants, magazines for data processing managers and so on.

(c) The size of *circulation* or *audience* for a particular medium is important, but there is no value in reaching a wide audience if they are not potential customers for the product being advertised. Expensive cameras, for example, are more profitably advertised in photography magazines (with small, specialist readership) than in national newspapers (which have a larger circulation). A high street butcher or car dealer should advertise locally (for example in local newspapers or the cinema) rather than over a wider area. Industrial goods would be advertised in a trade magazine, should advertising be required.

(d) It may be too expensive to try and reach an entire potential market with an advertising campaign; too wide a choice of media will probably bring diminishing returns on the money spent.

3.17 The advertiser will want reliable information about the audiences for each medium in order to help in the choice of media for an advertising campaign. Research into audiences is provided by the following:

(a) for major newspapers and magazines – the National Readership Survey or JICNARS (the Joint Industry Committee for National Readership Surveys);

(b) for television – JICTAR (the Joint Industry Committee for Television Advertising Research);

(c) for radio – RAJAR (Radio Joint Audience Research);

(d) for poster audiences – JICPAS;

(e) for the cinema – the Screen Advertisers' Association.

3.18 Another important consideration is *cost*. Advertising costs consist of:

(a) the cost of producing the advertisements;
(b) the cost of exposure in the media.

The costs of exposure are perhaps ten times the cost of production in consumer goods advertising.

3.19 The cost of a medium is measured by the 'cost per thousand' criterion. If a full page advertisement in a national newspaper circulating to 2 million readers is £7,000, the cost per thousand is £3.50.

3.20 Cost per thousand is a very simple measure, which should be interpreted with caution.

(a) There is no value in advertising female fashions to male readers, although males might account for half the readership of a newspaper; in other words, the advertisement might be reaching many people who will not be affected by it.

(b) Not all users of the medium will see the advertisement. Many TV viewers will leave the room during a commercial break; magazine and newspaper readers will not look at every advertisement.

3.21 Other factors in the choice of media are as follows.

(a) How many competitors use the medium? A company is likely to use a medium which is used by the competition. Competing advertising (in a magazine, for example) is likely to result in diminishing returns from the advertisements.

(b) What is the 'environment' of the medium – that is, the circumstances in which an advertisement is shown to its audience? As mentioned above, one of the features of television advertising is that a large number of people leave the room during a commercial break, or during short programmes for a charity appeal. Radio commercials are often sandwiched between music, and the problem here is to ensure that an advertising message is memorable and registers with the listener.

Posters are seen for brief moments, and are mainly useful as 'reminders' rather than as a medium for conveying an initial message. Newspaper and magazine advertisements are 'confined' by the static, limited space available to them, and they have to 'fight' with the news and features for the attention of the reader. Cinema audiences are largely 'captive' and are usually prepared to watch advertisements on the screen.

(c) What is the nature of the product? Some items are more suited to advertisements in a Sunday newspaper colour supplement and others to a trade journal.

(d) What is the message? The nature of the information might help to determine the choice of media, for example technical data would be suited to a technical journal. (Advertising copywriters will adjust the *wording* of a message to suit the medium, but they cannot change the nature of the information which the advertiser wishes to put across.)

Step 4: scheduling media

3.22 An advertiser will not restrict his campaign to one advertisement in a single newspaper or one appearance of an advertisement on television.

(a) An advertisement must be repeated because many of the target audiences will miss it the first time it appears.

(b) It has been found that a larger target audience is reached by advertising in several newspapers instead of just one, and in several media instead of just one.

The theoretical optimal level of advertising

3.23 It is generally undisputed that it is necessary to advertise. The problem facing management is just how much advertising maximises profits.

3.24 It is possible to construct a theoretical model showing an idealised solution. Such a model is shown below.

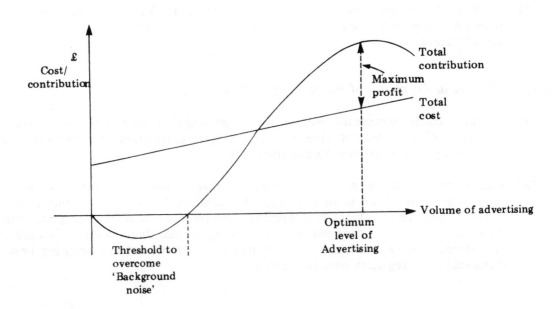

Assumptions: no scale discounts for volume of advertising

S shaped total contribution curve $(f = (x)^3)$

3.25 Market research and advertising agencies attempted with little success to produce computer simulations of models similar to the above in the mid 1960s. These attempts failed because economists always make the proviso *ceteris paribus* (all other things being equal) which in practice renders many theories impossible to prove or disprove. All other things rarely are equal - they change unexpectedly.

3.26 In reality exogeneous influences such as the marketing activities of competitors mask any underlying relationship between advertising spend and profits. The above model shows a threshold effect where more money is being spent on advertising but where consumers do not yet notice the campaign, perhaps because of the background noise effect of all the other, perhaps larger scale, campaigns. Once past this threshold consumers start taking notice and the contribution of advertising spend shows increasing returns to scale. This effect cannot be maintained indefinitely and whilst contribution still increases the effect moves into an area of diminishing returns. Where the slope of the total advertising cost is tangential to the total advertising contribution curve, the theoretical maximum benefit is achieved.

Step 5: setting the promotional budget

3.27 In an ideal world the budget for a campaign should be determined by a consideration of the four steps discussed so far. The budget needed is that which meets the objectives using the chosen media to convey the required message. In reality the constraint of what the organisation can afford is commonly paramount. It is noteworthy that in an economic recession it is often the advertising budget that is first to be cut when one could argue that it should be increased. The 'value for money' from advertising is not always appreciated by senior management, often because it is very difficult to quantify.

3.28 The promotional budget is often linked to sales using:

(a) a percentage of last period sales;
(b) a percentage of expected (target) sales;
(c) a percentage of past (or target) profit.

3.29 By using these methods advertising is determined by sales quantity rather than by revenue (quantity × price). When sales (past or present) increase then advertising expenditure will increase - when one could argue that it should decrease. Another approach is to match the advertising expenditure levels of rivals; again, there is little theoretical justification for this approach.

Step 6: measuring the success of advertising

3.30 An advertising campaign can only be termed successful if it generates profit for the company. However, it is almost impossible to measure the effect on sales and profits by any direct means. The problem is that advertising never takes place in a vacuum and other events in the market place, such as competitors' actions, changing attitudes and relative price changes, swamp the advertising effect. It is therefore necessary to observe changes earlier on in the buying process. The assumption being that favourable changes in awareness and attitude will result in higher sales and profits.

3.31 There is a paradox involved in trying to measure the effectiveness of advertising. The early stages in the process by which advertising generates sales are easy to measure (for example exposure by readership and/or viewer surveys) but are of little direct importance. The real effect that is of interest is obviously the net increase in sales. However, the sales effect can at best be inferred.

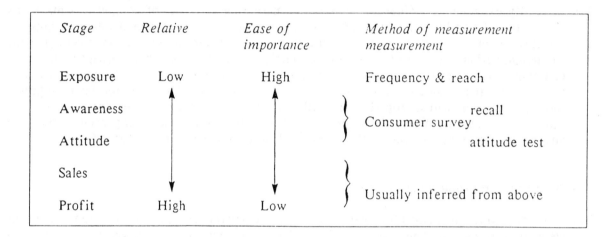

Stage	Relative importance	Ease of measurement	Method of measurement
Exposure	Low	High	Frequency & reach
Awareness			recall
			Consumer survey
Attitude			attitude test
Sales			
Profit	High	Low	Usually inferred from above

(a) *Exposure.* Exposure can be measured in terms of frequency (for example the number of times a TV advertisement is screened, the number of posters put up on hoardings) and the number of potential customers reached. One TV advertisement might reach 2 million people; by repeating the advertisement, the intention would be to reach people who missed the advertisement previously, but also to reinforce the message through repetition to people who have seen it before.

(b) *Awareness.* Awareness would have to be clearly defined as awareness of the existence of a product, or awareness of certain particular features of a product. Awareness could be measured by recall tests or recognition tests (see chapter 2).

(c) *Attitudes.* The aim of a campaign might be expressed in terms of 'x% customers should show a preference for Product A over rival products'; or 'y% of customers should show a favourable attitude towards the product or service'. Market research can be used to discover whether targets appear to have been achieved.

(d) *Sales (volume and/or revenue).* Advertising is often intended to increase sales. In the case of mail order advertising, where there is direct dealing between the seller and the consumer, often on application forms issued by the seller, the effect of a new advertising campaign on sales should be fairly easy to measure. In other cases, however, the effect of advertising on sales is not easy to measure.

(i) Advertising is only one part of a marketing mix. Other factors influencing sales might be price changes, whether retailers have stocked enough of the products to meet an increase in demand or whether competitors are also advertising rival products at the same time.

(ii) Advertising might succeed in maintaining a firm's existing market share, without actually increasing sales. There are obvious practical difficulties in estimating accurately what the fall in sales would have been if an advertising campaign had not been undertaken.

(e) *Profits*. The aim of an advertising campaign might be to increase profits, sales volume or revenue. The difficulties of measuring the effect of an advertising campaign on profits are therefore the same as those described in (c) above.

However, an advertising campaign must earn at least sufficient extra profits (contribution) to cover the costs of the campaign itself. Breakeven analysis can be used to calculate the volume of extra sales required to cover the (fixed) costs of the advertising. In monitoring the effects of a campaign, management might be able to judge whether this minimum increase in sales probably has, or probably has not, been achieved.

(f) *Enquiries*. Advertising might be aimed at generating extra enquiries from potential customers (for example mail order advertising, but also advertising for goods and services such as building services, double glazing, plumbing services and so on). Where possible, enquiries should be traced back to the advertisement. For example, a customer reply coupon in a magazine advertisement should be printed with an identification number or label, identifying the magazine and date of its issue.

4. SUCCESSFUL ADVERTISING

4.1 The *content* of an advertisement is determined largely by the objective of the advertising and the motivation of the potential customer. For example, it may be informative, or it may 'knock' competing products. Some advertising slogans succeed in becoming well known phrases. Emotions may be exploited (for consumer goods rather than industrial goods) to attract attention to the advertisement so that the message of the advertisement can be put across to a potential customer whose emotional interest has been aroused. An advertisement should present information which leads to a greater awareness of the product; using non-economic emotions (fear, humour) should be an attention-getter, but inciting these feelings should not be allowed to be the only effect of the advertisement.

4.2 The content of advertisements is regulated by the British Code of Advertising Practice and members of the public can make individual complaints to the Advertising Standards Authority (ASA). There are also many statutory controls, which for example, include the Trades Description Acts 1968, the Foods and Drugs Act 1965 and the Labelling of Food Regulations.

4.3 In certain classes of products that may be injurious to health it is virtually impossible to make any product claims in advertisements that are acceptable within the ASA's code of practice. Increasingly, therefore, advertisements for cigarettes and alcoholic drinks are designed to hold the viewer's attention, thus reinforcing the exposure to the brand image, without attempting to communicate any product benefits.

4.4 Advertising will be most successful if the following conditions apply.

(a) The product should have characteristics which lend themselves to advertising.

(i) It should be distinctive and identifiable (if it is not, a distinctive brand may be created).

(ii) It should stimulate emotional buying (emotive products such as medicine, insurance and cosmetics and products which can be made to arouse social instincts, such as cars, alcohol, cigarettes and household appliances, can be advertised with great effectiveness).

(iii) If at the point of sale a customer can refute an advertising claim simply by inspecting the product, advertising will achieve no sales at all.

(b) There should be consistency throughout the sales operation. Advertising, the activities of salesmen and dealers, branding, packaging and pricing should all promote the same product image.

(c) There should be co-operation between advertising staff and all other activities in the company. Product design, production, distribution, selling and financial operations should all combine to achieve customer orientation and maximum selling efficiency.

Advertising agencies

4.5 Most large scale advertising involves not just an advertiser and the media owners, but also an advertising agency. An advertising agency advises its client on the planning of a campaign and buys advertising 'space' in various media on behalf of its client. The success of advertising depends largely on the artistic skills of an agency's copywriters and artists but there is a 'scientific' approach to advertising which complements the artistic side.

4.6 An advertising agency is appointed by clients to conduct an advertising campaign on their behalf. In the UK they receive a commission (of 10% or 15%) from the owners of the media with whom they place the advertisements.

4.7 Large or medium sized agencies may be creative agencies (specialising in originating creative ideas, which are necessary for, say, TV advertising) or media buyers (whose specialist skills are in buying media space and air time). Advertising of industrial goods is usually handled by smaller 'industrial agencies' which have the accounts of chemical, transportation and engineering firms. Most of their work is in the sphere of sales promotions, such as direct mail, exhibitions and public relations.

Advantages of agencies

4.8 The advantages of advertising agencies are as follows.

(a) From the media owner's point of view:

(i) they reduce the number of organisations with whom they have to deal;

(ii) agencies are bound to conform to the British Code of Advertising Practice in order to obtain their commission.

(b) From the advertiser's point of view:

(i) an agency's specialised services are likely to be cheaper than an internal advertising department;

(ii) an agency will have broader contacts with ancillary services such as printers and photographers;

(iii) the advertiser receives expert advice (for example from the agency's account executive) free of charge;

(iv) agency employees have a broad experience in the field of advertising.

The advertiser and the agency

4.9 To take full advantage of the agency's services, the advertisement manager of the advertising company must:

(a) have a working knowledge of advertising;

(b) be able to negotiate with the agency so that the proposed campaign appears to achieve the marketing aims of the organisation;

(c) transmit whatever information is necessary to the agency which may be of value in furthering the advertising campaign in the best interests of the organisation (for example the annual report and accounts, copies of all the news releases and house journals, changes in products, packaging or distribution methods and news about R & D).

4.10 The depth of potential for distrust between client and agency is pointed up by a Media Audits survey of March 1992. More than half of the companies surveyed believe their agencies are overcharging them on their invoices. 42% think fraudulent practices are widespread. Nearly three-quarters would favour some form of payment by results. Two problems come immediately to mind.

(a) What is the value of a new idea? It is obvious, once conceived, yet how much time and skill went into the creativity? And what is that time and skill worth?

(b) How can a yardstick for payment be determined when communication objectives refer to behavioural changes in members of target audiences, when there is a limited research budget, and when the tangible results of promotion are likely to be spread over a considerable period?

The only solution is for both client and agency to work hard at establishing and maintaining mutual trust - and this means open books on both sides. Client and agency are both in business to make a profit: it is only good sense if each helps the other, with the minimum of secrecy.

4.11 The advertisement manager may be supported by specialist staff within the firm (for example an exhibitions manager, brand manager or product manager or a public relations officer) but he should be involved in all dealings between in-house specialists and advertising agency staff, to ensure that advertising campaigns are fully co-ordinated.

4.12 Before looking at other promotional activities we will discuss the role of 'branding' in the communications mix and product design.

Exercise 1

The trade journal of the advertising industry is *Campaign*. This is targeted at people working in ad agencies but although a lot of the gossip about individuals will go over your head, reading *Campaign* will give you a very strong flavour of the industry and some fascinating insights into what goes on behind the scenes. You will also become familiar with the industry's jargon and find articles that are directly relevant to your studies.

Your task, then, is to buy (and read) a copy of *Campaign* from time to time.

---

5. **BRANDING**

5.1 *Branding* is a very general term covering brand names, designs, trademarks, symbols, jingles and the like. A *brand name* refers strictly to letters, words or groups of words which can be spoken. A *brand image* distinguishes a company's product from competing products in the eyes of the user.

5.2 A brand identity may begin with a name, such as 'Kleenex', 'Ariel', but extends to a range of visual features which should assist in stimulating demand for the particular product. The additional features include typography, colour, package design and slogans.

5.3 Often brand names suggest desired product characteristics. For example, 'Fairy' gives impressions of gentleness and hence mildness.

5.4 The reasons for branding are as follows.

(a) It is a form of product differentiation, which makes customers readily identify the goods or services and thereby helps to create a customer loyalty to the brand. It is therefore a means of increasing or maintaining sales.

(b) Advertising needs a brand name to sell to customers and advertising and branding are very closely related aspects of sales promotion; the more similar a product (whether an industrial good or consumer good) is to competing goods, the more branding is necessary to create a separate product identity.

(c) Branding leads to a readier acceptance of a manufacturer's goods by wholesalers and retailers.

(d) It facilitates self-selection of goods in self-service stores and also makes it easier for a manufacturer to obtain display space in shops and stores.

(e) It reduces the importance of price differentials between goods.

(f) Brand loyalty in customers gives a manufacturer more control over marketing strategy and his choice of channels of distribution.

(g) Other products can be introduced into brand range 'piggy back' on the articles already known to the customer (but ill-will as well as goodwill for one product in a branded range will be transferred to all other products in the range). Adding products to an existing brand range is known as *brand extension strategy*.

(h) It eases the task of personal selling (face to face selling by sales representatives).

(i) Branding makes market segmentation easier. Different brands of similar products may be developed to meet specific needs of categories of users.

5.5 The relevance of branding does not apply equally to all products. The cost of intensive brand advertising to project a brand image nationally may be prohibitively high. Goods which are sold in large numbers, on the other hand, promote a brand name by their existence and circulation.

5.6 Where a brand image promotes an idea of quality, a customer will be disappointed if his experience of a product fails to live up to his expectations. Quality control is therefore an important element in branding policy. It is especially a problem for service industries such as hotels, airlines and retail stores, where there is less possibility than in a manufacturing industry of detecting and rejecting the work of an operator before it reaches the customer. Bad behaviour by an employee in a face to face encounter with a customer will reflect on the entire company and possibly deter the customer from using any of the company's services again.

5.7 The decision as to whether a brand name should be given to a range of products or whether products should be branded individually depends on quality factors.

(a) If the brand name is associated with quality, all goods in the range must be of that standard. An example of a successful promotion of a brand name to a wide product range is the St Michael brand of Marks and Spencer; and Kelloggs use their family brand name to promote their (quality) cereal products.

(b) If a company produces different quality (and price) goods for different market segments, it would be unwise to give the same brand name to the higher and the lower quality goods because this would deter buyers in the high quality/price market segment.

Branding strategies

5.8

Branding strategy	Description	Implies
Family branding	The power of the family name to help products	Image of family brand applicable across a range of goods
Brand extension	New flavours, sizes etc	High consumer loyalty to existing brand
Multi-branding	Different names for similar goods serving similar consumer tastes	Consumers make random purchases across brands

5.9 *Family brandings:* the power of the 'family' name to assist all products is often debatable. In the early 1970's, United Biscuits and the Cadbury Group experimented with the joint distribution and manufacture of a range of cakes under the Cadbury brand. The Cadbury name was found to be a potent brand but *only* for chocolate cakes within the range.

5.10 *Brand extension* denotes the introduction of new flavours, sizes etc. New additions to the product range are beneficial for two main reasons.

(a) They require a lower level of marketing investment (part of the 'image' already being known).

(b) The extension of the brand presents less risk to consumers who might be worried about trying something new. (Particularly important in consumer durables with relatively large 'investment' in a car, stereo system or the like.) Recent examples include the introduction of Persil washing up liquid and Mars ice cream.

5.11 *Multi-branding:* the introduction of a number of brands that all satisfy very similar product characteristics.

(a) This can be used where little or no brand loyalty is noted, the rationale being to run a large number of brands to pick up buyers who are constantly changing brands.

(b) The best example is washing detergents. The two majors, Lever Brothers and Proctor & Gamble, have created a barrier to fresh competition as a new company would have to launch several brands at once in order to compete.

Trademarks

5.12 A trademark is a legal term covering words and symbols. A legally protected mark can be a very valuable asset because:

(a) the legal protection can continue after patent protection runs out;

(b) competitors will be prevented from using a market leader's branding as a generic term for a class of products (as has happened with aspirin and cellophane).

5.13 However, even with trademark protection the impact of a market leader's branding may be weakened by consumers who perceive the brand name as a generic term.

(a) How many people 'hoover' with an Electrolux machine?
(b) Have you ever 'xeroxed' on a photocopier not made by Rank?
(c) Hence the message 'It's the real thing' from Coca Cola.

6.   SALES PROMOTION

6.1 Non-media advertising and *below the line* advertising (or activities) are alternative terms which mean sales promotion activities. Sales promotions are used extensively, because there is often a direct link between the promotion and short-term sales volume. For example, the offer of a free gift or a reduced price 'bargain' will be made dependent on the purchase of the product. A promotion offer might be a free gift if the consumer sends in three packet tops of the product; or a competition entry form might be printed on the product's packaging.

6.2 Sales promotional techniques have a more direct effect on usage than does advertising. As such sales promotions can be particularly useful in inducing trials by consumers of rival products, the three for the price of two offer being a sufficient inducement to wean the consumer away from purchasing their usual brand.

6.3 Examples of sales promotion activities are as follows.

(a) *Consumer promotions:*

 (i) free samples;
 (ii) coupon offers (money-off offers);
 (iii) price reductions as sales promotions;
 (iv) competitions;
 (v) free gifts (in exchange for, say, packet tops. These are known as 'free sendaway premiums');
 (vi) combination pack offers (two for the price of one);
 (vii) off-price labels;
 (viii) trading stamps;
 (ix) samples;
 (x) exhibitions and demonstrations (eg the Motor Show or Ideal Home Exhibition);
 (xi) catalogues (notably the large mail order catalogues of mail order firms);
 (xii) on-pack offers (ie free gifts which come with the product. This is sometimes used for first editions of new magazines).

(b) *Retailer or middleman promotions as a 'push policy':*

 (i) extended credit;
 (ii) merchandising facilities;
 (iii) contests for retailers or shop assistants;
 (iv) consumer promotions and advertising act as a 'pull policy' to attract dealer attention by means of consumer demand.

(c) *Sales force promotions:*

 (i) bonuses;
 (ii) contests between salesmen (based on volumes of sale);
 (iii) sales motivators - ie gifts linked to sales.

(d) *Industrial promotions:*

 (i) sales literature and catalogues;
 (ii) special discounts;
 (iii) exhibitions and trade fairs;
 (iv) events - eg invitations to customers to visit the Wimbledon Tennis Championships or the Open Golf Championship;
 (v) trade-in allowances;
 (vi) inducements (such as diaries and calendars).

6: PROMOTION

6.4 Sales promotions are essentially short-term sales measures and an advertiser planning a campaign should not be tempted to sacrifice long-term prospects (for example brand image built up through media advertising) in order to spend too much on short-term promotions. Although sales promotion is short-term in its effects, its objectives are broadly similar to those of above-the-line advertising:

  (a) to increase sales revenue by generating extra interest;
  (b) to attract new customers;
  (c) to encourage resellers to stock the item or increase their stocks;
  (d) to encourage slow moving lines;
  (e) to clear out stocks;
  (f) to counter the moves of a competitor;
  (g) to launch a new product;
  (h) to encourage the sales force to greater effort.

6.5 Sales promotion can also supplement media advertising. 'Although display advertising can be very effective in making consumers aware of the existence of a product, inertia frequently prevents consumer sampling and some additional incentive is required to persuade non-users to try it. Promotions are designed to provide this incentive.' (Baker)

At whom are sales promotion activities directed?

6.6 Sales promotion activities may be directed at any of the following.

  (a) People who do not currently use the product or service. The sales promotion will attempt to persuade them to try out the item.

  (b) Existing customers. The sales promotion will try to persuade them to use the product or service more frequently, or in larger quantities.

  (c) People who currently use rival products. The sales promotion will try to weaken their current brand loyalty and persuade them to try out the promoter's own brand.

6.7 If the target for a sales promotion is a particular segment of a market (for example young girls, young boys, mothers with small children) the type of promotion (the type of free gift for example) will be specifically designed to appeal to a particular type of person.

6.8 A target for a sales promotion campaign might be to boost the morale of the sales force. By offering some incentive to customers or consumers to purchase their products, a manufacturer will then be indirectly trying to influence his sales force by making their task of selling easier - by giving them something extra to sell with.

6.9 Some types of sales promotion will now be considered in a little more detail.

6: PROMOTION

Merchandising

6.10 A manufacturer of consumer goods usually relies on reseller organisations (rather than direct selling) to bring the goods to the point of sale with the consumer. This dependence on resellers for the sales volume of a product will be unsatisfactory to the manufacturer who may therefore try to take on some of the job of selling to the consumers. Manufacturer involvement in selling to consumers is achieved by advertising, packaging design or sales promotion offers. Another way of extending manufacturer involvement in selling is by means of merchandising.

6.11 Merchandising is a method by which the manufacturer tries to ensure that a retailer sells as many of his products as quickly as possible. The manufacturer therefore gives advice to the retailer, either from the sales force or from full time merchandising specialists.

6.12 Merchandising is concerned with putting the manufacturer's goods in the *right place* at the *right time*.

(a) *In the right place*. The right place means not just the stores and shops with the highest turnover, but also the best locations within the store. In self service stores, some shelves are in 'strategic' positions which attract greater customer attention, and merchandising staff attempt to secure these strategic positions for the manufacturer's products. Due to the costs of merchandising work, these efforts will usually be restricted to the larger, more profitable stores with a high turnover.

(b) *At the right time*. In most stores, there are some days when demand is at a peak. Merchandising staff should try to ensure that if a strategic location is only available for a limited time, then this time should include a period of peak demand. Similarly, it is important to ensure that seasonal goods (Christmas items or Easter eggs) receive prominent display at the right time of year.

6.13 In spite of the need to ensure that the costs of merchandising are justified by the benefits of greater sales volumes, a manufacturer might provide staff for a short period to exhibit, demonstrate and sell his products within a store on behalf of the retailer.

6.14 The term 'merchandising' may also be extended to include the special sales promotion devices such as premium offers, competitions, free samples, two for the price of one banded packs, free gifts, gift coupons, picture cards, children's contests, which are used by the manufacturer, not only to attract consumer interest, but also to persuade the retailer to give the product a prime location in the store.

6.15 As an aspect of sales promotion activity, merchandising is designed to give a short term boost to sales. It is essentially short term in its intended effect and the retailer will later move the product away from prime locations, or give it a reduced amount of shelf space.

6.16 Other items associated with merchandising activities are *point of sale material*. The point of sale is the shop where goods are sold, and point of sale material is used in sales promotion. It includes:

(a)   posters (for example holiday posters in travel agents' offices);
(b)   showcards (for example dispensers from which customers can take the product);
(c)   mobiles (display items suspended from the ceiling of, say, a supermarket);
(d)   dump bins or dumpers: a product is dumped into a bin, suggesting a bargain offer;
(e)   dummy packs;
(f)   metal or plastic stands (to display the birthday cards etc of one manufacturer, say);
(g)   plastic shopping bags;
(h)   'crowners' - the price tags or slogans slipped over the neck of a bottle.

6.17 In the UK merchandising tactics have gained ground at the expense of traditional advertising media (especially the press) in the sales promotion of bulk-bought materials.

Exercise 2

Everything that you have read about advertising, branding and sales promotion will sound very familiar, but would you have examples at your fingertips in an examination? Pick some products that you buy regularly or are interested in and make a point of tracking their advertising and promotion over a period of several months. Note how posters and shop displays back up TV campaigns, and see whether the campaign attracts any 'free' publicity in the form of press coverage, or references by public figures like TV comedians. Is the promotion talked about at work or in the pub? Has the slogan caught on and fallen into general usage?

The more you look, the more you will see.

Sales literature

6.18 A further aspect of sales promotion is the provision of sales literature such as specification sheets, catalogues, price lists, leaflets or brochures, wall charts, calendars etc. These are particularly useful for industrial goods (although catalogues are an important feature of mail-order business and one used by some chain stores such as Habitat and Mothercare).

Exhibitions and trade fairs

6.19 Britain has been fairly backward in its use of exhibitions and trade fairs and even the new Birmingham centre does not rival the foreign exhibition centres of Hanover or Geneva.

6.20 Exhibitions as a form of sales promotion may be:

(a)   public indoor exhibitions (the Ideal Home Exhibition);
(b)   trade indoor exhibitions (Commercial Motor, Hotelympia);
(c)   public and trade indoor exhibitions (the Boat Show, the Motor Show);
(d)   private indoor exhibitions (arranged by a single firm, with guests invited to attend);
(e)   agricultural shows;
(f)   overseas trade fairs, where national pavilions exhibit goods from a particular overseas country.

6: PROMOTION

6.21 The advantage of exhibitions to the visitor are that:

(a)   the products can be viewed and demonstrated;

(b)   a wide range of up to date products can be seen in one place and expert assistance is available for answering queries.

6.22 The advantages of exhibitions to the manufacturer are:

(a)   they attract many visitors who are potential customers; prospective customers are met quickly and cheaply;

(b)   they are a valuable public relations exercise;

(c)   they are useful for launching a new product, or testing a market;

(d)   they sell the product.

6.23 Disadvantages of exhibitions are:

(a)   they are costly to prepare and operate;

(b)   they take salesmen away from normal selling duties because exhibition stands must be permanently staffed.

6.24 Exhibitions are more naturally suited to some products than to others. Where demonstrations are particularly valuable to the prospective customer (for agricultural equipment for example) or at least visual inspection and expert information are required (for example motor cars) exhibitions are a valuable means of sales promotion.

7. PUBLICITY

7.1 Publicity is defined as being any form of non paid, non personal communication, and like advertising, it involves dealing with a mass audience. Although some components are 'paid for', we can also include *public relations* under this general heading since it is concerned more generally with building and maintaining an understanding between the organisation and the general public.

7.2 Publicity offers a number of benefits to the organisation - so long as it is *good* publicity. It has no major time costs, it provides access to a large audience and the message is considered to have a high degree of credibility. The information is seen as coming from an independent or quasi-independent source as opposed to from the company itself. However, it is also one of the more difficult forms of promotion to implement and to control since the presentation and timing of information about the organisation will be in the hands of particular publicity channels such as television and newspapers.

7.3 Traditionally, publicity and public relations were seen as being centred around producing regular, informative press releases and building up good contacts with journalists. As a consequence, its importance has often been underestimated. However, with increasing pressure on advertising space, time and costs, the importance of publicity seems likely to increase.

Sponsorship

7.4 It is becoming increasingly difficult to undertake any sporting activity which is not sponsored. Sponsorship has grown very rapidly in the last ten years, and this growth rate shows no signs of falling off. Insurance companies and tobacco companies have been at the forefront of this booming industry covering cricket, swimming, table tennis, horse racing, snooker and a host of other sports, and indeed arts, events.

7.5 In marketing terms, sponsorship can be seen as a form of marketing communication. It stands alongside media advertising, personal selling, public relations and other forms of sales promotion as a method by which companies can communicate with potential customers.

7.6 It seems unlikely that there is a direct link between sponsorship and increased sales. It can be argued that the objective of sponsorship should be communication and is therefore seen as one form of marketing communication. There are many other influences on sales, and it is extremely difficult to isolate the effects on them of specific marketing activity. There are, however, several other potential *advantages* of sponsorship, besides awareness creation in a wider audience than could be reached cost-effectively by other forms of advertising and the media coverage generated by the sponsored events.

(a) Distributor and customer relations. Hospitality facilities at sponsored events can be used with effect to create and maintain positive attitudes towards the company on the part of middlemen.

(b) The impact of sponsoring 'worthy' events can have a wide positive effect on the attitude of *potential customers* toward the company's services. It should then be easier for the company's salespeople to conver these prospects into sales.

(c) Sponsorship has wider implications in public relations terms. It demonstrates good *corporate citizenship* and it may also have a positive impact on the company's employees. This would seem to be more likely the more the sponsored event fits in with the desired image of the company. The image of 'solid dependability' and 'protectiveness' and 'traditional British values' which might be thought to be likely to appeal to those seeking insurance policies should fit with the types of event which insurance companies sponsor: cricket, tennis, golf and athletics, as well as national orchestras and other arts events, are likely to provide such image links. The images of 'youth', 'fun', 'creativity' and 'imagination' connected with pop concerts make them attractive sponsorship events for soft drinks manufacturers and other suppliers to young people.

8 NON-PROFIT ORGANISATIONS

8.1 Before moving on from the four Ps it is worth considering whether they apply outside a commercial, profit-centred environment. Examples of non-profit-organisations are charities, churches, libraries, the police and so on. You may find it helpful to think of local authorities as your main example, however, since they have perhaps the widest range of activities amongst non-profit organisations.

8.2 From a marketing stance, non-profit organisations (NPOs) have much in common with organisations whose primary aim is to make a profit.

    (a)   Both have products and/or services.

    (b)   Both have organisational structures designed to produce and distribute their products or services.

    (c)   Both have 'customers' who consume the products and services.

8.3   One of our key definitions of marketing as being concerned with meeting organisation objectives by providing *customer satisfaction* is therefore self-evidently applicable to all types of organisation, whatever their profit orientation. 'In a non-profit situation, a marketing orientation involves defining what the organisation is attempting to supply or achieve; equivalent to defining the market in the commercial sector. A public library does more than provide books. It also serves as a meeting place, a support to local schools and a source of information for a wide range of commercial activities. When seen through a marketing orientation, libraries are, for example, involved in providing "leisure" and "information". Librarians should seek to improve services which contribute to these areas when looking for new ways in which libraries can be used - one local authority has recently added toys to its "product" range!' *(Lancaster, Pearson and Reynolds)*

8.4   Thus each of the elements of the marketing mix is relevant to NPOs.

    (a)   The quotation above is just one illustration of the relevance of *product* and *place*.

    (b)   *Price* is perhaps the most problematic of the four Ps in this context, but if you think in terms of *value for money*, local authorities, for example, have been praised or condemned according to the level and quality of services provided as compared with the level of poll tax or council tax charged.

    (c)   *Promotion* is a key issue for NPOs in the 1990s. This is what the Citizens' Charter is all about.

Exercise 3

Start collecting examples of the efforts of NPOs to market themselves. Look for press advertisements, study your 'junk' mail more carefully, notice changes in the way public services are delivered and presented to you in your local area.

---

9.   CONCLUSION

9.1   Promotion comprises advertising, sales promotion, publicity and the sales force's activities. Firms use varying combinations of these activities depending on the nature of their business.

9.2   Promotional activity may have either a pull effect (whereby consumers ask distributors for the product) or a push effect (whereby distributors decide to stock it) or both.

6: PROMOTION

9.3 The AIDA model suggests that promotion moves consumers from awareness to interest to desire to action. Advertising may therefore be informative, persuasive or reminding. It must be able to differentiate the advertised product rather than advertise the generic product.

9.4 The six steps in a promotion campaign are:

(a) identify the target audience;

(b) specify the promotional message;

(c) select media;

(d) set the promotional budget;

(e) evaluate promotional effectiveness.

You should be able to discuss each of these steps, in particular the factors involved in selecting media, the factors affecting the promotional message and the difficulty of determining the optional amount of, and the effect of, advertising.

9.5 *Branding* is used to differentiate products and so build consumer and distributor loyalty. It is most relevant in marketing mass market items in competition with very similar generic products. A range of products of similar quality can be successfully branded. Branding strategies include family branding, brand extension and multi-branding. *Trademarks* may be used.

9.6 Sales promotion activities have a more direct but possibly shorter term effect on sales than does advertising. There are many techniques, which you should be able to list and discuss. Merchandising is a particularly important one, concerned with getting a firm's goods in the right place (such as in the middle shelf of a rack rather than the top or bottom) at the right time (such as late night shopping on Friday in a suburban supermarket). Sales literature, exhibitions and trade fairs are also important, but with a less immediate effect on sales.

9.7 Finally, promotion may include public relations exercises, including sponsorship. The purpose of this type of activity is not directly to increase sales but to increase and improve the profile of the firm and its products, particularly in its target market. This aspect of marketing is vitally important whatever the profit orientation of the organisation.

TEST YOUR KNOWLEDGE

Numbers in brackets refer to paragraphs of this chapter

1   What is a push effect, in promotional terms? (1.3)

2   Distinguish between advertising and sales promotion. (1.5, 1.8)

3   What is the AIDA effect? (2.1)

4   List three main types of advertising. (2.6)

5   What is the role of advertising in industrial markets? (2.15)

6   What is likely to be the effect of a health promotion campaign which tries to frighten its target audience into changing its behaviour? (3.13)

7   What are the pros and cons of advertising in (i) a regional newspaper; (ii) the trade press; and (iii) the cinema? (3.14)

8   Which organisation measures radio audiences? (3.17)

9   Why is cost per thousand a measure to be used with caution? (3.20)

10   What are 'frequency' and 'reach'? (3.31)

11   List the conditions for successful advertising. (4.4)

12   How can a firm make best use of an advertising agency? (4.9)

13   Why is branding used? (5.4)

14   Distinguish between family branding, brand extension and multi-branding. (5.8-5.11)

15   Give examples of sales promotion activities aimed at (i) the retailer; (ii) the sales force. (6.3)

16   What is merchandising? (6.11)

17   Give examples of point of sale material. (6.16)

18   Give reasons for engaging in sponsorship. (7.6)

Now try questions 12 to 15 at the end of the text

Chapter 7

BUYER BEHAVIOUR

This chapter covers the following topics.

1. Customer loyalty
2. What influences customer behaviour?
3. How do people buy?
4. Models of customer behaviour
5. Features of organisational buyer behaviour
6. The organisational buyer behaviour process

---

1. CUSTOMER LOYALTY

1.1 It is important that each customer who deals with an organisation is left with a feeling of satisfaction. This outcome is important since it can lead to increased purchases and/or to a willingness to pay higher prices and thus to higher profits. If customers are satisfied they may:

(a) buy again from the same supplier;
(b) buy more of the same item or of more expensive items;
(c) advise their friends to buy from the supplier.

1.2 Making a purchase necessarily involves taking a risk. Everyone likes to get value for money, but the risk in buying a new product or buying from a new supplier increases the risk of dissatisfaction. It is important that the supplier helps to reduce this risk for new customers so that they are more likely to become regular customers.

1.3 *Customer loyalty* is important for several reasons.

(a) It means that customers will support the supplier when times are hard, making it difficult for competitors to attract them away from their favoured supplier.

(b) Regular customers provide regular and reliable income and turnover.

(c) It is possible to build rapport with customers over time which helps the supplier understand their needs more easily, thus making the sales process more straightforward.

(d) Customer loyalty is a source of goodwill and will enhance the supplier organisation's image. It can be a source of very potent advertising in that loyal customers may recommend the supplier to their friends or colleagues.

1.4 *Customer dissatisfaction* is the reverse of customer loyalty in the sense that it may dissipate established goodwill and can adversely affect the company image. The added complication is that bad news travels faster than good news. It is easier by far for new customers to be put off by a negative recommendation than for a company to attract new customers with positive recommendations.

2. WHAT INFLUENCES CUSTOMER BEHAVIOUR?

2.1 Understanding customer behaviour can be of major help in effective marketing management. However, there are many influences on customer behaviour and so the outcome in terms of purchasing decisions can be very difficult to understand from a rational viewpoint. Emotional and rational influences intertwine and lead to purchase outcomes which can seem illogical even to the buyer. We are all purchasers, and even organisational buying is conducted by individuals who have their own preferences and preconceptions which still affect them in the work environment.

2.2 We will now consider influences on customer purchasing decisions, namely needs, motives, culture, socio-economic groups, family and other reference groups.

Needs

2.3 There are many classifications of need. The simplest is to split needs into two main types.

(a) *Physiological needs* concern physical well-being and include needs for food, drink, warmth, sex and sleep.

(b) *Psychological needs* concern emotional or mental wellbeing and include needs for belonging (to groups), acceptance (by those regarded as important) and affection (of others).

2.4 We are born with these needs. In addition, we learn other psychological needs as we grow in society. These are secondary or learned needs and include:

(a) appreciation (by others);
(b) respect (by others regarded as important);
(c) recognition (of accomplishments);
(d) achievement.

2.5 The academic Maslow conceived a hierarchy of needs in which he not only identified needs but also ordered them, thus suggesting that some are more important than others. This hierarchy is shown below.

Maslow's hierarchy of needs

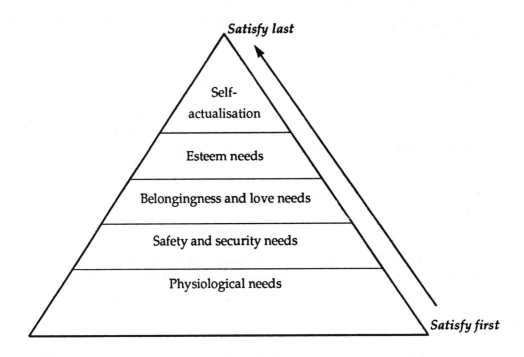

2.6 Maslow argued that lower order needs such as physiological needs must be satisfied before higher order ones such as self-actualization needs (making the most of your potential). Whilst these ideas are very appealing and have gained widespread interest there are major criticisms of his classification.

    (a)   Although research has tried to prove Maslow's hierarchy in practice, results have not been at all conclusive.

    (b)   Maslow's description of each category is vague and hence difficult to define precisely and test in practice. There has been widespread disagreement about how each should be defined.

    (c)   The hierarchy is too simplistic. Maslow later accepted that it can be possible for higher order needs to take precedent over lower order needs as the individual develops psychologically: for example the artist who paints (self-actualization) whilst starving in an attic (physiological need).

Nevertheless, Maslow's hierarchy is a useful way of examining people's needs and how they are translated into purchasing actions.

Motives

2.7 Motives sit between needs and action. A need motivates a person to take action. Motives are derived from needs. The differences between needs and motives are as follows.

    (a)   *Motives activate behaviour*. Being thirsty (need) causes (motivates) us to buy a drink (action). If the need is sufficiently intense, we are motivated to act.

(b) *Motives are directional.* Needs are general but motives specify behavioural action. A need to belong may lead to a motivation to join a badminton club.

(c) *Motives serve to reduce tension.* Essentially man aims to be in an equilibrium state. This aim is known as the concept of *homeostasis.* If we are too cold, we are motivated to reduce the tension in our bodies that this causes by seeking a source of warmth. If we are not accepted by those we regard as important, we aim to reduce the tension this causes by seeking to change our behaviour so as to gain acceptance by those we value. This tension is also known as *dissonance.* When it exists, we aim to reduce it.

2.8 For example, dissonance may arise when an item is purchased which does not give satisfaction. The buyer may feel that he has not 'done the right thing'. This tension has to be reduced. The buyer may convince himself that he has bought the right thing by rereading the sales brochure or revisiting the sales people who sold it to him. Alternatively, he may get rid of the item and reduce the tension in this way. Importantly, what remains is likely to be a negative image of the supplier.

Exercise 1

Have you ever bought something on impulse or been talked into buying something that you were not quite convinced that you needed? Try to remember how you reconciled yourself to the purchase.

Culture

2.9 Motives arise from needs and can lead to purchasing actions. However, motives do not tell us how consumers choose from the options available to satisfy needs. Other influences are clearly at work.

2.10 Culture represents a group's common interests. It is about values and characteristic ways of living in a society. Culture varies widely and has many influences as shown in the following diagram.

The impact of culture

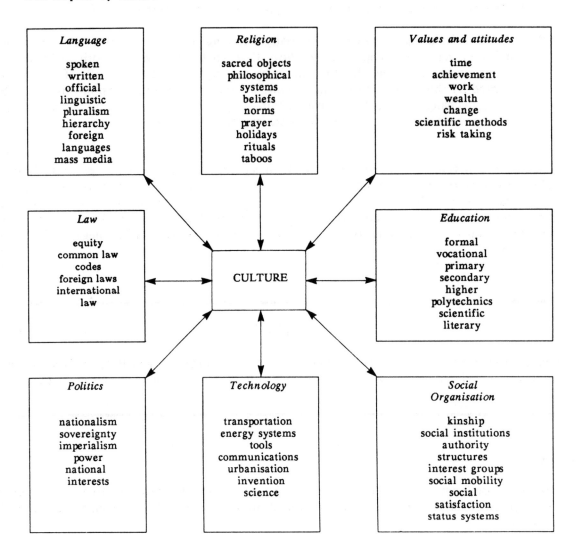

2.11 Culture varies between countries but also within countries (subculture). Not only do we have restaurants in the UK offering ethnic food (such as Chinese or Indian) but within the UK there are certain (although declining) regional differences in the food we eat - laver bread in Wales, lardy cake in the West and potato bread in Northern Ireland being examples.

2.12 Language differences raise obvious marketing implications when brand names have to be translated, often leading to entirely different (and sometimes embarrassing) meanings in the new language.

2.13 Cultural differences raise many purchasing issues influencing every facet of life. Cultural differences can affect purchasing in several ways.

> (a) *What* is bought (style, colours, types of goods/service)?
> (b) *When* are things bought (for example, is Sunday shopping approved of)?
> (c) *How* are things bought (bartering, haggling about price)?
> (d) *Where* are things bought (type of retail outlet)?
> (e) *Why* are things bought (influence of culture on needs and hence motives)?

Socio-economic groups

2.14 Marketing interest in socio-economic groups (as already discussed in Chapter 4) stems from the observable fact that members of specific groups have similar lifestyles, beliefs and values which can and do affect their purchasing behaviour.

2.15 Socio-economic classification is very commonly used in marketing and market research in the UK, yet it is simplistic. For example, in terms of disposable income (the take-home pay of workers) C2 members often have more money than do C1, which obviously affects buying capability. Also there is class mobility in that individuals and their families can move between groups, although their underlying influences may remain as they were or change only slowly.

2.16 Because of criticisms of the A - E classification more sophisticated measures of socio-economic group membership have been devised. An example (again, already discussed in Chapter 4) is the ACORN system (A Classification of Residential Neighbourhoods). This system introduces house type into the classification and every UK household has been classified in ACORN groups. Other work has cross-referenced ACORN with postcodes for every address in the UK making specific identification of customer types more flexible.

2.17 Further, more sophisticated, classifications based on socio-economic groups have been developed which add the person's activities, interests and opinions to the analysis. These analyses (known as psychographics) enable the identification of specific clusters of individuals who share similar activities, interests and opinions and hence, by association, purchasing behaviour. The 'He Man' cluster of young, aggressive, sporting men is one psychographic group. This group is a target group for lager advertising and sportswear, for example.

Family

2.18 Family background is a very strong influence on purchasing behaviour. It is in family groups that we learn how to be members of society and how to behave in different settings. Having learnt, it is difficult to forget. Family influences remain strong through the rest of our lives.

2.19 In the UK family structure is changing. There are more single person and single family households as the divorce rate has increased and as the population ages. There are now more single person households of young unmarried people than of older widows/widowers. The traditional nuclear family of husband, wife and two children beloved of TV advertisements actually represents a small proportion of all families.

2.20 The family is important in purchasing behaviour because it is often a 'purchasing unit' with one member (the buyer) buying on behalf of all members (users) but others in the family influencing the decision (influencers). Joint husband and wife purchasing decisions for major items are common.

Other reference groups

2.21 The family is a reference group in that in marketing decisions we use it as a reference point. Socio-economic groups are also reference groups in this sense. The immortal phrase 'keeping up with the Jones's' is a useful reminder of a further point: that other groups to which a person belongs or aspires can be strong influences on purchasing and other behaviour. Examples abound. Yacht clubs are synonymous with a particular style of dress (club blazer, for example) whereas working men's clubs conjure up different but no less potent images (such as the cloth cap). Different marketing approaches by suppliers would be necessary for each type of reference group.

Other influences on customer behaviour

2.22 There are other influences on customer behaviour in relation to suppliers.

(a) *Economic influences*
   (i)   Income
   (ii) Occupation
   (iii) Career prospects
   (iv) House type

(b) *Social influences*
   (i)   Family
   (ii) Socio-economic group
   (iii) Culture
   (iv) Reference groups
   (v)   Education

(c) *Psychological influences*
   (i)   Needs
   (ii) Motivation
   (iii) Personality

(d) *Sociopsychological influences*
   (i)   Attitudes

(e) *For organisational buyers: organisational influences*
   (i)   Company needs
   (ii) Inter-departmental rivalries
   (iii) Performance
   (iv) Buying committee/purchasing officer.

2.23 To get a better idea of how these factors can influence purchasing behaviour, we will continue by considering the major steps in the purchasing process.

3. HOW DO PEOPLE BUY?

3.1 People buy not because they want the product/service in itself but because they want to solve problems they have. These problems to be solved are rooted in the lifestyle of the buyer and are influenced by the factors we have discussed in this chapter.

3.2 There is an identifiable buying process which consumers follow through, either consciously and logically or, more often, unconsciously and intuitively. This can be summarised as follows:

(a) problem recognition;
(b) information search;
(c) evaluation of alternatives;
(d) purchase decision;
(e) post-purchase evaluation.

Problem recognition

3.3 The first stage in the process is problem recognition. The buyer must recognise a need and be motivated to solve it. A difference exists between the customer's desired state and his or her actual state, and this difference is sufficiently large to persuade the customer to act in order to solve the problem. The recognition, by the customer, of a problem (a need for a particular type of product or service) will be affected by the individual's personal characteristics, social position and relationships, economic circumstances and psychological make up.

Information search

3.4 The second stage involves seeking information which can be used in the decision making process as to how to solve an identified problem. Many sources of information exist and typically the more complex the problem, the more information will be sought. Sources of information include the following.

(a) Memory: if the purchase to be made is of a type which has been made before, then past experience is a potent influence.

(b) Family: reference may be made to past purchasing behaviour by the family unit. A child who has left home, for example, may buy the brands familiar from home.

(c) Friends: especially if a friend is a 'significant other', someone whose view on a particular type of product is respected (for example, a car enthusiast or a hi fi buff may be approached because their views on car or hi fi purchases are valued and seen as independent, and hence highly potent in influencing behaviour). Pharmacists are often asked to recommend patent medicines by mothers, a fact recognised by suppliers who try to convince pharmacists to recommend their brand.

(d) Sales brochures.

(e) Visits to sales outlets.

(f) Watching/listening to/reading advertising messages.

(g) Consumer advice sources, such as Which? magazine.

3.5 The process of collecting information regarding the possible purchases which could be made in order to generate a solution to a particular problem may be *internal*, based on past experience of a product/service, or may simply take the form of brand loyalty. Equally, though, the customer may undertake *external* searches, collecting information from manufacturers, distributors, other users, consumers' associations and so on.

3.6 Purchasers are at their most receptive to advertising messages at this stage. How to recognise and influence purchasers who are at this stage is an important decision, and making sure persuasive information is available is a key task.

Evaluation of alternatives

3.7 The third stage is to identify alternative solutions and to evaluate each option. This process may be as quick and simple as looking at competing brands on a supermarket shelf or it may take months if the purchase is important and the criteria are complicated (such as buying a car). Based on the evaluation of alternatives, the consumer will make a choice to buy, selecting that product which has the most satisfactory performance in relation to the evaluative criteria.

3.8 How the options are evaluated will involve both rational and emotional considerations. For example, a car can be evaluated on rational criteria such as price, economy, range of extras and performance but also on emotional criteria such as style, colour quality, image and personality.

3.9 The prime task for suppliers is to get their product on the customer's shortlist of options.

Purchase decision

3.10 The fourth stage is the purchase decision. The customer will see this decision as finding a solution to the problem he has identified. It is important that suppliers also take this view and thus express all communications to customers in terms with which the customer can identify.

3.11 Based on the evaluation of alternatives, the customer will make a choice to buy, selecting that product which seems to have the most satisfactory performance in relation to the evaluative criteria. In the absence of sudden or unexpected changes in the customer's circumstances or in the market place, the purchase decision will lead to actual purchase. It is of course possible that the decision will be not to buy or to postpone purchase until a later date.

Post-purchase evaluation

3.12 The process does not end with the purchase decision. Buyers reappraise their decision.

(a) If customers are satisfied with their experience of using the product or service then the next time a similar problem arises, they may short-circuit the decision process and buy the same product or use the same service. They become loyal customers.

(b) If a customer is dissatisfied, then not only will the same supplier not be used again but the customer may disseminate negative reports about the supplier and/or its products to others.

4. MODELS OF CUSTOMER BEHAVIOUR

4.1   We have now considered influences on customer behaviour and introduced one type of model of the purchase process.

4.2   The use of models for buying behaviour is an attempt to express simply the fundamental elements of a complex process. Such models try to express the interrelationship of those variables which are significant in influencing the outcome of a purchase motivation. Their aim is to help the marketing manager to understand the buying process so as to use a marketing strategy which is most applicable to the specific situation.

4.3   Thus the simple model discussed earlier in this chapter attempts to simplify and clarify the purchase decision process by showing it as a series of sequential steps. This type of model is useful to the marketing manager in trying to influence the process. For example, advertising and promotional activity is aimed at the information search stage and after sales service is aimed at the post-purchase evaluation stage.

4.4   The other major type of model is the theoretical model which tries to show the interrelationship between the various behavioural and economic factors which are involved. The aim is to give the marketing manager a better understanding of the buying process. Here is an example of a well known theoretical model, the Howard-Sheth model of consumer behaviour.

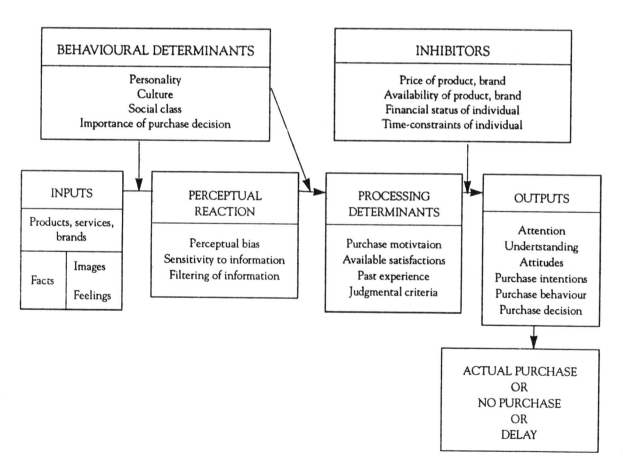

4.5 The Howard-Sheth model has a number of elements.

Inputs
Information inputs about the alternative services available include both rational and emotional elements. Thus, the interest rate structure information for a particular type of savings account at a bank or building society (rational or factual data) can be an input, as can the customer's reaction to the organisation's logo (emotional or irrational factor).

Behavioural determinants
These elements (covered earlier in this chapter) include the existing predispositions of the purchaser which have been influenced by culture, socio-economic group, family and personality factors, amongst others. This element will have a larger role for big or otherwise significant purchase decisions.

Perceptual reaction
Information from inputs is not accepted at face value but interpreted. For example, an individual is likely to value information more highly if it has been actively sought than if it has been passively received (from TV advertisements for example). The credibility of information varies according to the credibility of the source, perceived authority and content of the information. The customer will filter out information which is thought to be unimportant or which lacks credibility.

Processing determinants
These are the factors affecting how the information gathered is evaluated. They include motivation (based on perceived needs), the available satisfactions relevant to the purchase motivation and the individual's past experience of the supplier's services. The individual will also have some judgemental criteria with which to evaluate the alternatives. These personal criteria are clearly vital in the process. Organisations can use market research methods to try to identify these criteria so as to try to influence the individual.

Inhibitors
There are external constraints on actual or potential purchase behaviour. For example, for the purchase of a car, constraints could include:

(a) the rate of interest charged for a loan;
(b) legal constraints on credit terms;
(c) the price of petrol and performance criteria of different models of car;
(d) time constraints, such as the duration of a special offer.

Outputs
The outcome of the complex process of interacting elements may be a purchase decision, a decision not to buy or a decision to delay buying.

4.6 The Howard-Sheth model has a number of advantages over other models.

(a) It has been validated for practical examples of purchases.
(b) It indicates the complex nature of the buying process.
(c) It emphasises the need for marketing managers to analyse the satisfactions which customers seek in relation to the purchase of goods or services.
(d) It emphasises the need to gain a clear understanding of individual purchase motivations.
(e) It points to the importance of external constraints on the process.
(f) It suggests that customer satisfactions occur on a number of levels and in a number of forms at the same time. For example, both rational and emotional satisfactions are likely to be sought.

Thus the Howard-Sheth model can help the marketing manager to obtain useful and practical insights into customer behaviour.

Exercise 2

Using the Howard-Sheth model explain what the inputs, behavioural determinants and so on might be in making the following purchases.

(a)   A new suit
(b)   A packet of cigarettes
(c)   A meal in a restaurant not visited before
(d)   A microwave oven
(e)   A novel
(f)   A weekend break

---

5.   FEATURES OF ORGANISATIONAL BUYER BEHAVIOUR

5.1   All organisational buying decisions are made by individuals or groups of individuals, each of whom is subjected to the same types of influences as they are in making their own buying decisions. However, there are some real differences between personal and organisational buying decision processes.

(a)   Organisations buy because the products/services are needed to meet wider objectives: for instance, to help them to meet their customers' needs more closely. However, as individuals do not buy products and services for themselves but for the benefits they convey, it could be argued that both are forms of derived demand.

(b)   A number of individuals are involved in the typical organisational buying decision. Again, a personal buying decision may involve several family members, for example, and so may not be very different in some cases.

(c)   The decision process may take longer for corporate decisions: the use of feasibility studies, for example, may prolong the decision process. Tendering processes in government buying also have this effect.

(d)   Organisations are more likely to buy a complex total offering which can involve a high level of technical support, staff training, delivery scheduling, finance arrangements and so on.

(e)   Organisations are more likely to employ buying experts in the process.

5.2   There are many examples of different types of organisational buying behaviour ranging from simple reordering (for example, of stationery supplies) to complex purchasing decisions (such as that of a consortium to build a motorway with bridges, tunnels, for example). Although it is difficult to identify a useful overall categorisation scheme there are common features which can be discussed.

(a) Who buys? Is it an individual or a committee? What is the job title of the buyer? Who influences the process?

(b) How does the organisation buy? Are there discernible stages in the buying process?

(c) Why does the organisation buy? What are the factors which influence the decision process and what is the relative importance of these factors?

Complexity of organisational buying

5.3 One system of categorisation for corporate buying decisions, devised by Howard and O'Shaughnessy, is based on the complexity of organisational buyer behaviour. They identify three types.

(a) *Routinised buyer behaviour*. This category is the habitual type, where the buyer knows what is offered and is buying items which are frequently purchased. It is likely that the buyer has well developed supplier preferences and any deviation in habitual behaviour is likely to be influenced by price and availability considerations.

(b) *Limited problem solving*. This category is relevant to a new or unfamiliar product/service purchase where the suppliers are nevertheless known and the product is in a familiar class of products, for instance a new model of car in a company fleet.

(c) *Extensive problem solving*. This category relates to the purchase of unfamiliar products from unfamiliar suppliers. The process can take much time and effort and involve the need to develop criteria with which to judge the purchase, for example the construction and refurbishment of new offices where previously buildings were looked after by managing agents.

Large organisational buyers

5.4 An extra dimension in the organisational buying process occurs where the customer involved actually or potentially represents a significant proportion of the total sales of the supplier. For marketing purposes the relationship between the supplier and the large customer needs to be managed well. In addition, it is possible that independent intermediaries such as consultants are involved in the process, adding complexity. It is important to identify the dimensions of what is a complex buyer-seller relationship so that the supplier can try to plan and control the relationship.

5.5 In a Canadian study of buyers of industrial equipment (Banting 1976) the dimensions of the supplier-customer interface (where there is direct distribution) in order of importance were as follows.

1	Delivery reliability	8	Replacement guarantee
2	Promotional activity	9	Wide range
3	Technical advice	10	Pattern design
4	Discounts	11	Credit
5	After sales service	12	Test facilities
6	Representatives	13	Machinery facilities.
7	Ease of contact		

5.6 A study by Schary (1982) of head office buyers for a major UK food product group produced the following hierarchy of customer service elements:

1	Product availability	7	Pricing
2	Prompt quotation	8	Merchandising
3	Representatives	9	Product positioning
4	Order status	10	Invoice accuracy
5	Distribution system	11	New product introductions
6	Delivery time	12	Advertising

5.7 Whilst most commentators dismiss the interface between customer and supplier as being primarily concerned with a price-quality trade-off, the above lists illustrate the wide range of dimensions which are considered important in practice by the organisational buyer.

Choosing a supplier

5.8 In practice there are two types of dimension to the relationship between organisational buyer and supplier.

(a) Formal dimensions include objectively measurable supplier characteristics such as price, credit terms, delivery speed, documentation and product training.

(b) Informal dimensions include subjectively evaluated supplier characteristics such as technical product responsiveness, producer credibility, perceived sales representative quality and perceived ease of contact.

5.9 The reason for making the distinction between formal and informal dimensions is to emphasise the role which marketing can play in the supplier's attempt to influence the interface. In addition the distinction emphasises the importance of customer service in the supplier's marketing mix .

5.10 From a marketing perspective, the role of the sales representative is vital to the supplier. As the human face of the supplier company, the sales representative is a key figure in establishing the relationships between the supplier and the customer.

5.11 Much of the research work on organisational buyer behaviour stresses the rationality with which buyers defend their purchasing decisions. It is much more difficult to identify and evaluate the weight of informal dimensions of the interface than it is to deal with objectively measurable dimensions.

5.12 A further complication is that links between supplier and industrial customers can occur at different levels in the organisation. Indeed, for one off purchases the decision makers in the buying organisation need to be identified at an early stage in the marketing process.

6. THE ORGANISATIONAL BUYER BEHAVIOUR PROCESS

6.1 A number of models have been devised to try to encapsulate the essence of the organisational buying process. Here we consider two.

Wind's model: a model of industrial source loyalty

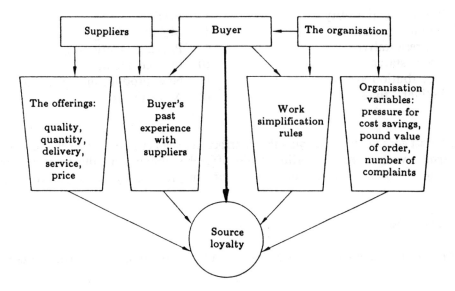

6.2 This model stresses *source loyalty:* in other words, the tendency for customers to continue to rely on the same supplier unless there are good reasons not to do so. These reasons are classified by Wind as:

(a) the offerings and dimension of the relationship with the customer;

(b) the past relationship with the supplier;

(c) organisational variables such as the degree of pressure for cost savings, the number of complaints;

(d) ways in which the organisational customer thinks the task can be simplified, such as convenience of access to the supplier, inertia and resistance to change.

Webster and Wind's model: a model of organisational buyer behaviour

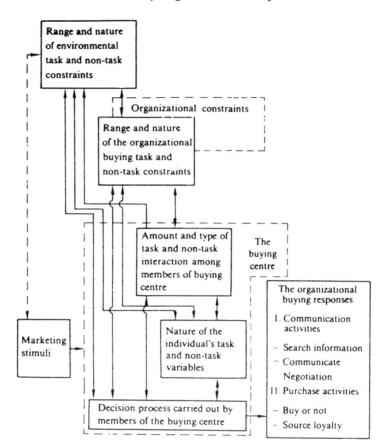

6.3 Webster and Wind together see organisational buyer behaviour as influenced by a number of sets of variables.

(a) The *individual characteristics* of the members of the buying centre, such as personality and preference, must be considered. These factors are similar to personal buying processes.

(b) The *relationships* between members of the buying centre are also important.

(i) The *user* may have influence on the technical characteristics of the equipment (and hence the cost) and on reliability and performance criteria.

(ii) The *influencer* is particularly useful where the purchase relies on technical knowledge. Unlike personal purchasing behaviour where opinions may be sought from colleagues, friends and family, competitive pressures and trade secret constraints may limit the sharing of information between companies. In this environment the salesman can be a respected technical link with the buyer and so be able to influence the purchasing process. Trade journals and trade associations or professional bodies can often be a good sources of influential information in addition to salesmen of the supplying company. Also, there is a tendency not to copy competitors but to seek one's own solution and thus demonstrate independence.

(iii) The *buyer* or *decider*. As already noted, decisions are, in the final analysis, made by individuals or groups of individuals. These individuals have personal idiosyncrasies, social pressures and organisational and environmental pressures. Thus each has a set of rational factors (task variables) and non-economic factors (non-task variables).

(iv) The *gatekeeper* who controls the flow of information about the purchaser may be senior or junior but is important because he/she influences the communication flow within the organisation.

(c) *Organisational characteristics* including the buying and organisational task, the size and structure of the organisation, the use of technology and so on. The relationships of the buyer within the organisation are particularly important. This post can be senior or junior and can involve power struggles with user departments. To retain and to try and increase organisational status, the buyer might use a variety of techniques designed to stress the buyer's role over that of financial or operational specialists.

   (i) Role-orientated tactics involve keeping to the formal rules of the organisation where these rules work in favour of the buyer's intentions.

   (ii) Role-evading tactics involve passive resistance to the rules where these rules do not work in favour of the buyer's intentions.

   (iii) Personal-political tactics involve manipulating the relationship between informal and formal relationships in the process.

   (iv) Educational tactics include using persuasive techniques.

(d) Environmental factors such as the physical, technological, economic and legal factors which affect general competitive conditions.

Decision-making unit

6.4 We can see that there are four main sets of variables influencing organisational buyer behaviour:

(a) individual characteristics in the buying centre;
(b) group characteristics in the buying centre;
(c) organisational characteristics; and
(d) environmental factors.

These four sets of variables interact in the decision process carried out by members of the buying centre. This is the *decision making unit* (DMU) of the buying organisation. In marketing terms the DMU is a vital target for the supplier's marketing initiatives. The size and structure of the DMU will vary between organisations, over time in the same organisation and for different types of purchase.

6.5 The marketing department of a supplier aiming at corporate clients therefore needs to be aware of:

(a) how buying decisions are made by the DMU;
(b) how the DMU is constructed; and
(c) the identities of the most influential figures in the DMU.

The decision process and the DMU

6.6 The diagram shows the decision process and the role of members of the DMU at each stage. Of course the process will vary according to the type of purchase being made.

A decision process model of industrial purchase behaviour

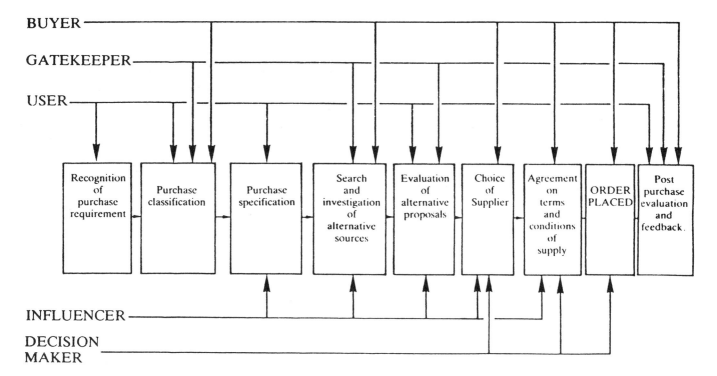

6.7 The organisational buying process is complex and needs careful marketing action if the outcome is to be influenced favourably.

7. CONCLUSION

7.1 In this chapter we have looked at the factors affecting buyer behaviour, moving from the consumer to the more complex case of the organisational buyer. In both instances, it is well worth building customer loyalty because this will build a solid customer base which should safeguard turnover and profits. It will also enhance the supplier's standing with potential customers and should enable the supplier to meet customer needs more precisely by using the more extensive knowledge of the customer base which can be garnered.

7.2 Customers have physiological and psychological *needs*, which Maslow suggested can be arranged in a hierarchy, although this is rather a simplistic analysis. Needs *motivate* people to act, but if action fails to satisfy a need, then *dissonance* results. An unsatisfactory purchase results in customer dissatisfaction.

7.3 Other factors affecting customer behaviour are culture, socio-economic classification, family influences and economic, social and psychological characteristics.

7.4 There are various needs in existence which attempt to explain how these variable factors affect the buyer process. One simple model suggests that the steps in the process are:

(a) problem recognition;
(b) information search;
(c) evaluation of alternatives;
(d) purchase decision;
(e) post-purchase evaluation.

Suppliers must therefore try to convince potential buyers of their need for the benefits provided by a particular product or service, and of the particular merits of the supplier's own offering. However, in the event of post-purchase dissatisfaction, a good after sales service will help to reduce, if not eliminate, customer dissatisfaction.

7.5 The Howard-Sheth model is a more complex model which attempts to link rational and emotional factors affecting the buying process.

7.6 Organisational buyer behaviour depends on the individual characteristics of the buyer, the user and others involved in the decision, such as technical experts. Howard and O'Shaugnessy suggest that there are three types of organisational buying: routinised buyer behaviour, limited problem solving and extensive problem solving. Suppliers need to consider what type of purchase their customers are engaged in and what factors will affect the purchase. It is important to ascertain the membership of the decision-making unit (DMU) and how the DMU is to make decisions.

TEST YOUR KNOWLEDGE
Numbers in brackets refer to paragraphs of this chapter

1 Give four reasons why customer loyalty is to be valued. (1.3)

2 Outline Maslow's theory of the hierarchy of needs and list the arguments against it. (2.5, 2.6)

3 Why is the family an important factor influencing buyer behaviour? (2.18-2.20)

4 What sources of information may be used in making a purchasing decision? (3.4)

5 What is the Howard-Sheth model of consumer behaviour? (4.4) What are its advantages? (4.6)

6 List the most significant differences between consumer and organisational buying decision processes. (5.1)

7 Limited problem solving relates to the purchaes of unfamiliar products from unfamiliar suppliers. True or false? (5.3)

8 What is the DMU? What is its importance? (6.4-6.6)

Now try question 16 at the end of the text

Chapter 8

SALES MANAGEMENT AND SALES FORECASTING

This chapter covers the following topics.

1. Introduction
2. Personal selling: general considerations
3. The personal sales process
4. Sales force management
5. Sales force organisation
6. Trends in personal selling
7. Sales forecasting

---

1. INTRODUCTION

1.1 In this chapter we will look at aspects of the work of the sales department, which nowadays, as we have already seen, is usually a subsection of the marketing department.

1.2 The sales department will include employees responsible for making sales, either over the telephone, or by going out personally to canvass potential customers. It is the sales manager's job to find ways of increasing sales and the obvious way is to motivate the sales force. In this chapter, therefore, we will be looking at the advantages and disadvantages of the most common ways of organising and remunerating the sales force.

1.3 Another important responsibility of the sales department is to forecast sales, and we will conclude this chapter by looking at the various techniques available for doing this.

2. PERSONAL SELLING: GENERAL CONSIDERATIONS

The sales force

2.1 The sales force is an important part of the communication mix. It engages in 'personal' selling, as compared with the 'non-personal' selling of advertising and sales promotion activities.

2.2 Each individual probably has his own ideas of the 'typical' personal sales representative, but it is interesting to consider the wide range of face to face sales activities which exist. Types of selling include:

(a) delivery staff who also sell (the classic example being a milkman);

(b) sales staff within the premises of the sales organisation (such as a shop assistant);

(c) travelling sales representatives, who require limited technical knowledge (for example soap, food and drink);

(d) sales staff who need technical expertise to sell their product, probably selling to a small number of potential industrial customers (for example salesmen of computer hardware or software systems);

(e) sales staff who need to create a sale through their selling methods where an established market does not exist (for example door-to-door selling of encyclopaedias and insurance policies).

2.3 To be an effective sales person, it is necessary to recognise problems of potential customers and to offer help in solving them. The buyer-seller relationship is critical, and it is the immediacy of this relationship of face to face selling that helps to 'make a sale'.

2.4 Given that the term 'sales person' covers a wide range of selling activities, it may be apparent that the desirable personality of the sales person is likely to vary from one type of selling to the next.

(a) Shop assistants are expected to conform to the shop's norms for appearance (so that, for example, Harrods staff should look smart and conventional), easily recognisable (for example, because they wear a uniform or stand behind a counter), and polite and pleasant.

(b) Travelling sales representatives must be able to strike up an instant rapport with potential customers. Shopkeepers welcome fast talkers and sales reps who bring news and gossip to accompany their sales 'patter'.

(c) A travelling sales representative dealing in consumer goods might also need to be able to convince shopkeepers and managers of the advantages of a sales promotion, in order to win more shelf space or a prominent display position in a store or supermarket. Sales promotion skills are therefore essential.

(d) A sales representative for industrial goods will expect to sell his product on its technical merits (or other comparative advantage). Persuading the customer by rational suggestions will require technical expertise, pamphlets and reference to other industrial users. Customers may be 'persuaded' over a business lunch. This style of selling, because of its special nature, is probably well suited to a more sober personality.

2.5 Recruitment and training programmes should operate to ensure that the right type of person is employed to do the job of selling.

The task of selling

2.6 The task of selling involves the following.

(a) *Communicating the advantages of a product* to the customer, to develop the target customer's 'product and market knowledge'.

(b) *Securing a sale.*

(c) *Prospecting* for additional customers. This involves searching for prospective customers, perhaps visiting them several times, and then making a sales 'pitch'.

(d) *After-sales service.* Queries and complaints will arise and must be dealt with to the customer's satisfaction, in order to win repeat sales;

(e) *Gathering information* about what the customer wants.

2.7 The selling tasks above are those of the travelling sales representative; selling tasks of the sales department may include:

(a) product delivery (remember the milkman);

(b) order taking inside the seller's store;

(c) order taking 'outside' by a field sales force;

(d) order taking by telephone;

(e) building up goodwill (such as by merchandising work);

(f) the provision of technical or engineering advice to customers, perhaps in helping a customer to draft specifications for a product;

(g) 'creative' selling of tangible products (such as door to door brush salesmen);

(h) 'creative' selling of intangible products (for example people involved in the sale of services such as banking, or insurance).

Personal and non-personal selling

2.8 Since the work of the sales force is only one element in the sales mix, greater dependence on advertising and sales promotion will mean a lesser dependence on direct selling. At one extreme, direct mail firms do not need any sales force. It is unlikely, however, that sales staff - even shop assistants - could sell without some advertising or sales promotion back-up.

2.9 A *sales plan* or *budget* should attempt to co-ordinate personal and non-personal selling, so that:

(a) the sales staff have sufficient sales literature to show to prospective customers;
(b) their task is aided by a sales promotion activity;
(c) advertising campaigns are used to prepare the ground for sales effort.

2.10 Although the emphasis of the above is the co-ordination of elements in the *sales mix*, the marketing effort as a whole will call for a co-ordination of all the elements in the *marketing mix* - product, price and place as well as promotion. Indeed, one of the tasks of a manufacturer's sales force might be to extend the reseller network by obtaining new reseller customers, so that the selling effort would be directed towards improving the 'place' in the marketing mix. Another example of co-ordinating the mix is the need to ensure that the sales force has a product to sell, so that stocks must be available and delivery dates promised should be adhered to.

Size of the sales force

2.11 An important problem is to decide the optimum size of the sales force. Provided that an organisation has sufficient resources to increase its output and distribution, the sales force could be increased up to the point where the marginal costs of extra sales effort begins to exceed the marginal revenue from the incremental sales. Effectively, however, the overall size of the sales organisation is restricted by the resources available to the company and by company policy, and by the balance in the sales mix between personal and non-personal selling.

2.12 Differing views exist as to whether sales staff should be given an equal workload (which relates to the number of calls and the size of customer) or whether they should be given sales territories of equal sales potential (regardless of geographical area) in order to optimise their efficiency. There are practical considerations here: the sales rep asked to cover South-East London will have less travelling to do between calls than the rep asked to cover the North of Scotland. The fact that these areas may have the same sales potential is less relevant.

2.13 Every organisation will have some idea about what it can afford to spend on selling. In practice 'rules of thumb' are usually applied. If it is decided that selling expenses should not exceed, say, 10% of sales and if a sales representative, with selling expenses and commission, costs, say £30,000 per annum, turnover of £300,000 per annum would then be required to support each representative. So, if a company budgets annual turnover of, say, £6 million, then the total sales force could then not exceed 20 staff.

The figures above are hypothetical, but should indicate to you about how a rule of thumb judgement can be made about the maximum economic size of a sales force, based on annual turnover and selling costs. Obviously, a complex sales force organisation would be inappropriate for a firm with only a relatively low sales turnover.

The selling organisation

2.14 The type of selling organisation will be influenced by various factors.

(a) Intensity of competition, and possibly the structure of a competitor's selling organisation, will affect a company's own sales organisation structure. If, for example, specialisation appears to give a marketing advantage to a rival product, a company might need to use specialised selling itself.

(b) If it is decided that personal selling by sales representatives is the most efficient way to sell, the quantity and quality of the sales force will reflect this decision (so low dependence on advertising may result in a greater reliance on personal selling).

(c) Whenever possible, specialisation of the sales force should be introduced (whether by function, product, type of customer, outlet or market).

(d) The extent to which dealers are used will affect organisation. If a company sells only to a limited number of multiple stores and wholesalers, a small sales organisation will be sufficient.

(e)   Generally, there is direct selling for industrial goods but sales are often confined to a few customers, so that the number of orders is small but their value high, and consequently:

(i)   the number of orders/size of sales force ratio is low;
(ii)   the value of orders/size of sales force ratio is high.

3.   THE PERSONAL SALES PROCESS

3.1   Many guides have been written on ways of improving the performance of personal selling. In this section, the main stages of the personal sales process (for example, for a sales interview) are highlighted with some common guidelines for each stage.

Stage 1: prerequisites

3.2   Before a salesperson begins work, a number of prerequisites should have been met.

(a)   The salesperson should have a *good knowledge* of the company and its products and service.

(b)   The salesperson should know the *limits of negotiation* within which the deal can be made regarding price, delivery terms, volume and cash discounts, credit and other relevant items.

(c)   The salesperson should feel that he has top *management support.*

(d)   The salesperson should feel a *respected* member of the organisation in order to have self-respect.

Stage 2: gain the customer's attention

3.3   Here the aim is to define the customer's need by identifying the problem which the customer is buying the product or service to solve. (Refresh your memory about buyer behaviour by looking back to Chapter 7 at this point.) A good salesperson should aim to follow these eight steps to attract and keep the customer's attention.

(a)   Don't mention the product until the *need* is identified.
(b)   Try to identify how the *decision* is to be made (such as by consideration of alternatives).
(c)   *Gain attention* quickly before the client loses interest.
(d)   Have a *good first sentence* (which is not 'Can I help you?').
(e)   Show he can *solve the problem.*
(f)   Ask *positive questions* (Have you? Can you? Are you?, not 'Haven't you?' etc).
(g)   *Avoid external distractions* (TV, telephone, other people).
(h)   Maintain *eye contact.*

Stage 3: create interest

3.4   This stage involves making the prospect interested in the product. At this stage, a good salesperson tries to match the product to the needs of the customer. The salesperson should:

(a)   *demonstrate* the product or service to let the prospect see for himself how it works;
(b)   get information from the prospect about his *needs*;

(c)   involve him in *conversation*;

(d)   not simply let the prospect look at brochures and so *lose his attention*, enabling the prospect to say 'I'll read it and come back later'.

Stage 4: stimulate the desire to buy

3.5   Here the salesperson should be seeking proof that the product does match the customer's needs. The customer accepting that it does so is the proof which is being sought. The salesperson should:

(a)   sell the idea or problem solution, not the product itself;

(b)   get the customer to decide on *principles* and sort out the *details* later;

(c)   *involve the customer* in the process;

(d)   remember that *repetition can reinforce*;

(e)   try to satisfy the customer's *special requests;* this involves him more closely and makes him feel special;

(f)   *anticipate events* - talk as though the sale is concluded and discuss after-sales issues (but do not write out the order until he agrees to buy);

(g)   show that the purchase is seen as *inevitable*, because radiating conviction can induce the prospect to buy;

(h)   invite the client to spell out remaining *objections* and then clear them up;

(i)   if no decision is made, if appropriate *keep in touch* with the prospect and try to make a further appointment (which should always be kept).

Stage 5: conclude the sale

3.6   The final part of the process can be the most difficult: the client must make the final decision, the salesperson cannot do it for him. The salesperson should:

(a)   ask questions that require *positive answers* whilst making sure that negative answers allow the sale to continue;

(b)   know what to say *whatever the response* of the prospect;

(c)   offer alternatives which are *positive* ('would you prefer this one or that one?');

(d)   *invite the prospect to agree* several times, moving closer to the sale each time.

3.7   These sales stages are bound to be generalisations and tend to imply a *non-specialist buyer*. Selling to a *specialist buyer* (such as an organisational buyer) is a more sophisticated process although similar principles can be of some use.

Exercise 1

Choose a product that interests you and about which you have a reasonable amount of technical knowledge - a car, a musical instrument, a domestic appliance or the like. Now try to write out a dialogue between a potential buyer of such a product and a good salesperson, using the guidelines shown above.

---

4. SALES FORCE MANAGEMENT

4.1 A sales force may be organised in several different ways, including:

(a) territorial design;

(b) a specialised structure of the sales force with salesmen specialising in:

    (i) types of product;
    (ii) types of outlet (which is a form of specialisation by customer).

Many companies use a combination of these different types of sales force organisation. These will be evaluated later in this chapter.

Recruitment

4.2 It is quite obvious from our discussions regarding the role of personal selling that the effectiveness of sales staff selection and training is paramount to the success of the company. Determining the size of the sales force depends on the way in which selling is organised within the company. The individual abilities that a salesperson should have will depend on what the job entails (the job description). These abilities will differ from company to company with some general traits that would be required by all sales staff. *General traits* might include the ability to communicate effectively verbally and in writing. More *job specific traits* might include a knowledge of the industry or the production processes of buying organisations.

4.3 *Training* plays a great part in the effectiveness of sales personnel and training courses should typically contain the following elements:

(a) why customer care is important;

(b) how to deal with the public and the importance of treating customers as individuals whose needs are important;

(c) how to deal with complaints and difficult customers;

(d) the importance of individual staff to the organisation to make staff feel part of a team and to build up the value of their contribution towards the achievement of organisational objectives;

(e) the benefits of good service;

(f)   product knowledge;

(g)   the development of ideas for improving service quality;

(h)   the importance of relationships with customers, colleagues and managers.

Remuneration

4.4   Remuneration can be an important and influential way in which to motivate sales staff. There are three basic types of sales remuneration.

(a)   *Fixed salary*. Sales staff on fixed salary are more likely to view the sales function as a whole. This means that they consider after sales service as an important aspect of their job or give information to people they do not consider probable customers. It is also easier for management not to have to make the decision as to how much commission to pay. The main drawback is of course there is no *direct* financial incentive to increase sales and exceptionally good salespeople may prefer commission payments. The fixed salary method of payment is often used in the industrial sector where high priced goods are purchased with technical after sales service built into the purchase.

(b)   *Commission only*. Here there is obviously a strong incentive to sell the company's products since income is totally dependent upon sales performance. This can lead to a rather short-term view of the selling function. This method provides little financial security for sales staff although is very flexible for management as costs are directly related to sales volume.

(c)   *Salary plus commission*. This is the 'middle ground' position and if implemented correctly should give the benefits of both the other two systems without the problems.

4.5   Financial rewards are not the only way in which companies can motivate their sales force and it is to other motivation techniques we now turn our attention.

Motivation

4.6   Many theories of motivation have been developed by academics who have studied organisational behaviour. It is not appropriate here to look at any of these in detail and so we shall simply give an overview of the common types of motivation in the selling function. *Monetary rewards* can make the salesperson myopic towards customer orientation, which we have discovered is at the heart of marketing. Selling in itself can be a lonely occupation where there is little commitment to the organisation. One way to overcome this is to involve sales staff as *groups* and to discuss company objectives and strategies with them. *Non-monetary rewards* can be more appreciated than monetary ones, for example a holiday for two given as a prize to the top performing sales person. Higher management can motivate sales personnel to a great extent. Simply being supportive and listening to complaints or comments can go a long way in the motivation of personnel.

5.   SALES FORCE ORGANISATION

5.1   Management therefore have a role to play in the motivation of sales people. They also have to organise the sales function, which can be done in a number of ways.

8: SALES MANAGEMENT AND SALES FORECASTING

Efficiency and sales force planning

5.2 As with any aspect of marketing and selling, it is the job of marketing management to organise resources so as to maximise the efficiency of selling (and thus to reduce the costs of selling).

5.3 It has already been suggested that design of the sales territory will influence selling efficiency.

   (a) A sales person needs an area of *adequate sales potential*. Semlov (1959) has suggested that if sales areas have unequal potential, the extra productivity of the salesman in an area with better area potential will be more than offset by the decline in productivity of the salesman with the worse area potential.

   (b) A salesman should not be given a sales area which is beyond his *workload capabilities;* equally, there must be sufficient sales potential in the area to motivate the salesman.

   (c) The lower costs of *territorial organisation* should be considered against the possible loss of custom which might result as a failure to *specialise*. A sales force structured by type of customer or by product may cost more than a simple territorially based sales force, but it could be capable of winning many more sales.

5.4 A further aspect of sales territory design is *sales call planning*. Given that a sales area must have adequate sales potential and workload, it should be possible to plan the number of calls a salesman should be able to make over a period of time. 'Standards' should exist for the average number of calls per day, or average miles travelled per day; and by planning the salesman's workload, it should be possible to prevent time lost through inefficient routing, or spending too long with difficult or reluctant customers.

5.5 A useful cost efficiency ratio which may be used is:

$$\text{Budgeted sales} = \frac{\text{Sales budget}}{\text{Average cost per call*}} \times \text{Average sales value per call*}$$

and

$$\text{Actual sales} = \frac{\text{Actual selling costs}}{\text{Average cost per call**}} \times \text{Average sales value per call*}$$

   * budget
   ** actual.

5.6 *Operational research techniques* may help to prepare sales call plans. It is also worth remembering that telephone calls by a salesman (*telemarketing*) might on occasions be just as effective as a personal visit.

Territorial design

5.7 Eventually, all large sales organisations involve a territorial breakdown. Where there is no specialisation, the sales organisation may be based entirely on *geographical* divisions.

    (a)   There may be a *pyramid organisation* structure with top management at head office, sales supervisors controlling the sales force in a region, and a salesman or sales force for each territory in a region.

    (b)   The span of control of a sales supervisor is influenced by:

        (i)   the amount of work to be done;
        (ii) the physical conditions under which it is done (such as how much travelling is involved);

    (c)   The amount of supervision required depends on two factors.

        (i)   The initiative which individual sales staff are allowed (if they can arrange delivery dates, price and production possibilities, they must have easy communication access back to their immediate superiors).

        (ii) The size of sales commission will determine how much salesmen are willing to work without the need to be supervised.

    (d)   The size of each sales territory should be such that the amount of time wasted by sales staff in travelling is not excessive; there should be a good 'frequency of call' rate.

5.8 The purpose of a *territorial sales force design* is:

    (a)   to reduce travelling time and costs;
    (b)   to enable the sales staff to get to know their customers and sales areas;
    (c)   to motivate sales staff by giving them autonomy over their area;
    (d)   to give sales staff an equal workload or equal sales potential;
    (e)   to keep the organisation and administration simple.

5.9 It is most suited therefore, to the sale of products in a homogeneous range (because it is important for the salesman to know his products as well as his customers). If the range of products is wide, and technically complex, it is unlikely that an individual sales person will be able to learn enough about them to sell them effectively.

5.10 The size of the sales area will depend on the expected workload for each sales person, or the sales potential of any area. An organisation might need several sales areas in South East England whereas the whole of Scotland might be a single area.

Specialised structures

5.11 Specialisation may be introduced into a sales organisation, and may take any of the following forms (or combination of several).

(a) *Specialisation by function:* for example, advertising group, market research group, new production group, sales/production liaison group, sales training and personnel section. This type of specialisation is more relevant to the marketing and selling department as a whole rather than to the sales force itself.

(b) *Specialisation by the nature of goods:* the more complex the nature of the goods to be sold and the more knowledgeable the customer, the more it is necessary to employ sales staff with a skilled knowledge of the product.

(c) *Specialisation by the range of goods*

    (i) If a company manufactures a range of goods, its sales staff may specialise in a section of the range; for example, in the sale of a range of office equipment some salesmen may specialise in calculators and others in document copiers.

    (ii) It is also possible to employ *product managers* who specialise in a product or range of products and who advise the sales force who sell the entire range without specialising. This type of organisation has drawbacks because it may be difficult to decide to what extent product managers should simply be advisers and how much authority they should be allowed over sales executives.

    (iii) Sales staff must know their products; therefore if the company's product range is broad and complex, product specialisation may be desirable. Several sales staff would be required to cover the same sales area.

Disadvantages of product specialisation are that:

    (i) travelling time and expenses are higher than with a territorial sales organisation;

    (ii) one customer buying two different products from the same company might have to deal with two different salesmen;

(d) *Specialisation by range of market:* by market segments. Examples of specialisation by market segment are:

    (i) home and overseas sales;
    (ii) industrial and non-industrial sales;
    (iii) male and female markets (eg clothiers);

The *advantage* of market specialisation is that salesmen get to know the needs of a particular market segment.

The *disadvantages* of market specialisation are:

    (i) travelling time and costs;

    (ii) potential problems for product designers when different market segments begin to show differing requirements;

    (iii) the potentially complex organisation structure, such as possible problems of identifying boundaries between one segment of the market and another, especially when new market segments are evolving.

(e) *Specialisation by range of customers:* in selling industrial goods, a specialised sales force should be organised so that each sales person deals with a small number of potential customers in order to foster a better understanding of the motivation of the customers. This could be vital for securing large or valuable industrial orders.

The *advantages* of specialisation by types of customer are as follows:

(i) the sales force will be more alert to the specific needs of each type of customer;

(ii) in selling industrial goods, knowledge about the customer's industry and needs might be crucial in winning sales over the bids of competitors.

(f) *Specialisation by range of outlets:* with changing patterns of consumer and wholesale buying, such as the growth of multiple stores and superstores, specialisation by sales staff in dealing with different types of outlet may improve a manufacturer's selling efficiency.

5.12 A combination of these different types of sales force designs can be used. For example, sales staff might specialise in a type of customer or type of product within a sales area or in a type of product for a restricted number of potential customers.

Exercise 2

Imagine that you have responsibility for organising the sales force for each of the following items (in turn, not together!)

(a) Daz (soap powder)
(b) Escalators
(c) Yachts

In each case how would you design your sales force?

Evaluation of sales force performance

5.13 Evaluation should be made of the sales function as a whole and for individual sales personnel. Performance should be measured against objectives which may be *quantifiable* such as the number of new accounts or more *qualitative* such as customer satisfaction.

After sales service

5.14 After sales service is especially important in industrial markets where technical service may be required long after purchase. Much of the work on after sales service involves producing instruction manuals and the like. The overall product offering (including heavy industrial manufacturing equipment) has a service element included. This can be pre-sale (for example, design and installation services) or postsale (for example, maintenance and training services).

After sales service is one way in whch organisations can build a competitive advantage and is increasingly valued by the customer. An increased awareness of developing service quality can lead to:

(a) *Greater customer retention rates and customer loyalty*. If customers are satisfied with the service the supplier provides, they are less likely to switch to another supplier.

(b) *Attraction of new customers from word of mouth recommendation*. Customers are more likely to recommend a high quality service to their friends, family and business colleagues than they are a poor quality service. If, in conversation, the topic of quality of service arises, the opportunity for recommendation may be taken up if the customer is satisfied by the service. Such recommendations are much more potent than other forms of promotion because the customer is seen as an objective judge.

(c) *Greater market share*. This advantage flows from the first two. If maintained, higher levels of customer care can lead to greater market share. Higher levels of service quality are more difficult for competitors to copy; price competition can be matched by rivals quickly but a system of higher service quality takes much longer to embed into the rival's operating procedures and so increased market share is maintained for longer.

(d) *Improved employee morale*. Higher service quality means fewer customer complaints and higher levels of satisfaction with the service. Service personnel are more likely to gain job satisfaction if not faced by a constant stream of complaints and abuse. Employees are thus more likely to have positive attitudes to their jobs, to feel more professional and to be more committed to their organisation. As a result staff turnover is likely to be lower and fewer mistakes are likely to be made; both of these in turn lead to higher service quality and lower costs (in training, for example). As a group of staff work together over time, team spirit develops and the group cohesion further reduces staff turnover and associated costs.

(e) *Insulation from price competition*. If customers evaluate suppliers in terms of *value for money* rather than purely in cost terms then service quality is more difficult for competitors to copy. As noted above it is relatively easy for competitors to reduce their prices in the short term. It is not so easy to improve their service quality in the short term. Thus, higher service quality is likely to insulate the supplier from price competition.

(f) *Lower advertising and promotion costs*. As noted above, word of mouth recommendation is much more potent than paid for advertising in gaining new business; it is also cheaper. Thus the supplier may see gains in numbers of customers without the need to increase advertising and other promotion costs.

(g) *Lower operating costs*. Cost can be saved in a number of ways:

   (i)   from reduced staff turnover;
   (ii)   in training and retraining costs;
   (iii) in rectifying transaction mistakes;
   (iv)   in administrative costs;
   (v)   from customer complaints being reduced.

(h) *Increased productivity* should flow from these advantages and should lead to increased financial performance and profitability.

6. TRENDS IN PERSONAL SELLING

6.1 Personal selling is still the most important element in the sales mix for the selling of industrial goods and for sales to government markets. Similarly, personal selling plays an influential role in sales to reseller markets. However, the rapid increase in labour costs (and travelling costs) especially during the 1970s inevitably turned management attention to the cost effectiveness of sales staff, with the following results.

(a) In many shops, there has been a switch to self-service displays and a reduction in the selling role of shop assistants.

(b) Advertising is used in advance of a sales campaign, so that salesmen do not have to start 'cold' with prospective customers.

(c) Selling by telephone (or at least, obtaining initial customer reactions by telephone, with a follow up personal visit if a sale might be in prospect) is a way of cutting down travelling time and selling costs. Salesmen can reach more prospective customers by telephone than by personal visits - even if they work in a very restricted geographical area.

(d) Sales managers pay more attention to sales call planning and sales territory design. Sales call planning should help to reduce the average cost per call, and efficient sales territory design should enable a higher average sales value per call to be achieved.

(e) The growth of large retail chains (notably supermarket chains) with a central buying department has meant that the manufacturer must now sell to a small group of purchasing managers instead of to a large number of individual stores. Although personal selling is an important feature of selling to these retail chains, the number of salesmen required to do the job is much less than in selling to individual shops.

6.2 Personal selling is probably one of the most expensive forms of promotion in terms of cost per person contacted. The extent to which sales staff are used varies with different products and different markets, but there are few occasions when some element of personal selling is not needed. The use of personal selling is probably most extensive in industrial markets where the number of buyers is small, the value of the account potentially large and there is often a demand for a specialised or customised product. A particular strength is that personal selling allows for feedback in communication process.

6.3 Although there is often a tendency to think of sales people as pursuing a hard sell and pressurising clients to buy, it should be remembered that the objectives of sales staff can vary quite considerably. They will be involved in some element of *prospecting*, which is concerned simply with making contact with potential customers and providing them with information for current or future use. Obviously, the process of persuading customers to make a purchase is important, but so is the provision of after sales service/advice to consumers and the collection of data regarding the consumers' views of the product.

6.4 Personal selling is perhaps most important when dealing with *corporate clients*. This group of customers will have quite specific needs and requirements, and in general understanding the nature of a complex service will be less of a problem than is the case with personal customers. The corporate customer will be more concerned with obtaining a service which will meet a specific set of needs. The role of the salesman will then be one of identifying the needs and tailoring a service to meet those needs rather than concentrating on improving customer understanding of the standard product range.

6.5 Compared with other forms of promotion, the main advantage which personal selling possesses is that it is a *two way* form of communication which gives the *customer* the opportunity to query aspects of the product and the *sales staff* the opportunity to deal with the specific needs of each customer. As a result, the message itself becomes much more flexible and service provision can more easily be tailored to the needs of the consumer. However, as a consequence, it is rather more expensive and requires a high degree of expertise both among the management who co-ordinate and motivate sales staff, and among the sales staff themselves who require a variety of interpersonal skills combined with in-depth knowledge about the organisation's product range.

6.6 Although there are always some individuals who are natural communicators and naturally good in the selling function, a number of general principles can be identified which will contribute to the success of personal selling.

(a) Given the significance of contact with individual staff, it is clearly important to ensure that sales staff develop *good personal relationships* with their customers.

(b) Alleviating any doubts which the customer may have requires a *professional orientation* on behalf of sales staff to illustrate their competency and familiarity with all *aspects of the relevant products*.

(c) This in turn requires the organisation to ensure *good training and motivation* for such staff.

(d) Finally, the personal selling approach should ensure that the actual purchase decision is made easy and minimal demands are imposed on the customer.

7. SALES FORECASTING

7.1 Sales forecasting is a key element in budgeting and in long-term strategic planning, both essential disciplines in running a business of any size. Without an accurate idea of a business's future sales it becomes difficult to make any meaningful plans for the short term, let alone the longer term.

7.2 Companies must be aware of factors both inside and outside their control so they can plan effectively for the future. Sales figures do not simply depend on how well the sales force is performing or even how well the product fits customer requirements. In the long run performance will depend on the general economic climate, the level of technology and rate of technological change, to name just a few factors. Forecasting is a tool which, when used correctly, enables management to make informed decisions about the future.

7.3 There is a vast array of forecasting techniques that can be applied to sale forecasting but here we will only deal with a small number. Some forecasting methods are very basic, for instance using last month's sales figures to predict this month's. Others are very complex such as some econometric models. The use of computers has aided the development of forecasting techniques.

7.4   Managers should be aware of the different types of product that exist to serve a particular market before attempting to forecast demand. For example, a coffee producer must decide which forecast suits his objectives: a forecast for the total coffee market, the decaffeinated coffee market or the instant coffee market. The manager must also make a decision about the geographical area the forecast should cover. Companies can estimate sales at different levels of marketing effort and expenditure.

7.5   Assumptions will have to be made about the marketing environment, which are the external uncontrollable factors such as the economic, technological and political environment. Companies can attempt to make forecasts for these factors. Sales forecasting should not simply take into account competitor sales so market shares can be established. Government statistics in industry sectors can be used to evaluate past sales and base forecasts on future sales. Specialist research companies issue market reports (eg Mintel) that can be used to assess present positions.

7.6   Companies often arrive at sales forecasts in three stages:

(a)   environmental forecast;
(b)   industry forecast;
(c)   company sales forecast.

7.7   There are three basic ways forecasts can be made. The first surveys the opinions of consumers, sales people or experts within the field. For example, an economist's opinion may be sought to give an assessment of future interest rate levels. The second method looks at what people do if the product is made available. For example, a supermarket may make a new flavoured yoghurt available in a small number of stores and analyse the sales to test whether to distribute the yoghurt throughout its stores. The third method looks into the past to evaluate what was purchased and when. The method which is used to estimate sales will depend upon product characteristics. The *product life cycle* which was discussed in Chapter 4 can be a useful tool in sales estimates. The shape and length of the PLC will depend upon the frequency of purchase. Companies should estimate first time and replacement/repeat sales.

7.8   The diagram below shows some examples of forecasting requirements of a company, illustrating how many different forecasts are needed in addition to sales forecasts.

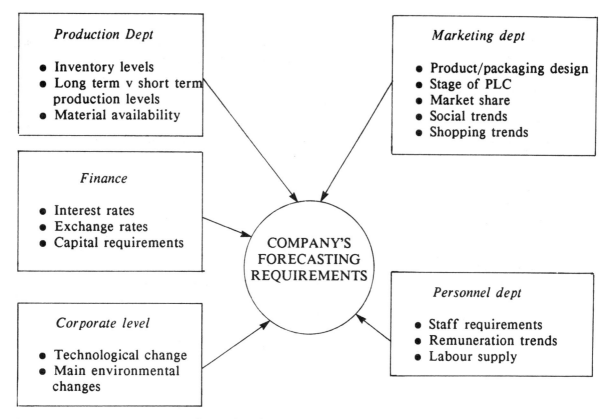

7.9 Forecasts should take the following into account.

(a) *Accuracy*. Although this seems obvious the level of desired accuracy can differ. The longer the time span involved generally the less accuracy is possible.

(b) *Time period*. Short-term forecasts can be made to allow for the smooth production and delivery of products. Longer-term forecasts are usually used to help managers make strategic decisions.

(c) *Detail*. The level of detail required by a forecast will differ amongst functional departments. Production will want a very detailed assessment of the future demand for the product to enable them to make necessary adjustments.

Forecasting techniques

7.10 There are many different forecasting techniques available at different levels of complexity. Here we shall be evaluating the three broad categories of forecasting methods: time series, causal and qualitative techniques.

Time series forecasts

7.11 Historical (past) data is analysed and trends or patterns are projected into the future. This type of analysis is, of course, more useful in stable industries that have been in existence for some amount of time. This means that data is available and is relatively reliable. In essence it is a short-term technique rather than a long-term one.

7.12 Statistical techniques are available that take into account seasonal variations, such as occur, for example, in the sales of fireworks. In the long term, fireworks may be used in more displays and entertainments throughout the year rather than the traditional Guy Fawkes night. Where the seasonal sales pattern is not expected to continue unchanged for the foreseeable future, in the longer term time series analysis may be less useful. Statistical methods that are used to make projections into the future include moving averages or weighted moving averages and exponential smoothing. More complex approaches are Chow's and the Box Jenkins methods.

Causal models

7.13 Causal models use equations to explain the relationship between a dependent variable (the one being forecast) and a number of independent variables. Past data can be used in the model and with the use of computers complex models can be evaluated. Causal models are linked to probability so a forecast may be that there is a 95% chance that sales will achieve a certain target. They are useful for longer term forecasting as independent variables can be altered and their impact noted. An example of a causal model can be seen below, where demand for electricity may depend upon a number of independent variables.

$$\text{Demand for electricity} = aPE + bPA + cEA + dPD$$

Where   PE = price of electricity
                   PA = price of alternative energies
                   EA = electricity appliances already in operation (so locked into supply)
                   PD = past demand of electricity

                   a, b, c and d are weights attached to each independent variable according to their importance.

7.14 The mathematical technique of regression analysis is used to analyse causal models. Macroeconomic forecasting uses causal models to predict economic growth rates, for example. Demand for goods can also be forecast using causal models, and these can take into account many diverse aspects such as advertising and demand for complementary or substitute goods.

Qualitative forecasting

7.15 Qualitative forecasting techniques do not depend on historical data as the quantitative methods (time series and causal) do. Qualitative techniques are used either where quantitative data is unavailable or for long-term forecasts. They are used mainly in technological forecasting, corporate planning and monitoring changes in consumer tastes and culture. There are two types of qualitative forecasting: *explorative* and *normative*. *Explorative techniques* start with the current state of affairs and attempt to predict changes. *Normative techniques* start with a desired state of affairs in the future and work back to consider ways in which to get there. So, for example, qualitative techniques can attempt to forecast new product adoption, technological change and innovations. Examples of individual techniques are Delphi, Morphological analysis and relevance trees.

8.   CONCLUSION

8.1   The sales force has many varied responsibilities but perhaps the most important is communication with customers, often after a sale is made as well as before. Few firms use no personal selling but the size and complexity of the sales force depend on the size and nature of the business. Direct mail and telesales are alternatives to (or complementary approaches to use with) employing sales representatives to meet customers face to face.

8.2   The sales force should be knowledgeable about the firm and its products, and also loyal. It is therefore essential to motivate and reward sales staff adequately, using training, sales conferences and bonus/commission schemes and competition. There should not be an undue reliance on sales commission as a motivator as this encourages short termism. Non-monetary rewards may be highly valued.

8.3   The sales force should be organised with a view to maximising sales and minimising costs. Each sales person should have an area of adequate sales potential and within his workload capability. Sales call planning is a useful control measure. Territorial sales design is very common but some degree of specialisation may also be beneficial, either by product or by type of customer.

8.4   After sales service is very important, particularly in industrial markets, as it builds customer loyalty and improves employee morale.

8.5   Sales forecasting is an essential discipline, although it is difficult to forecast accurately. Both external and internal factors must be considered. The longer the period covered by the forecast, the less accuracy can be expected. Forecasts can be made using time series analysis, causal models or qualitative techniques.

TEST YOUR KNOWLEDGE

Numbers in brackets refer to paragraphs of this chapter

1   What does the task of selling involve? (2.6)

2   If a firm expects its sales force to cost 5% of sales, what value of sales should a sales rep costing £35,000 a year generate? (2.13)

3   How can a sales person create interest in a sale? (3.4)

4   What topics would sales training courses typically cover? (4.3)

5   What are the pros and cons of paying sales staff by fixed salary? (4.4)

6   What is the function of sales call planning? (5.4)

7   Why might specialisation be introduced into a sales force? (5.11)

8   List the advantages of providing a good after sales service. (5.14)

9   What effect has the rising cost of labour had on personal selling? (6.1)

10 How do time series forecasts work? (7.11-7.12)

Now try questions 17 and 18 at the end of the text

Chapter 9

PLANNING, EVALUATION, ORGANISATION AND CONTROL

This chapter covers the following topics.

1. Marketing strategy
2. The planning cycle
3. Marketing planning and strategy
4. Strategy formulation
5. Market segmentation
6. Positioning products and brands
7. The marketing plan

---

1. MARKETING STRATEGY

Introduction

1.1 Marketing has traditionally been seen as a separate functional activity with a primarily *tactical* role to play in business development. However, this view is largely being replaced by the recognition that marketing has a key *strategic* role to play. *Strategic planning* sets or changes the *objectives* of an organisation. *Tactical planning* is concerned with decisions about the efficient and effective use of an organisation's resources to achieve these objectives and strategic targets.

1.2 In addition, consumers are becoming more sophisticated and quality conscious. To deal with such rapid change, it becomes important for an organisation to adopt a planned approach to its business to guide its development in an increasingly unknown and uncertain future. Effective planning will enable any organisation to adopt a *proactive* stance to its markets and to anticipate changes to ensure that it sustains a competitive position. Given the uncertainty which prevails, it is crucial that plans are flexible and adaptable.

1.3 The development of *corporate strategic plans* is intended to guide the overall development of an organisation. Within that framework specific plans regarding marketing strategies will be determined. These plans, to be effective, will inevitably be interlinked and interdependent with those for other functions of the organisation. This chapter focuses on the development of *marketing plans,* recognising that these will contain both strategic and operational components. The strategic component of marketing planning focuses on the direction which an organisation will take in relation to a specific market or set of markets in order to achieve a specified set of objectives. Marketing planning also requires an operational component which details specific tasks and activities to be undertaken in order to implement the desired strategy.

1.4 Developing such a planned, strategic approach ensures that the marketing efforts of any organisation are consistent with organisational goals, internally coherent and tailored to the needs of identified consumer markets. It should also ensure that the resources available within the organisation are allocated in a systematic manner consistent with specified objectives.

Strategies

1.5 Within any organisation, strategies develop at several levels. *Corporate strategy* deals with the overall development of an organisation's business activities, while *marketing strategy* focuses specifically on the organisation's activities in relation to the markets served. Strategy can take many forms; two commonly identified ones are deliberate and emergent strategies.

(a) *Deliberate strategies* exist as the result of conscious, planned activities.

(b) *Emergent strategies* are the outcome of activities and behaviour which develop unconsciously but which fall into some consistent pattern.

In practice, it is frequently the case that most strategies which are pursued by firms are part deliberate and part emergent. To the extent that they are deliberate, they are typically the outcome of some planning process which is concerned with guiding the development of the business.

1.6 In the context of developing a marketing plan, the notion of strategic marketing can be seen as having three key components:

(a) the designation of specific, desired objectives;
(b) commitment of resources to these objectives;
(c) evaluation of a range of environmental influences.

A key feature of strategy is that it does not just focus on organisational *efficiency;* arguably, its more important function is that of enabling the organisation to be *effective*. Where strategy and planning are concerned, *efficiency* simply relates to doing a task well, but *effectiveness* relates to doing the right task - having the right products in the right markets at the most appropriate times.

1.7 However, an organisation can only be effective if it is aware and responsive to the environment in which it operates. In a sense, it can be argued that marketing is by definition 'strategic', since to be able to market a product successfully ultimately requires that the firm has the right type of product and is operating in the right markets.

1.8 It should also be emphasised that the concept of strategy has a dynamic component. We have stressed the importance of strategy in enabling an organisation to be effective, but to be truly effective that organisation should not only be 'doing the right things now', it should also be aware of and prepared to anticipate future changes to ensure that it will also be 'doing the right things in the future'. Planning and strategy do not give the organisation the ability to predict the future. Rather, planning enables managers to think through the possible range of future changes, and hence be better prepared to meet the changes that actually occur.

2. THE PLANNING CYCLE

2.1 The process of developing marketing strategies and marketing plans has already been described as being closely related to the development of overall corporate strategies and corporate plans. The nature of this link will be made clearer if we consider their relative positions in the planning cycle. The first stage of a typical planning cycle begins with the collection of information by planners from all areas of the organisation. This will include financial and production data, but arguably one of the most important sources of such data will be the marketing department. Much of the information collected will be factual but there will also often be information in the form of opinions and attitudes, since this is the opportunity for individual functional departments to make an input to the corporate planning process. This phase is often described as *'bottom up' planning* since the main information flow is from lower to higher levels of management.

2.2 The second phase of the planning cycle involves the organisation and analysis of the information which has been collected in order to formulate an overall *corporate plan*. This will specify the objectives which the organisation wishes to achieve in the short, medium and long term, as well as specifying the way in which it intends to achieve them. The plan at this level will focus on broad aspects of overall corporate development and thus provides a framework within which specific functions such as marketing can develop their own plans. This phase is typically referred to as *'top down' planning* since the flow of information is now from senior to junior levels.

2.3 This combination of 'bottom-up' and 'top-down' planning enables senior levels of management - specifically, corporate planners - to provide a coherent structure for the organisation's development. The benefits of this structure are as follows.

(a) A framework is provided to enable managers to think ahead and anticipate change.

(b) Patterns of resource allocation within the organisation are clearly identified, which should minimise the extent of inter-departmental conflict. At the same time, because there is an important input to the planning process from functional managers, the plan will benefit from the specific experience of these managers who are closest to markets or functions within the organisation.

2.4 Finally, we should remember that although the planning cycle has been presented as having two discrete phases, in practice it is a continual process. Annual plans will be developed to guide short-term developments, but these will be generated within the framework of medium and long-term plans which will themselves be updated as the operating environment changes.

3. MARKETING PLANNING AND STRATEGY

3.1 The key requirement from any format for a marketing plan is that it should follow a logical structure, from historical and current analyses of the organisation and its market, on to a statement of objectives, then to the development of a strategy to approach that market, both in general terms and in terms of developing an appropriate marketing mix, and finally to an outline of the appropriate methods for plan implementation. The issues of implementation often appear briefly at the end of any discussion of marketing plans; and yet, arguably, the process of monitoring and controlling marketing activities is the most crucial factor in determining whether a plan is successful or not.

3.2 The main function of the plan is to offer management a coherent set of clearly defined guidelines, but at the same time it must remain flexible enough to adapt to changing conditions within the organisation or its markets. The stages in strategic planning are as follows.

Development of the organisation's mission statement

↓

Statement of objectives

↓

Situational analysis

↓

Strategy development

↓

Specific plans

↓

Implementation

Company mission statement

3.3 The company mission statement is simply a statement of what an organisation is aiming to achieve through the conduct of its business; it can even be thought of as a statement of the organisation's reason for existence. The purpose of the mission statement is to provide the organisation with focus and direction. The precise nature of the corporate mission depends on a variety of factors. Corporate history will often influence the markets and customer groups served - thus, in the banking sector Credit Agricole retains strong links with its farming depositors, while Coutts concentrates primarily on high income consumers in its retail banking activities.

3.4 Corporate culture and organisational structures may also influence the approaches to markets and customers. The commonest approach to determining the corporate mission is to rely on the product/market scope. The mission statement is then essentially based on customer groups, needs served and technology employed. This approach may be of particular use from the perspective of marketing since it forces managers to think of the customer groups and the particular set of needs/wants which the firm is looking to satisfy.

3.5 It is not sufficient, for example, for a bank to identify its mission as being 'banking' - it would be more appropriate to identify that mission as being, for example, 'meeting consumer needs for financial transactions.' A mission statement of this nature can offer guidelines to management when considering how the business should develop and in which directions. With the benefits of a clear mission statement, future growth strategies can rely on what are regarded as distinctive competences and aim for synergies by dealing with similar customer groups, similar customer needs or similar service technologies.

Statement of objectives

3.6 Objectives enter into the planning process both at the corporate level and at the market level. Corporate objectives define specific goals for the organisation as a whole and may be expressed in terms of profitability, returns on investment, growth of asset base, earnings per share etc. These will feed down through the planning process and will be reflected in the stated objectives for marketing, branch and other functional plans. Clearly, the objectives specified for marketing will not be identical to those specified at the corporate level and an important component of the marketing planning process is the translation of corporate (often financial) objectives into market specific marketing objectives. These may take the form of targets for the size of the customer base, growth in the usage of certain facilities, gains in market share for a particular product type etc. Whatever the status of a set of objectives, they must conform to three criteria; they must be achievable, they must be consistent and they must be stated clearly and preferably quantitatively.

3.7 Once a clear statement of the corporate mission has been achieved and corporate objectives have been determined, this information, in conjunction with further detailed analysis of the environment, provides the input for the next stage in the planning process.

Situation analysis

3.8 Although environmental factors will have affected the mission statement and the identification of objectives, a much more comprehensive analysis is required for the development of overall and market specific strategies. Situation analysis requires a thorough study of the broad trends within the economy and society, as well as a detailed analysis of markets, consumers and competitors. In particular, it may involve some consideration of the nature and extent of *market segmentation*. It also requires an understanding of the organisation's internal environment and its particular strengths and weaknesses. Market research and external databases provide the main source of such information relating to the external environment while an audit of the organisation's marketing activities provides information on the internal environment. The use of a *marketing information system* provides the ideal system for processing and analysing this type of data, while techniques such as SWOT analysis (see below) are of use in organising and presenting the results of such analysis.

Exercise

Look at the statement below, which the National Westminster Bank publishes (untitled) every year on the first page of its annual report and accounts. Is it a mission statement or a statement of objectives? What do you think is NatWest's aim in publishing it?

The NatWest Way is to bring:

QUALITY TO OUR CUSTOMERS

We value our customers as the foundation of our business. Our relationships with customers and suppliers are based on principles of respect and mutual benefit.

We aim to develop profitable and lasting relationships. We want to build on what we do well and to innovate to meet changing customer needs.

QUALITY TO OUR INVESTORS

We have a long term responsibility to everybody who has a stake in the Group to operate with care, efficiency and at a profit.

Our objective is to earn the profits needed to provide a consistent increase in the value of our shareholders' investment, obtain the highest credit ratings and finance the development of our business.

QUALITY TO OUR PEOPLE

We respect each other's experience and skills and value the contribution each of us makes to the NatWest team. We recognise that pride and enjoyment in the job come from commitment, leadership by example and accomplishment.

Our goal is to work together to reward, train and develop people in ways that acknowledge performance and individual abilities.

QUALITY TO THE COMMUNITY

We recognise that our actions must acknowledge our responsibilities for the well-being and stability of the community.

We aim to support the community through the involvement of our people and the contribution of 1% of our Group profits.

Strategy development

3.9 The process of strategy development is a key link between corporate level plans and market level plans. In developing strategy, most large organisations will have important *resource allocation* decisions to make. With a variety of products and divisions financial and human resources must be allocated in a manner consistent with the achievement of corporate objectives. Some areas will be designated for expansion, others perhaps for contraction. This process of resource allocation is a key component of corporate strategy and it indicates the direction in which specific markets or products are expected to develop. It therefore provides direction for the development of *market level plans.*

3.10 Market specific plans indicate the organisation's intentions with respect to particular markets, or in some cases, particular products. They are closely tied to the corporate plan through the statement of objectives and the resource allocation component in strategy development. Situation analysis must continue at the market level to supply further information on patterns of competition, consumer behaviour and market segmentation. This will provide input to the development of marketing objectives and market specific strategies.

3.11 The market specific variables which are typically under the control of the marketing department are, as we have already seen, product, price, promotion and place. The development of the marketing mix is guided by the need to ensure that the product is appropriate to the market in terms of its features, its image, its perceived value and its availability.

3.12 The level of marketing expenditure will be determined largely by resource allocation decisions at corporate levels, but nevertheless a statement of the budget required and the way it is to be spent will be an important component of any marketing plan.

Implementation

3.13 This requires an identification of the specific tasks which need to be performed, the allocation of those tasks to individuals and the establishment of a system for monitoring their implementation - identifying the nature of any short term marketing research which needs to be undertaken to determine how appropriate the product is, the nature of customer reactions etc. The implementation procedure may also include some elements of contingency planning. However well thought out the marketing plan may be, the market is always changing. Consequently, certain planned activities may turn out to be inappropriate or ineffective; it is important to be aware of these and be in a position to respond - to modify the strategy as new information becomes available.

3.14 We will now take a more detailed look at how strategies can be formulated.

4. STRATEGY FORMULATION

4.1 In developing a marketing strategy, the company is seeking to find the most appropriate position in its operating environment. This may involve adjusting the nature of the company's strategy to fit into the existing market environment, although in some cases it may involve attempting to change the environment to fit with the company's strategy. The resulting strategy must enable the bank to meet the specific needs of its consumers and to do so more effectively than its competitors.

9: PLANNING, EVALUATION, ORGANISATION AND CONTROL

SWOT analysis

4.2 This simple technique provides a method of organising information in identifying possible strategic direction. The basic principle of SWOT analysis is that any statement about an organisation or its environment can be classified as a Strength, Weakness, Opportunity or Threat. An *opportunity* is simply any feature of the external environment which creates conditions which are advantageous to the firm in relation to a particular objective or set of objectives. By contrast, a *threat* is any environmental development which will present problems and may hinder the achievement of organisational objectives. What constitutes an opportunity to some firms will almost invariably constitute a threat to others.

4.3 A *strength* can be thought of as a particular skill or distinctive competence which the organisation possesses and which will aid it in achieving its stated objectives. These may relate to experience in specific types of markets or specific skills possessed by employees. A strength may also refer to factors such as a firm's reputation for quality or customer service. A *weakness* is simply any aspect of the company which may hinder the achievement of specific objectives such as limited experience of certain markets/technologies, extent of financial resources available.

4.4 This information would typically be presented as a matrix of strengths, weaknesses, opportunities and threats. There are several points to note about presentation and interpretation. First, it should be remembered that effective SWOT analysis does not simply require a categorisation of information, it also requires some evaluation of the relative importance of the various factors under consideration. In addition, it should be noted that these features are only of relevance if they are perceived to exist by the consumers. Listing corporate features that internal personnel regard as strengths/weaknesses is of little relevance if they are not perceived as such by the organisation's consumers. In the same vein, threats and opportunities are conditions presented by the external environment and they should be independent of the firm.

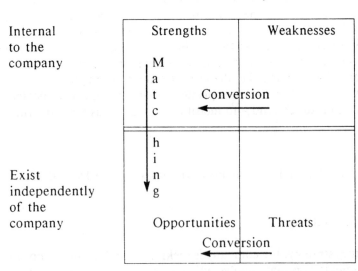

SWOT Analysis

4.5 Having constructed a matrix of strengths, weaknesses, opportunities and threats with some evaluation attached to them, it then becomes feasible to make use of that matrix in guiding strategy formulation. The two major strategic options are as follows.

(a) *Matching*
     This entails finding, where possible, a match between the strengths of the organisation and the opportunities presented by the market. Strengths which do not match any available opportunity are of limited use while opportunities which do not have any matching strengths are of little immediate value from a strategic perspective.

(b) *Conversion*
     This requires the development of strategies which will convert weaknesses into strengths in order to take advantage of some particular opportunity, or converting threats into opportunities which can then be matched by existing strengths.

4.6   Although SWOT provides some guidance on developing a match between the organisation's environment and its strategic direction, it is also necessary to consider more specific aspects of strategies such as how best to compete, how to grow within the target markets etc. To aid this process there are a number of analytical techniques which can be used; the role of these techniques is not to offer definitive statements on the final form that a strategy should take, but rather to provide a framework for the organisation and analysis of ideas and information. No one technique can always provide the most appropriate framework and those discussed below can and should be regarded as complementary rather than competitive.

Competitive strategies

4.7   Initially, a key factor is that management must identify the way in which it will compete with other organisations and what it perceives as the basis of its competitive advantage. The American strategist Michael Porter argues that the strategy adopted by a firm is essentially a method for creating and sustaining a profitable position in a particular market environment. The profit made by the firm depends first on the nature of its strategy and second on the inherent profitability of the industry in which it operates. An organisation in a basically profitable industry can perform badly with an unsuitable strategy while an organisation in an unprofitable industry may perform well with a more suitable strategy.

4.8   The profitability of an industry depends on the structure of the industry and specifically on five key features:

(a) bargaining power of suppliers;
(b) bargaining power of consumers;
(c) threat of entry;
(d) competition from substitutes;
(e) competition between firms.

4.9   Developing a competitive strategy requires a thorough analysis of these factors and from this analysis the organisation must decide whether to compete across the entire market or only in certain segments *(competitive scope)* and whether to compete through low costs and prices or through offering a differentiated product range *(competitive advantage)*. This decision can lead to four possible strategies as outlined below.

Competitive strategies

COMPETITIVE SCOPE

BROAD ... NARROW

	COST LEADERSHIP Eg specialist mortgage supplier	COST FOCUS Eg regional building society with savings and mortgage facilities only
	DIFFERENTIATION LEADERSHIP Eg National/International bank with money transmission, mortgage and insurance products	DIFFERENTIATION FOCUS Eg Insurance broker offering wide range of financial advice

(Left axis: COMPETITIVE ADVANTAGE; inner axis: COSTS / DIFFERENTIATE)

Source: Ennew, C T, Watkins, T and Wright M (1990) Marketing Financial Services, Heinemann

(a) *Cost leadership*

The strategy is to attempt to control the market through being the low cost producer. Typically, the product is undifferentiated, although differentiation cannot be ignored, since the cost savings for the consumer must compensate for the loss of product features, while the discount offered by the firm should not be so high as to offset cost advantages.

(b) *Differentiation*

The strategy is to offer products which can be regarded as unique in areas which are highly valued by the consumer. It is the products' uniqueness and the associated customer loyalty that protects the firm from competition. However, the price premium received must outweigh the costs of supplying the differentiated product for this strategy to be successful; at the same time, the customer must feel that the extra features more than compensate for the price premium.

(c) *Focus/nicheing*

This strategy uses either costs or differentiation but rather than serving the entire market, the organisation looks to operate only in particularly attractive or suitable segments or niches. Differentiation focus is the most common form of focus strategy and implies producing highly customised products for very specific consumer groups.

An important feature of this approach is the need to avoid being 'stuck in the middle' – trying to be all things to all consumers. The firm trying to perform well on costs and on differentiation is likely to lose out to firms concentrating on either one strategy or the other.

Growth strategies

4.10 A common framework for the analysis and determination of growth strategies is Ansoff's Product/Market matrix which suggests that the strategy decision rests on whether to use new or existing products in new or existing markets. This produces four possible options which are outlined below.

(a) *Market penetration*

This involves selling more of the existing products in existing markets. Possible options are persuading existing users to use more (so a credit card issuer might try to increase credit card use by offering higher credit limits or gifts based on expenditure); persuading non-users to use (for example, by offering free gifts with new credit card accounts); or attracting consumers from competitors. It should be noted that market penetration will, in general, only be viable strategy where the market is not saturated.

(b) *Market development*

This entails expanding into new markets with existing products. These may be new markets geographically, new market segments or new uses for products. With the advent of the Single European Market, the opportunities for market development in the European Community are likely to increase significantly in some (although not all) areas of business. As a strategy, it requires effective and imaginative promotion, but it can be profitable if markets are changing rapidly.

(c) *Product development*

This approach requires the organisation to operate in its existing markets but develop modified versions of its existing products to appeal to those markets. Recent developments in the mortgage market provide a good example of product development as the traditional standardised mortgage account is rapidly being supplemented by variants which offer lower starting rates, special terms for particular types of customer, particular mixes of fixed and flexible repayment rates etc. A strategy of this nature relies on good service design, packaging and promotion and often plays on company reputation to attract consumers to the new product. The benefits are that by tailoring the products more specifically to the needs of some existing consumers and some new consumers the organisation can strengthen its competitive position.

(d) *Diversification*

The three strategies described above tend to be relatively low risk, since the organisation is operating in areas in which it has some experience. By contrast, the fourth strategy - *diversification* (new products, new markets) is much more risky because the organisation is moving into areas in which it has little or no experience. As a consequence, the instances of pure diversification are rare and its use as a strategic option tends to be in cases when there are no other possible routes for growth available. The diversification strategies which have been observed in the financial services sector typically involve the introduction of new (as opposed to modified) products for the same broad market.

5. MARKET SEGMENTATION

5.1 'Market segmentation is the subdividing of a market into distinct subsets of customers, where any subset may conceivably be selected as a target market to be reached with a distinct marketing mix.'
(Kotler)

5.2 Customers differ in various respects - according to age, sex, income, geographical area, buying attitudes, buying habits etc. Each of these differences can be used to segment a market.

Steps in the analysis of segmentation

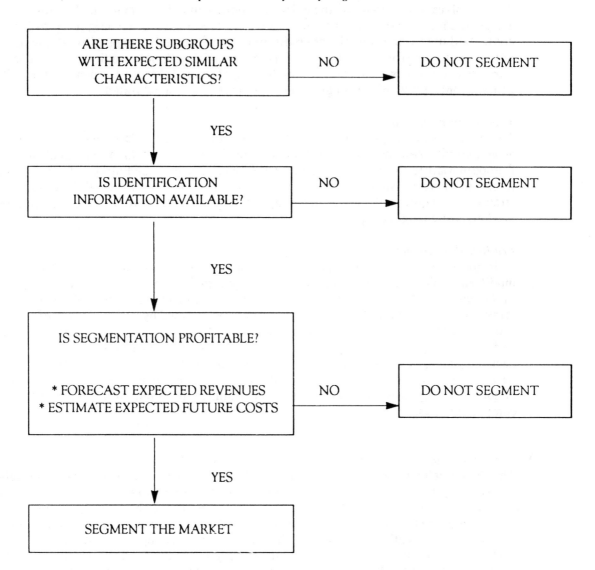

Market segmentation and marketing planning

5.3 A market is not a mass, homogeneous group of customers, each wanting an identical product. Market segmentation is based on the recognition that every market consists of potential buyers with different needs, and different buying behaviour. These different customer attitudes may be grouped into segments and a different marketing approach will be taken by an organisation for each market segment.

5.4 Market segmentation may therefore be defined as 'the subdividing of a market into distinct and increasingly homogeneous subgroups of customers, where any subgroup can conceivably be selected as a target to be met with a distinct marketing mix'. 'The danger of thinking in terms of single, mass homogeneous markets has been recognised. Market segmentation, as an approach, emerged from the recognition of this danger.' (Tom Cannon *Basic Marketing: Principles and Practice 1980*).

5.5 The important elements in this definition of market segmentation are as follows.

   (a) Although the total market consists of widely different groups of consumers, each group consists of people (or organisations) with common needs and preferences, who perhaps react to 'market stimuli' in much the same way. For example, the market for umbrellas might be segmented according to the sex of the consumers. Women might seem to prefer umbrellas of different size and weight. The men's market might further be subdivided into age (with some age groups buying few umbrellas and others buying much more) or occupation (eg professional classes, commuters, golfers). Each subdivision of the market (each subsegment) will show increasingly common traits. Golfers, for example, appear to buy large multi-coloured umbrellas.

   (b) Each market segment can become a target market for a firm, and would require a unique market- ing mix if the firm is to exploit it successfully. In other words, recognition of segmentation will enable a company to adopt the proper approach to selling to a given group of potential customers, which will be more successful than an undifferentiating market approach to all customers.

5.6 A total market may occasionally be homogeneous but this is likely to occur only rarely. At one time, for example, the Coca Cola Company successfully sold one type of drink in one bottle size to a mass market (although it has since recognised market segments in the soft drinks market). Sometimes consumer differences may exist, but it may be difficult to analyse them into segments. A segmentation approach to marketing succeeds when there are identifiable 'clusters' of consumer wants in the market.

The bases for segmentation

5.7 An important initial marketing task is the identification of segments within the market. There are many different bases on which segments can be analysed; one basis will not be appropriate in every market, and sometimes two or more bases might be valid at the same time. One basis or 'segmentation variable' might be 'superior' to another in a hierarchy of variables; for example, market segments may exist on the basis of sex; subsegments may then be age group within sex and subsubsegments may be geographical region within age group within sex. On the other hand, if a market can be segmented both by marital status (unmarried, married) and by sex then the market might be divisible into $2 \times 2 = 4$ separate segments (married men, unmarried men, married and unmarried women).

5.8 Segmentation may to some extent be a matter of subjective analysis by marketing management, but the following are typical market segments.

   (a) *Geographical area:* for example, the needs and behaviour of potential customers in South East England may differ from those in Scotland or Italy. For example, commercial radio stations may compete with national radio stations by broadcasting items of local interest; and in the past, the market for beer and cider could be segmented on a regional basis, between, for example, the North ('mild' beer), the South (lager) and the South West (cider).

   (b) *End use:* for example, paper used in office will vary in quality depending on whether it is used for formal letters and reports, informal working or for typewriter carbon copies. Paper is also bought by consumers, who have their own uses for the product. 'Use' in the consumer market might refer to leisure or work use: for example, the men's shirts market can be divided into leisure wear, formal wear and shirts to wear at work with suits or jackets.

(c) *Age:* a useful age division might be 0 - 3 years, 4 - 6 years, 7 - 11, 12 - 19, 20 - 34, 35 - 49, 50 - 64 and over 64.

(d) *Sex.*

(e) *Family size or family life cycle:* for example, young and single, young and married with no children, with 1, 2 or more children, older and single, older and married with 1, 2 or more children. The age of the children might also be introduced into the segment analysis of the family.

(f) *Income:* useful, for example, in segmenting the market for housing.

(g) *Occupation:* for example, the market for men's suits might be segmented according to occupation.

(h) *Education:* to segment by education may be relevant to the marketing of newspapers), for example.

(i) *Religion or religious sect:* this form of segmentation may be important for marketing by charities. Also, there would be little point in advertising non-kosher foods in the Jewish Chronicle, for example.

(j) *Race* may affect the market for music, cosmetics, newspapers and so on.

(k) *Nationality* affects the market for food, as just one example.

(l) *Social class.* The marketing analysis of consumers into socio-economic groupings is an important one because these groupings appear to provide reliable indicators of different consumer attitudes and needs for a wide range of products.

(m) *Lifestyle.* Differences in personality, socio-economic groupings and the like can be condensed into a few categories of life style. It may therefore be possible to segment a market according to these lifestyle categories (such as interest in second hand or new motor cars).

Lifestyle dimensions

Activities	Interests	Opinions	Demographics
Work	Family	Themselves	Age
Hobbies	Home	Social issues	Education
Social events	Job	Politics	Income
Vacation	Community	Business	Occupation
Entertainment	Recreation	Economics	Family size
Club membership	Fashion	Education	Dwelling
Community	Food	Products	Geography
Shopping	Media	Future	City size
Sports	Achievements	Culture	Stage in lifecycle

*Source: Joseph Plummer,
'The Concept and Application of Lifestyle Segmentation',
Journal of Marketing (January 1974), pp 33-37*

(n) *Buyer behaviour:* the usage rate of the product by the buyer, whether purchase will be on impulse, customer loyalty, the sensitivity of the consumer to marketing mix factors (price, quality and sales promotion).

5.9   There are other possible bases for segmentation connected with the use or usefulness of the product. The market for various foods, for example, can be segmented into 'convenience foods', such as frozen chips and TV dinners, or 'wholesome foods'. Such models focus on the range of benefits that are perceived by different customer groupings when using or consuming a particular brand.

Benefit segmentation of the toothpaste market

Segment name	Principal benefit sought	Demographic strengths	Special be-havioral char-acteristics	Brands dis-proportion-ately favored	Personality character-istics	Lifestyle character-istics
The sensory segment	Flavour, product appearance	Children	Users of spearmint flavoured toothpaste	Colgate, Stripe	High self-involvement	Hedonistic
The sociables	Brightness of teeth	Teens, young people	Smokers	Macleans, Ultra Brite	High sociability	Active
The worriers	Decay prevention	Large families	Heavy users	Crest	High hypochondriasis	Conservative
The independent segment	Price	Men	Heavy users	Brands on sale	High autonomy	Value-oriented

Segmentation of the industrial market

5.10 Segmentation applies more obviously to the consumer market, but it can also be applied to an industrial market. An important basis for segmentation is the nature of the customer's business. Accountants or lawyers, for example, might choose to specialise in serving customers in a particular type of business. An accountant may choose to specialise in advising and auditing retail businesses, and a firm of solicitors may specialise in conveyancing work for property development companies.

5.11 In much the same way, components manufacturers specialise in the industries of the firms to which they supply components. In the motor car industry, there are companies which specialise in the manufacture of car components, possibly for a single firm.

Examples of segmentation

5.12 A few illustrative examples follow, but you should appreciate that these examples merely try to indicate an approach to the more general problem.

  (a) *Adult education.* The market for adult education (say, evening classes) may be segmented according to:

      (i)   age (younger people might prefer classes in, say, yoga);
      (ii)   sex (women might prefer self defence courses);
      (iii) occupation (apprentices may choose technical classes);
      (iv)   social class (middle class people might prefer art or music subjects);
      (v)   education (poorly educated people might prefer to avoid all forms of evening class);
      (vi)   family life cycle (the interests of young single people are likely to differ from those of young married people with children).

  (b) *Magazines and periodicals.* In this market the segmentation may be according to:

      (i)   sex (Woman's Own);
      (ii)   social class (Country Life);
      (iii) income (Ideal Home);
      (iv)   occupation (Accountancy Age, Computer Weekly);
      (v)   leisure interests;
      (vi)   political ideology;
      (vii) age ('19', Honey);
      (viii) lifestyle (Playboy).

  (c) *Sporting facilities:*

      (i)   geographical area (rugby in Wales, ski-ing in parts of Scotland, sailing in coastal towns);
      (ii)   population density (squash clubs in cities, riding in country areas);
      (iii) occupation (gymnasia for office workers);
      (iv)   education (there may be a demand from ex-schoolboys for facilities for sports taught at certain schools, such as rowing);
      (v)   family life cycle or age (parents may want facilities for their children, young single or married people may want facilities for themselves).

5.13 It must be stressed that identifying the significant basis or bases for segmentation in any particular market is a matter of 'intuition' or 'interpretation' so that a new company entering a market may be able to identify a potentially profitable target market that no other firm has yet recognised. The examples in the previous paragraph merely suggest a few bases for segmentation in each case, and the various suggestions should not be expected to be mutually exclusive, nor should they necessarily carry equal weight or importance.

Target markets

5.14 Because of limited resources, competition and large markets, organisations are not usually able to sell with equal efficiency and success to the entire market: that is, to every market segment. It is therefore necessary for the sake of efficiency to select target markets. The marketing management of a company may choose one of the following policy options.

(a) *Undifferentiated marketing:* this policy is to produce a single product and hope to get as many customers as possible to buy it; that is, ignore segmentation entirely.

(b) *Concentrated marketing:* the company attempts to produce the ideal product for a *single* segment of the market (eg Rolls Royce cars, Mothercare mother and baby shops).

(c) *Differentiated marketing:* the company attempts to introduce several product versions, each aimed at a different market segment (for example, the manufacture of several different brands of washing powder).

5.15 The major disadvantage of *concentrated marketing* is the business risk of relying on a single segment of a single market; for example, the de Lorean sports car firm ran into irreversible financial difficulties in 1981-82 when the sports car market contracted in the USA. On the other hand, specialisation in a particular market segment can give a firm a profitable, although perhaps temporary, competitive edge over rival firms (such as Kickers specialising in leisure footwear).

5.16 The major disadvantage of *differentiated marketing* is the additional cost of marketing and production (more product design and development costs, the loss of economies of scale in production and storage, additional promotion costs and administrative costs and so on). When the costs of further differentiation of the market exceed the benefits from further segmentation and target marketing, a firm is said to have 'overdifferentiated'. Some firms have tried to overcome this problem by selling the same product to two market segments (so, for example, Johnson's baby powder is sold to adults for their own use; in the fairly recent past, many hairdressing salons switched from serving women only to serving both sexes).

5.17 The choice between undifferentiated, differentiated or concentrated marketing as a marketing strategy will depend on the following factors.

(a) How far can the product and/or the market be considered homogeneous? Mass marketing may be 'sufficient' if the market is largely homogeneous (eg safety matches).

(b) Will the company's resources be overextended by differentiated marketing? Small firms may succeed better by concentrating on one segment only.

(c)   Is the product sufficiently advanced in its 'life cycle' to have attracted a substantial total market? If not, segmentation and target marketing is unlikely to be profitable, because each segment would be too small in size.

5.18 The potential benefits of segmentation and target marketing are as follows.

(a)   *Product differentiation:* a feature of a particular product might appeal to one segment of the market in such a way that the product is thought better than its rivals. To other customers in different segments of the market, there may be no value in this distinguishing feature, and they would not buy it in preference to a rival product.

(b)   The seller will be more aware of how product design and development may stimulate further demand in a particular area of the market.

(c)   The resources of the business will be used more effectively, because the organisation should be more able to make products which the customer wants and will pay for.

6.   POSITIONING PRODUCTS AND BRANDS

6.1   Brands can be positioned against competitive brands on product maps that are defined in terms of how buyers perceive key characteristics.

6.2   Yoram Wind identifies a comprehensive list of these characteristics.

(a)   *Positioning by specific product features.* This is the most common approach to positioning, especially for industrial products. Price and specific product features are used as the basis for positioning. Most car advertisements stress the combination of product features available and may also stress what good value for money this represents.

(b)   *Positioning by benefits, problems, solutions, or needs.* The emphasis is on benefits, which is generally more effective than positioning on product features without referring to the benefits. Pharmaceutical companies position their products to doctors by stressing effectiveness and side effects. Other examples include Crest, which positions its toothpaste as a cavity fighter, and DHL, which uses its worldwide network of offices as a basis for its positioning.

(c)   *Positioning for specific usage occasions.* This approach is related to benefit positioning but uses the specific occasion as the major basis for the positioning. Johnson's Baby Shampoo is, thus, positioned as a product to use if you shampoo your hair every day, and Hennessy Cognac is for special occasions.

(d)   *Positioning for user category.* Examples here include 7-Up's use of the Fido Dido character to target urban adolescents. Age has been used as a basis for positioning by Saga Holidays, by many breakfast cereal producers (compare the target markets for Kellogg's Rice Krispies and Special K) and by Affinity shampoo for women over 40.

(e)   *Positioning against another product.* Although Avis never mentions Hertz explicitly in its advertising, its positioning as Number 2 in the rent-a-car market is an example of positioning against a leader.

(f) *Product class disassociation*. This is a less common basis for positioning, but it can be effective when introducing a new product that is different from standard products in an established product category. Lead-free petrol is positioned against leaded petrol.

(g) *Hybrid basis*. Often, a positioning strategy will be based on several of these alternatives, incorporating elements from more than one positioning base. The Porsche positioning, for example, is based on the product benefits as well as on a certain type of user.

6.3 A basic perceptual map is to plot brands in perceived price and perceived quality terms.

6.4 Price and quality are important elements in the marketing mix, but they will not, in the customer's opinion, be considered independent variables. A 'high' price will usually be associated with high quality and equally low price with low quality. Thus, while everybody would like to buy a bargain brand, there is a problem to overcome. This is a question of belief: will customers accept that a high quality product can be offered at a low price?

6.5 In the mid 1950s, the BBC ran an experiment on its live In Town Tonight programme. A journalist stood at Piccadilly Circus offering passers by the opportunity to buy £1 notes for ten shilling notes (50 pence in decimal currency). He reported over the live broadcast, that nobody, so far, had taken up the offer. Almost immediately, the journalist was swamped with individuals trying to trade 'ten bob' notes for pounds. All that had been needed was for potential customers to be reassured that there was no catch and that a genuine bargain was on offer.

6.6 Where would you place MFI in quality/price space? MFI would claim to be in the 'bargain' quadrant. Many potential customers think that they are at the lower end of the economy segment. MFI's practice of frequent sales and discounts has the effect of overcoming at least some of the difficulties resulting from individuals using price as a surrogate for assessment of quality. Thus the price label shows the higher pre-discounted price and the low sale price. The assumption is that customers will use the pre-sale price to confirm promotional claims about quality.

6.7 Public concern about the use of such promotional pricing has led to the introduction of restrictions on the use of these techniques. Stores now have to provide evidence that the promotion is part of a genuine 'sale'.

Identifying a gap in the market

6.8 Market research can determine where customers think that competitive brands are located.

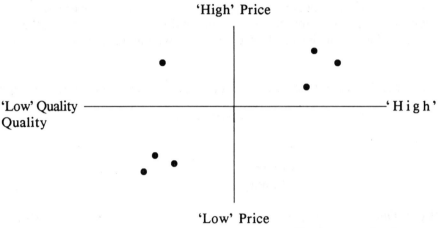

Restaurants in Anytown

6.9 In the hypothetical model above, there appears to be a gap in the market for a moderately priced reasonable quality eating place. This is shown between clusters in the high price/high quality and the low price/low quality segments.

6.10 However, it would be necessary to sound a note of caution before rushing off to set up such an establishment. Why does the gap exist? Is it that no entrepreneurial restauranteur has noticed the opportunity? Or is it that, while there is sufficient demand for gourmet eating and cheap cafes, there are insufficient customers to justify a restaurant in the middle range segment? More research would be needed to determine which of these conditions apply.

6.11 Perceptual maps can also be drafted to plot how customers perceive competitive brands performing on key product user benefits. Kotler provides the following hypothetical examples. He starts by considering the various products that serve the US breakfast market.

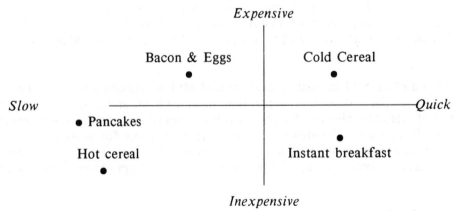

Product-positioning map:
Breakfast market

6.12 Within the breakfast market, a producer might be interested in entering the instant breakfast market. It would then be advisable to plot the position of the various instant breakfast brands.

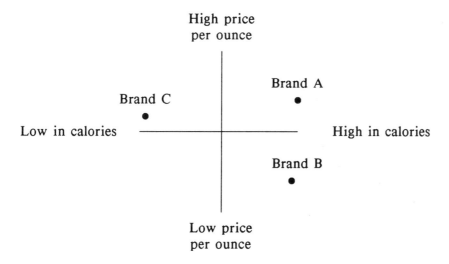

Brand-positioning map
(Instant breakfast market)

(Kotler, *Marketing Management*)

6.13 The above analysis now shows an apparent gap for a modest priced slimmers brand. Once again, it would be necessary to establish whether or not there exists sufficient demand for such a product to ensure that its production would be profitable.

6.14 When Ford launched the Fiesta, market research showed that whilst potential customers thought highly of the new car's performance and considered it economical, there were problems with perceptions of safety. This was inevitable given that its small size was seen as a minus point with regard to safety in the event of collision. Ford knew their product to be safe and so, when the Fiesta was relaunched, targeted the advertising copy line to change people's perception. One such advertisement showed the Fiesta braking in wet conditions. Another showed an expectant mother being delivered to hospital on time in spite of having to make an emergency stop when some idiot stepped out onto a zebra crossing.

Example of segmentation and positioning strategy: Texas Instruments

6.15 Texas Instruments, the US electronics manufacturer, aimed until 1985 to be the market leader in the world's semiconductor industry, competing with Japanese companies for the biggest share in the mass market for 'commodity' microchips, such as dynamic random access memory chips (the data storage chips used in every type of computer). Other US chip manufacturers had long since given up competing in the mass market, and had concentrated on custom-made and original design chips for specific customers or specific uses, which earn a higher profit margin on sales.

6.16 In 1985, prices of dynamic random access memory chips (DRAMs) fell sharply, and Texas Instruments went from record profits to record losses. The company reassessed its marketing strategy, and made the following policy decisions.

(a) It should remain in the DRAM business, because the technological know how obtained in this industry would spill over into other parts of TI's business, and help to keep the company in the forefront of technological developments. However, it was no longer to be an objective to be the world's market leader in the DRAM business. Sales growth was no longer a number one priority.

(b) Some cost cutting in its DRAM business was necessary. In 1985, TI's workforce was cut by 10%, and two semiconductor factories were closed down. A strategy for reorganisation and improving productivity was therefore pursued.

(c) The company recognised the need to adopt a more marketing oriented approach, since customers were now expecting better service from microchip manufacturers. The philosophy that superior technology will sell itself was abandoned, and instead the company began to recognise that customers didn't necessarily want the 'best' microchips; they wanted the chips that would solve their particular processing problems. The president of TI was reported as saying:

> 'There is a new emphasis across the corporation on strengthening our customer relationships. This will be a key to our long-term success. We must and will be market-oriented. Profitability will only come as a result of identifying and satisfying the real needs of our customers.'

(d) The company began to focus more attention on four specific segments of the market:

   (i) the market for microchips tailored to the needs of specific customers - custom-made chips;

   (ii) the microprocessor market for 'application processors' - microprocessors for special uses such as graphics and local area networks;

   (iii) developing highly integrated standard logic chips;

   (iv) the market for microchips for military uses.

6.17 Cost-cutting measures were introduced into other areas of TI's business, oil exploration and home computers. Long-term strategy involves the development of two programmes of R & D, in artificial intelligence and factory automation, with large research and development budgets being allocated. The president of TI has again been quoted as follows:

> 'Artificial intelligence and industrial automation both have the potential of becoming important businesses to TI. But a significant, additional advantage will come from our ability to focus these skills, strengthen them and infuse them back into our core businesses.'

Competitive positioning

6.18 Competitive positioning concerns 'a general idea of what kind of offer to make to the target market in relation to competitors' offers' (Kotler). Important considerations in competitive positioning are product quality and price, and Kotler identified a 3 × 3 matrix of nine different competitive positioning strategies.

Product	High price	Medium price	Low price
High	Premium strategy	Penetration strategy	Superbargain strategy
Medium	Overpricing strategy	Average quality strategy	Bargain strategy
Low	Hit and run strategy	Shoddy goods strategy	Cheap goods strategy

Fragmented industries and market segmentation

6.19 The fragmentation of industries and proliferation of market segments tends to occur when the following conditions apply.

(a) There are low entry barriers, and so new firms can enter the market relatively easily.

(b) There are few economies of scale or learning curve effects, and so it is difficult for big firms to establish a significant overall cost leadership.

(c) Transport and distribution costs are high, and so the industry fragments on a geographical basis.

(d) Customer needs vary widely.

(e) There are rapid product changes or style changes, which small firms might succeed in reacting to more quickly than large firms.

(f) There is a highly diverse product line, so that some firms are able to specialise in one part of the industry.

(g) There is scope for product differentiation, based on product design/quality differences or even brand images.

7. THE MARKETING PLAN

7.1 The marketing plan in detail consists of several inter-related decisions.

(a) *Sales targets* must be set for each product and each sales division (with sub-targets also set for sales regions, sales areas and individual salesmen). Sales targets may be referred to as sales quotas.

(b) The *total marketing budget* must be set.

(c) Given an overall marketing budget, resources (cash) must be allocated between:

(i) salaries and other staff costs;
(ii) above the line expenditure (advertising);
(iii) below the line expenditure (sales promotion items, price reduction allowances etc).

(d) The overall sales target set by top management will incorporate *sales price decisions;* but within the formulation of the marketing plan there is likely to be some room for manoeuvre and an element of choice in the pricing decision. In other words, top management will decide on a 'rough pricing zone' and a specific price within this zone will be fixed later within the marketing plan.

(e) Expenditure on marketing will also be allocated to different products or services within the organisation's product or service range. Some products might justify additional marketing expenditure; whereas others, nearing the end of their life cycle, may lose a part of their previous allocation.

7.2 Market plan decisions - about sales targets, total marketing expenditure budget, the marketing mix and the allocation of expenditure to products - are the main elements of *marketing programming*. They are very much inter-related, and a marketing plan should not be set without proper consideration of alternative choices.

The marketing budget

7.3 Strategic marketing decisions are an integral part of the corporate plan. Top management must set an overall sales strategy and a series of sales objectives; only then should a more detailed marketing plan be prepared.

7.4 There are three types of annual budget planning for a marketing budget:

(a) top down planning involves the setting of goals for lower management by higher management;

(b) bottom up planning exists where employees set their own goals and submit then to higher management for approval;

(c) 'goals down - plans up' planning is a mixture of the two styles, whereby top management sets overall goals and employees lower in the organisation hierarchy then set plans for achieving those goals. This type of planning is well suited to the formulation of sales budgets.

7.5 Budgeting for sales revenue and selling costs is plagued with uncertainty. The variables are so many and so difficult to estimate, even within a wide tolerance (largely because of competitive action and changing customer habits and tastes) that both setting budgets and budgetary control on the marketing side are different from the more 'mechanical' approach which can be adopted with other budgets.

7.6 However, it is plainly unsatisfactory to engage in minute cost control systems in production, and then hope that all other costs (eg research, distribution, sales) will look after themselves. A sales and marketing budget is necessary because:

(a) it is an element of the overall strategic plan of the business (the master budget) which brings together all the activities of the business;

(b) where sales and other non-production costs are a large part of total costs, it is financially prudent to forecast, plan and control them;

(c)   the very uncertain nature of factors which influence selling makes the need for good forecasts and plans greater, and it can be argued that if budgets are to be used for control, the more uncertain the budget estimates are, the more budgetary control is necessary.

Matching forecast demand with estimated available capacity

7.7   One of the problems in setting budgets is matching the forecast demand from customers with the estimated available capacity. There are three aspects to this problem.

(a)   It is difficult to make an accurate forecast of demand.

(b)   It is difficult to predict available capacity accurately too, given uncertainties about:

(i)   efficiency and productivity levels;
(ii)   the availability of staff, or cash;
(iii)   the likely down-town or time lost through industrial disputes;
(iv)   whether overtime or double shift working will be available;
(v)   the likelihood that changes in equipment (eg introduction of new equipment and replacement equipment) will take place in the budget period.

(c)   There are often practical difficulties in matching demand with capacity. Demand might be seasonal, and if services or non-standard products are required, it will not be possible to build up inventories in periods of slack demand in anticipation of periods of high demand.

7.8   In order to match demand with capacity, management must be flexible, and be prepared to take action:

(a)   to suppress demand if it exceeds capacity, by raising prices, for example;
(b)   to stimulate demand if there is excess capacity, such as by advertising or price reductions;
(c)   to reduce excess capacity by selling off surplus assets;
(d)   to supplement production when there is undercapacity by subcontracting work to other organisations, and perhaps to take steps to increase capacity (by acquiring new premises, equipment and labour, or by negotiating for more overtime from existing employees).

The advertising budget decision

7.9   This is an important feature of the marketing budget. The theory behind setting an advertising budget is the theory of *diminishing returns*. For every extra £1 of advertising spent, the company should earn an extra £x of profit. Further expenditure on advertising is justified until the marginal return £x diminishes to the point where £x < £1.

7.10 Unfortunately, the marginal return from additional advertising cannot be measured easily in practice because:

(a)   advertising is only one aspect of the overall marketing mix;
(b)   advertising has some long-term effect, which goes beyond the limits of a measurable accounting period;
(c)   where the advertising budget is fixed as a percentage of sales, advertising costs tend to follow sales levels and not vice versa.

7.11 Research has shown that in the UK, most advertising budgets are fixed by some rule of thumb, non-scientific methods, such as:

(a) a percentage of the previous year's sales;
(b) a percentage of the budgeted annual sales;
(c) a percentage of the previous year's profit.

There is no reason, however, why advertising costs should relate directly to either total turnover or profits. Given that large amounts of expenditure may be incurred on advertising, these arbitrary guesswork systems reveal an alarming lack of proper financial control.

7.12 Other methods of setting the advertising budget include the following.

(a) Fixing advertising expenditure in relation to the expenditure incurred by *competitors*. This is unsatisfactory because it presupposes that the competitor's decision must be a good one.

(b) *The task method*. The marketing task for the organisation is set and an advertising budget is prepared which will help to ensure that this objective is achieved. A problem occurs if the objective is achieved only by paying out more on advertising than the extra profits obtained would justify.

(c) *Communication stage models*. These are based on the idea that the link between advertising and sales cannot be measured directly, but can be measured by means of intermediate stages (increase in awareness, comprehension, and then intention to buy). An example of such a model is Colley's *DAGMAR* model (Defining Advertising Goals for Measured Advertising Results). A major problem with the use of such models is that it is not yet clear how the use of indices of customer opinion will enable management to set an effective advertising budget.

7.13 Recommended practice for fixing advertising cost budgets would be the use of:

(a) *empirical testing* (for example, in a mail order business or in retail operations, since it may be possible to measure the effect of advertising on sales by direct observation);

(b) *mathematical models* using data bout media and consumer characteristics, desired market share, and using records of past results. Regression analysis can be conducted to find out the likely cost of advertising (through several media) to achieve a given target.

Control

7.14 Once the plan has been implemented, the task of management is to control the use of resources. Aspects of control include:

(a) a comparison of actual sales against the budget;

(b) a comparison of actual marketing costs against the budgeted expenditure levels and against actual sales;

(c) analysis of the profitability of individual products, and distribution outlets;

(d) strategic control, ie checking whether the company's objectives, products and resources are being directed towards the correct markets.

Allocation of costs

7.15 The allocation of *direct selling costs* to products, type of outlet and so on is fairly straightforward, but *indirect costs* such as administration overheads must be allocated on an arbitrary basis (such as to products by value of sales). This aspect of cost allocation should be carefully considered when deciding whether to eliminate an unprofitable expenditure from selling or distribution.

(a) The cost of distributing goods to a distant area may seem to be relatively unprofitable; but if, by not selling the goods in this area, there will be unused production capacity, the products which are produced and sold will have to bear a higher proportion of fixed costs which will still be incurred.

(b) The allocation of fixed selling costs to products may make a product seem unprofitable, but the product may still be making a *contribution* to those fixed costs.

Example: allocation of costs

7.16 A business incurs £100,000 fixed costs per annum. It produces and sells two products, A and B.

	A £	B £
Per unit of product		
Sales price	10	8
Direct costs of production and sale	5	5
Contribution	5	3
Fixed (indirect) cost allocation	3	3
Profit	2	0

7.17 It may seem not to be worthwhile to produce product B at all. However, if sales of product A are insufficient to make £100,000 in contribution (in other words, if sales of product A are less than 20,000 per annum), then the business will make a loss overall. So, for example:

	£
Contribution from product A	
(assume sales of 18,000 units per annum) @ £5 per unit	90,000
Fixed costs	100,000
Loss	(10,000)

7.18 If at least 3,333 units of product B could be sold, then the loss would be wiped out because another £10,000 of contribution would be earned. In accountants' terms, the business would *break even:* cover its costs but make no profit.

7.19 Eliminating unprofitable selling and distribution expenditure is sound commercial practice, but the concept of avoidable and unavoidable costs should be used in deciding what is unprofitable. If the removal of one part of selling costs relieves a company of a cost which is higher than the contribution towards profit gained from it, then this part of selling activity can and should be eliminated. The unavoidable fixed costs of production as well as selling and distribution should be taken into account in any such decision.

Marketing audits

7.20 Top management is responsible for ensuring that the company is pursuing optimal policies with regard to its products, markets and distribution channels. Carrying out this responsibility is known as strategic control of marketing, and the means to apply strategic control is the marketing audit.

7.21 A marketing audit does not exist in the compulsory formal sense that an external financial audit does. For proper strategic control, however, a marketing audit should:

(a) be conducted regularly;

(b) take a comprehensive look at every product, market, distribution channel, ingredient in the marketing mix and so on and should not be restricted to areas of apparent ineffectiveness such as an unprofitable product, a troublesome distribution channel, or low efficiency on direct selling;

(c) be carried out according to a set of predetermined, specified procedures: it should be systematic.

The 'auditors' should, where possible, be independent, so that their findings and suggestions for remedial action are not coloured by their own particular job interests.

The audit procedure

7.22 A marketing audit should consider the following areas.

(a) *The marketing environment*

(i) What are the organisation's major markets, and what is the segmentation of these markets; what are the future prospects of each market segment?

(ii) Who are the customers, what is known about customer needs, intentions and behaviour?

(iii) Who are the competitors, and what is their standing in the market?

(iv) Have there been any significant developments in the broader environment (eg economic or political changes, population or social changes).

(b) *Marketing objectives and plans*

(i) What are the organisation's marketing objectives and how do they relate to overall objectives? Are they reasonable?

(ii) Are enough (or too many) resources being committed to marketing to enable the objectives to be achieved; is the division of costs between products, areas etc satisfactory?

(iii) Is the share of expenditure between direct selling, advertising, distribution etc an optimal one?

(iv) What are the procedures for formulating marketing plans and management control of these plans; are they satisfactory?

(v) Is the marketing organisation (and its personnel) operating efficiently?

(c) *Marketing activities*

(i) A review of sales price levels should be made (looking at, for example, supply demand, customer attitudes or the use of temporary price reductions).

(ii) A review of the state of each individual product (its market 'health') and of the product mix as a whole should be made.

(iii) A critical analysis of the distribution system should be made, with a view to finding improvements.

(iv) The size and organisation of the personal sales force should be studied, with a view to deciding whether efficiency should be improved (and how this could be done).

(v) A review of the effectiveness of advertising and sales promotion activities should be carried out.

8. CONCLUSION

8.1 In this final chapter, we have looked at marketing strategy and at tactical methods for maximising sales, most notably segmentation. We concluded by looking at the components of the marketing plan and at how managers can assess the effectiveness of their strategy and detailed plans by the use of marketing audit.

8.2 Use of strategic planning enables organisations to be *effective*, not just efficient. Information is gathered and used to develop a corporate plan, covering short, medium and long-term goals and acting as a framework within which specific functions such as marketing can develop their own plans.

8.3 Techniques used in strategy formulation include situation and SWOT analysis. The latter enables an organisation to choose whether to *match* its strengths to available opportunities or to *convert* its weaknesses into strengths or its threats into opportunities.

8.4 *Competitive strategies* can only be developed after thorough evaluation of an organisation's industry and involve deciding:

(a) whether to compete across the whole market or only in certain segments *(competitive scope)*;
(b) whether to compete through low costs/prices or by offering a differentiated product range *(competitive advantage)*.

You should learn the matrix in paragraph 4.9 showing the four main competitive strategies (cost leadership, cost focus, differentation leadership and differentiation focus).

8.5 Another widely known approach is to use the Ansoff Product/Market matrix to determine *growth strategies*. This should also be learnt (paragraph 4.10). It produces four strategies: market penetration or development, product development and diversification.

8.6 *Market segmentation* is a more complex and costly strategy to adopt than a mass market approach; but, where it is worthwhile, it should result in increased total sales and profits because products/services will be more likely to appeal to the target segments and pricing policy can be more sophisticated. There are many possible bases for segmentation, which you should learn. Some relate to the target consumer and others to the product.

8.7 Product/brand positioning may be determined in several ways, most commonly by highlighting specific product features, including price. Price and quality are very important in consumer perceptions of a product and analysis of existing products in a market can be used to identify gaps.

8.8 The *marketing plan* should include:

(a) sales targets;
(b) total marketing budget analysed between above the line, below the line and other items.

Budgeting is an essential financial discipline but a particularly tricky problem in marketing given the difficulty in determining both likely demand and likely cost of achieving a given sales target. The rules of thumb commonly used in setting promotional budgets (such as a percentage of budgeted or past sales or profit) are unsatisfactory because they are arbitrary.

8.9 *Marketing audits* are a means of applying strategic control to ensure that marketing policies are optimal. They should be carried out regularly, comprehensively and as far as possible objectively. The audit should consider the marketing environment existing marketing objectives and plans, and marketing activities.

TEST YOUR KNOWLEDGE

Numbers in brackets refer to paragraphs of this chapter

1   What is an emergent strategy? (1.5)

2   Outline the stages in strategic planning. (3.2)

3   What is situation analysis? (3.8)

4   SWOT analysis looks at strengths, weaknesses, opportunities and threats. Which are internal and which external? (4.2-4.4)

5   What five factors affect the profitability of an industry? (4.8)

6   A cost focus strategy attempts to control the market through being the low cost producer. True or false? (4.9)

7   Differentiate between market and product development. (4.10)

8   Diversification is a low risk strategy. True or false? Give reasons for your answer. (4.10)

9   When should market segmentation be used? (5.2)

10   List as many bases for market segmentation as you can. (5.8)

11   What is concentrated marketing? (5.14) What are its risks? (5.15)

12   A bargain brand is perceived as low price, high quality. True or false? (6.3)

13   A small town has no bookshop. Why should a potential bookseller think twice before rushing in to set one up? (6.10)

14   What seven conditions tend to give rise to fragmentation of industries and proliferation of market segments? (6.19)

15   What is above the line expenditure? (7.1)

16   Why is a sales and marketing budget necessary? (7.6)

17   List the problems encountered in setting a sales budget. (7.7)

18   What is the task method? (7.12)

19   Explain why the DAGMAR model may be useful in budgeting for advertising costs. (7.12)

20   What should be the scope of a marketing audit? (7.22)

Now try questions 19 and 20 at the end of the text

ILLUSTRATIVE QUESTIONS

AND

SUGGESTED SOLUTIONS

ILLUSTRATIVE QUESTIONS

F indicates a question set in the Fundamentals of Marketing paper and P a question set in the Practice of Marketing paper.

1   MARKETING ORIENTATION
F6/90

How does marketing orientation differ from product orientation?

2   THE MARKETING MIX
F6/90

What are the elements of the marketing mix? Outline some of the factors to be considered for a company to arrive at an appropriate marketing mix.

3   PRIMARY AND SECONDARY RESEARCH
P12/90

Using examples, distinguish between primary and secondary research. Explain the limitations of using secondary research in practice.

4   THE MARKET RESEARCH PLAN
P6/90

Outline the structure and content of a market research plan designed to examine the trade opinion of your competitors.

5   SAMPLING
P12/90

As a national distributor of office stationery to 2,000 commercial accounts you need to examine customer reaction to company policy to discontinue the practice of providing gifts to buyers as an incentive to purchase. To conduct this research:

(a)   select and justify an appropriate form of sampling;
(b)   state how the sample is to be selected;
(c)   explain how the data will be collected in a form suitable for analysis by management.

6   DISTRIBUTION
F12/90

Distinguish between selective, intensive and exclusive methods of distribution.

7   MAIL ORDER SELLING
F6/90

Describe and account for the growth in mail order selling.

8   PHYSICAL DISTRIBUTION MANAGEMENT
F12/90

What is the role and function of physical distribution management in connecting products to consumers?

9   THE PRODUCT LIFE CYCLE   F12/90

Describe the stages in the Product Life Cycle.

10   SCREEN, POSITION, MIX AND ELIMINATE   F6/90

Distinguish between product screening, product positioning, product mix and product elimination.

11   PRICING   F12/90

Write brief notes on:

(a)   cost plus pricing;
(b)   market skimming pricing;
(c)   marginal cost pricing;
(d)   market penetration pricing.

12   SALES PROMOTION   P6/90

As promotions manager of a well established UK manufacturer of women's beauty products, explain how you would use sales promotion to support the national launch of 'Chico'. This is a new fragrance targeted at B, C1, 18-45, experimentally minded women who are prepared to try a new perfume.

13   NOTES ON PROMOTION   F12/89

Write brief notes on the following:

(a)   unique selling propositions;
(b)   the promotional mix;
(c)   point of sales display;
(d)   publicity.

14   PUBLIC RELATIONS   P12/90

Discuss the statement that public relations can reduce the effects of corporate crisis upon an organisation's publics.

15   AGENCY/CLIENT RELATIONSHIPS   P6/90

The achievement of advertising campaign objectives depends upon effective agency/client relationships. Discuss.

16   THE CONSUMER MOVEMENT   F12/90

Describe how the consumer movement can influence marketing operations.

ILLUSTRATIVE QUESTIONS

17 SALES REPS AND SALES MANAGERS   P6/90

Making the transition from sales representative to sales manager can be traumatic. Explain the tensions involved and suggest ways in which such personal promotion can be achieved effectively.

18 SALES FORECASTING   P12/89

Why do companies forecast sales? Explain briefly *three* methods of sales forecasting in use.

19 OBJECTIVES, STRATEGIES AND CONTROL   P12/89

Using a product of your choice, distinguish between objectives, strategies and control as key elements in the annual marketing plan.

20 OVERSEAS EXPANSION   P12/90

What advice would you give to a company seeking expansion through overseas market entry?

1   MARKETING ORIENTATION

Product orientation as a business philosophy can take two forms, *product orientation* and *sales orientation*. In the last half of the nineteenth and the beginning of the twentieth century business was mainly *production oriented*. Demand for new products was high, due to the mass production methods that reduced prices and increased output. The products that were produced and the prices paid for them depended on the production methods and raw materials that were available. Typical of this ethos is Henry Ford's statement 'you can have any car you like as long as it is black'. A production orientation looks at what the company can produce rather than what the customer wishes to purchase. Promotion is not considered to be of great importance. Good quality products are supposed to 'sell themselves', and if they do not this is usually blamed on the sales staff or on the customers themselves! Improvements are concentrated on the productive efficiency of the company. Companies that follow a production orientation are often called 'marketing myopic'. Senior management in this type of company often have production backgrounds. If demand is buoyant this approach can be reasonably successful but can be difficult to sustain in the long run. Some firms still are production oriented, for example some high technology industries.

Sales oriented companies are also basically product oriented. In the 1920s and 1930s the downturn in economic activities made firms realise they did not face an insatiable demand for their products and products do not simply sell themselves. Promotional activities came to be of more importance than under a production orientation but the main focus in a sales oriented business is selling the products that have been produced. Again the products and sales figures are important rather than any aspect of customer satisfaction. Companies which are sales oriented are often typified by 'hard sell' tactics. Examples still occur of sales oriented companies, especially in home improvements or insurance sectors. It should be remembered that selling is an important function of the marketing mix. The basic assumption of a selling orientation is that customers will not seek out your products and they actually have to be sold to them, which is closer to a market orientation than a production orientation. However, a selling orientation does not build brand loyalty and is a rather short-term vision of the market place.

Marketing orientation is often called *customer orientation*. Instead of products and the selling of products being of central importance, the consumer is the focus of the marketing oriented firm. This takes a longer term view of business and profitability. A marketing oriented company sets out to define what the customer actually wants and then produces goods that fill those wants. Companies then make what customers want to buy rather than produce what they are good at or have traditionally supplied.

To be truly marketing oriented the firm should practice consumer orientation at all levels and within all functions of the organisation. This means that from Managing Director to shop floor workers all staff should have the customer in mind. Marketing should not simply be a functional department that organises the promotional aspects of the firm, but practised as a philosophy by all departments whether they be finance, production or marketing. This will change the objectives of all departments: for example, if the production department is customer oriented it may only produce short runs of certain products, whereas from a purely production point of view, it might prefer longer runs.

The organisational changes necessary for a company to move from being product oriented to marketing oriented are difficult for companies to make because they are not simply bureaucratic but require retraining and reorganisation at all levels. Usually a would be marketing oriented firm has a marketing director high up in the organisation's hierarchy, but this must be more than a token gesture if a true marketing orientation is to be achieved.

Within a customer oriented firm there is a great need for marketing research as this is the main way in which customer needs are identified. These needs may not simply be the obvious need that the product fills, but the less obvious needs that encompass the total product offering. For example, a car fulfils the need for transportation but there are many more personal and social needs that are filled by the particular model of car.

Markets are dynamic: they are constantly changing. Customer orientation means that these changes can be monitored and perhaps acted upon before the competition. Customer orientation also fosters the idea of brand loyalty. If you are satisfying customer needs, and are monitoring those needs for changes, then customers are less likely to go elsewhere for products. A marketing orientation takes a much longer term view of business than a product orientation.

Recently there has been an interest in what has been termed *societal marketing*. What the customer wants may not be in his best interest in the long run (eg smoking) or in society's best interest. Societal marketing aims to move from a simple marketing orientation to one that assesses the environmental and long-term consumer interest. In practice, of course, this is unlikely to make much headway unless backed by government legislation, but in the UK the Body Shop is one example of a company whose marketing orientation has a strong societal bias.

In conclusion, a product orientation makes the needs of the producer central, but marketing orientation makes the consumer central. For a company to be truly marketing oriented it should adopt a marketing orientation throughout the whole organisation and not simply treat it as a divisional role.

2 THE MARKETING MIX

A company's marketing mix includes all the tools that come under the organisation's control to affect the way products and services are offered to the market. Borden coined the phrase 'the marketing mix' from the idea that business executives were mixers of ingredients. From observing industries and individual firms it can be seen that there are wide ranging applications of the tools of marketing. The elements of the marketing mix are often described as the 'four Ps', Product, Price, Place and Promotion. It includes all the policies and procedures involved in each of these elements. This can be on a strategic level: for instance, whether to adopt a penetration or skimming pricing policy for a new product. It can also be on a more tactical level, for instance special price discounts. Each element is looked into in more detail below.

Product
Decisions to be made regarding products include the product lines that are produced, product improvements, new product development and which market(s) to sell them in, including whether to adopt a market segmentation approach.

Pricing
Decisions include the appropriate price level to adopt, the specific prices, price strategy for new products and price variations.

Place
The 'place' aspect of the four Ps is often also called 'channels of distribution'. This includes the way in which goods are passed from the manufacturer to the final consumer.

Promotion

Promotional aspects include personal selling, advertising, publicity and sales promotions. Each of these must be looked into to give an overall consistent message to the public. For example, it is not good to stress service quality in advertising if the actual personal selling of the organisation is not of high calibre. Decisions have to be made on the amount of time and money spent, media selection, desired image and length of campaign.

This is obviously not an exhaustive list. Some elements of the marketing mix do not easily fall exclusively into one category. Packaging, for example, has promotional aspects and product aspects.

There are many factors that come into play when the organisation is considering the most appropriate marketing mix. Some of these are market forces and some are product specific.

Many product areas are dominated by players that excel in one area of the marketing mix. A market may be typified by price competition for example, whereas in another branding may be of importance. This dominance of one aspect of the marketing mix will have an influence on competitors in the industry. This does not mean to say that all firms within the industry successfully differentiate themselves from the competition by focusing on neglected areas of the marketing mix. The stage in the product life cycle also has an influence on the appropriate marketing mix. In the introductory stage any design problems with the actual product should be solved. Price will depend on the costs of developing the product and the strategy regarding required market share. Promotion may concentrate on creating awareness and distribution may be selective. Throughout the other stages in the product life cycle the objectives of the marketing mix may change and the growth and maturity stage product differentiation, image building and quality may be concentrated on; whilst in the decline stage rationalisations may occur.

Other factors that should be taken into account when designing a marketing mix include the following.

Buyer behaviour

The behaviour of consumers and the behaviour of intermediaries should be taken into account. The actual number of buyers in a market is important as is the motivation for purchase and their buying processes. It is of no use to provide products by mail order, for example, if there is a strong resistance from buyers to purchasing products in this way. Whether the firm is providing goods or services will have an influence on buyer behaviour, as will whether the purchaser is in the consumer or industrial market. All these aspects will have an influence on marketing mix decisions.

Competitors

To a certain degree this has been dealt with above. However, the influence of competitors on marketing mix decisions is far reaching. Companies must analyse competitor strengths and weaknesses and their likely response to any marketing tools used.

Government

The government impose some controls on marketing that would affect decisions made regarding the marketing mix. These include regulations on advertising (eg cigarette ban), product specifications, pricing and competitive practices.

Company specific

All the above factors have to be taken into account when designing an appropriate marketing mix. However, it is easy to overlook one important consideration, that is company resources. The amount of money and staffing resources that marketing is allocated will determine to a large extent the elements of the marketing mix that are viable. The efficiency and effectiveness of marketing programmes need to be constantly monitored and built into the marketing planning process for the future.

All these factors should be taken into account when marketers are designing marketing mix programmes taking into account the size and resources of the organisation.

3 PRIMARY AND SECONDARY RESEARCH

Research can be classified as either primary or secondary. Secondary research consists of existing research material and is often termed desk research. Primary research is new original data collected specifically for a purpose.

Secondary research is often conducted before primary research because of the high cost of primary research and the time it takes to conduct. Secondary sources include:

(a) *Internal data sources*. For example, sales figures, financial data, customer complaints and past research reports. Internal data sources are often a neglected area of marketing research. Sometimes the way the data is collected can make an important difference to their use in marketing research.

(b) *Government sources*. There are many publications from government departments that are useful secondary research sources. The 'Guide to Official Statistics' (HMSO) and 'Regional Statistics' (HMSO) are useful publications that will aid the researcher to discover what statistics are available and where they can be found. Government departments also publish data that may be of use to the market researcher: for example, 'Housing and Construction Statistics' and 'Family Expenditure Survey Reports'. Government departments in other countries also publish statistical data as do organisations such as the EC.

(c) *Other publications*. There is a vast array of additional data sources available to the researcher. Many trade associations publish data for the industry. Yearbooks and directories are published in many industries. Professional institutions also provide members with information. The general and trade press also can be useful sources of information on trends and competitors. There are a number of commercial research companies that can also be used. Well known examples in this area are Mintel, MEAL (Media Expenditure Analysis), Euromonitor and the Economist Intelligence Group. Industry surveys from a financial viewpoint are conducted by some brokerage firms.

Secondary research can be expensive if all these reports are purchased. It may be in the company's best interests to join one of the main commercial libraries for example at London or Manchester Business School. Secondary data has a number of limitations which will be dealt with later, first we will turn our attention to primary research.

Primary research can be classified into three areas: experimentation, observation and questionnaires/interviewing. Experimentation is often used in the fields of scientific or technical research, as it usually involves testing in a laboratory situation where variables can be controlled. Within marketing however this is very difficult to do as there are many behavioural and situational variables that affect purchase decisions. Experimental research in marketing involves the testing of changes to one aspect of the marketing mix to monitor response. A supermarket may be contemplating the introduction of a new dessert and therefore introduce it in a representative sample of outlets to observe sales. Price sensitivity can be monitored using experimental research, as can the acceptability and effectiveness of advertisements.

Observing consumers' buying behaviour can also be a useful primary data collection method. Bias in the research is kept to a minimum in this method because of the distance between researcher and subject. Audits can be made of products in stock in sales outlets, or traffic and pedestrian flows can be monitored to assess the viability of sites. Consumers' shopping behaviour can be monitored using video cameras, EPOS systems and personal observation. Also of importance when assessing the level of service the company is providing is observing the behaviour of staff.

Questionnaires and interviewing are the most common methods of primary data collection. Questionnaires can be structured and administered by post or by person or semi-structured and administered verbally either face to face or by telephone. Interviews are usually based on a semi-structured questionnaire and can be individual or in groups. Great care is needed on the design of questionnaires to make sure that the information gained is what was really required.

To be successful, research should ideally use more than one technique. Secondary data can be used, for example, as an industry overview and to suggest areas where primary research is required. Although comparatively cheap secondary research does have limitations. It can give an overview of an industry but many of the details that are important to marketing management are missing. There may not be a great deal of secondary information available in certain industry sectors, so primary research becomes more important. If there is data available for the industry as a whole it is not specific to any one company. In practice some of the secondary data sources can be quite difficult to obtain. The choice of research methods obviously depend on the objectives of the research. If you wish to find out the consumer attitudes to your product, secondary internal sources can be used to a certain degree but primary research would give a more detailed and useful picture. Primary research is not without problems though, as specialist staff need to be used to administer and analyse primary data. However, the main limitation of secondary research is that it does not specifically relate to the company's consumers.

4 THE MARKET RESEARCH PLAN

There are a number of factors that have to be considered before a research plan can be designed. Whether or not the research should be done in house or through an agency will depend on the capabilities of the marketing department. The budget that is available will determine the methodology chosen to a certain degree. Any time constraints will also have an effect on the method chosen. The research plan should firstly set out clear objectives. In this case the objective will be 'to investigate the opinions and attitudes towards our trade competitors'.

Secondary research would have to be undertaken in order to assess the marketplace.

Secondary research - sources of information

Before an analysis of competitors can be started they have first to be identified. This can be done by looking at directories and yearbooks, asking present and past customers, keeping a 'weather eye' on trade press and asking sales representatives. Company profiles can then be used to give descriptions of the company in terms of size, profitability, past performance, corporate culture and image. Information that will be required to draw up these profiles can be found in annual reports (available from Companies House), trade press and published commercial reports in the area.

Primary research

The primary research should cover three areas. It should make an assessment of awareness of your company and its competitors. The image, opinions and attitude towards competitors (include your company also to get a comparative picture) should then be investigated. It should also look at the buying practices of the respondent, although not in a great deal of detail, simply enough to make recommendations in this area. Sales representatives could be used to gain information on competing firms although they will not really have the necessary skills to do this adequately and would probably not be objective.

The internal capabilities of the company should be taken into account when deciding whether to undertake the research in house or to employ a specialist marketing research company. The sample selected will depend greatly on the type of industry the company competes in. If the industry is dominated by a small number of large firms, a different sampling method should be used than for an industry characterised by a large number of small firms. If there are only a few buyers of the product in the market, then it is possible to research all the buyers. If there are a large number, then a representative sample must be chosen.

The primary research recommended is a questionnaire that would be administered by an interviewer. If the budget did not allow for this, then questionnaires could be mailed. However, when asking about awareness it is better that an interviewer is present. Also the responses to the first section (on awareness) will determine the companies that will be asked about in the second section (comparing attributes). Many firms will not be averse to discussing competitors in this way as they see it as encouraging competition. Before the interviewer calls, it is necessary to discover in each company who the right person to interview would be. This person should be an important member of the buying group, who will have the authority to answer questions. Researchers should telephone beforehand to make an appointment with the correct person. The identification of respondents can be made either by telephone or by consulting sales representatives.

The questionnaire should be designed with care and should include:

(a) A section evaluating the respondent's awareness of competitors in the industry and your own company.

(b) A section to give information on the opinions on your company and competitors. This should be scaled; for example, a rating from poor to excellent can be used for the companies the respondent is aware of along the following dimensions.

   (i)   Quality of service (pre sale)
   (ii)   Quality of after sales service
   (iii) Delivery time
   (iv)   Delivery reliability
   (v)   Product range
   (vi)   Price
   (vii) Value for money.

   Following on from this, the competitors' images can be assessed by asking respondents to rate each company along certain dimensions. This can be done by having statements that are scaled from 'agree strongly' to 'disagree strongly' and include statements such as 'the company is a traditional type of supplier' or 'the company follows the market leader'.

(c) A section that analyses the way in which purchases are made for this type of product in the company. Questions that should be asked include: how many people are involved in buying? Is there an informal or formal buying procedure?

Analysis

The analysis that is appropriate will depend on the sample size. If a very small number were interviewed, then little statistical analysis can be carried out. For larger samples questionnaires should be coded for ease of analysis. This will also mean that cross tabulations can be performed on data. For example, quality can be cross tabulated with price. General percentages should be analysed before undertaking any advanced quantitative techniques.

Report preparation

The research report should then be presented in a way that can be quickly and easily understood. It should not include detailed statistical analysis but should include the pertinent points and conclusions and recommendations.

Included in the research plan should be an envisaged time scale for each aspect of the research as shown below.

Time scale of research

	Week
Secondary research	1-2
Design sample frame	2-3
Primary data collection	3-6
Analysis	6-8
Report preparation	8-10

Limitations

Limitations of the research should be acknowledged. Budget and time limitations are obviously important. The identification of the sample is another area in which limitations are likely to exist. Unless there are a very small number of competing suppliers there is not going to be a 100% response rate. Including more respondents would alter the findings of the research.

5   SAMPLING

(a)   In an industrial market it is often possible to obtain data from all members of the market. In this case it would be possible to survey all 2,000 firms, although it would not be practical to do so because of time and money constraints. Therefore it is necessary to obtain a sample that will estimate the characteristics of the population. The accuracy of a sample will depend on how the sample is chosen, the variability of the population and the size of the sample. In general the larger the sample the more accurate the results. In an industrial market the buyers are often very different sized firms. A single industrial buyer may be very large, in so far as it accounts for a large volume of sales in that market. A random sample may not pick up a large buyer, or if it was selected and it was treated the same as small buyers in the sample, then the results could be distorted. If the market is characterised by large buyers a random sampling technique may not be appropriate. The main types of sampling techniques are outlined below.

Random sample
A random sampling technique is one in which all members of a population have an equal chance of being selected. A random sample starts with a sampling frame. That is a list of all members of the population. In this case it would be the 2,000 firms. A random sample can then be made by using either a lottery method or random number table.

Non random sample

As stated earlier random samples can be problematical for industrial markets. The main methods of non random sampling are systematic sampling, stratified sampling, multistage sampling, quota sampling and cluster sampling. It is not appropriate here to discuss each of these methods in more detail. We shall concentrate on the techniques that are most relevant to the example. Stratified sampling divides the population into strata that are distinct in some way from each other. In this case, the population could be divided into size of orders or industry type. A random sample from each group will then be selected. Quota sampling could also be used. Surveys are undertaken until a certain quota is met. Again this method is useful in industrial markets because it allows the population to be divided into groups so taking into account the diversity of buyers.

Before a sampling method is selected the researcher should investigate how many buyers there are in the population (in this case 2,000), and whether any large buyers dominate the market. If there are no dominant buyers then a random sample can be obtained and errors calculated mathematically. If there are dominant buyers a non random sample should be used. In the case of our example, a quota sampling technique would satisfy the objective of the research and probably the industry characteristics.

(b)   The sample should be selected by dividing the buyers into large, medium and small buyers. This is done not simply looking at the size of the company but rather looking at their importance in the market for office stationery. Then an assessment should be made as to the number in each category. The researcher should take a certain number from each category to fulfil the quota in a random way. This number should reflect the spread of buyers throughout each of the categories. Within each company selected the person receiving the gift should be identified, which can be done either through internal records or by asking sales representatives. A total sample of around 500 should be adequate to assess buyers' opinions of buyer incentives. This may seem quite a high number and will obviously depend on the characteristics of the industry, although the methodology selected for this survey is relatively cheap and quick allowing more responses to be gained.

(c)   In this case data can be quickly and easily gathered using a telephone survey. The information is not confidential and can be gathered by a few simple questions. The main problem in this type of survey is finding out whether the buyers are actually telling the truth! They may overstate the importance of gifts being made to them in the buying decision because they do not want the gifts to be withdrawn. A telephone survey could ask the following:

(i)   What is your role in the buying procedure?
(ii)   What is your opinion of the gift scheme?
(iii)   Does it affect your choice in any way?
(iv)   Would any other incentives be more appreciated?
(v)   What was the last gift you received from the company?

As much of the information as possible should be gathered in a way that allows a quantitative analysis to be made. For example, the answer to the question 'does it affect your choice in any way?' can be recorded in a distinct way using, yes, no, maybe categories. Then the percentages in these categories can be calculated. However, if the analysis was simply left at this, valuable information could be lost. For example, if the answer to the question about buyers' opinion of gifts was negative, this might mean either they felt it was a bribe or that the gifts were too inexpensive! So asking a number of questions to elicit the reasons for a certain response should be incorporated in the research and recorded. In this way management can see at a glance numeric responses to certain questions, but also have some qualitative data in which to put the research into context and make informed decisions.

6 DISTRIBUTION

A major element in distribution strategy is the degree of market coverage that is desired for a product. Linked to this question is the required support the distribution strategy needs from the producer. In order to serve existing and future customers to the required standard the company must decide how many outlets should be established in an area and what services channel members can offer. Market coverage is often termed 'distribution intensity' and refers to the number and size of outlets in a particular area. There are three basic choices in the method of distribution: selective, intensive and exclusive.

Exclusive distribution means appointing outlets for an area to distribute your goods exclusively. Exclusive distribution restricts the number of outlets where the goods are available. This exclusivity can be in the overall type of channel chosen, for example selecting department stores rather than supermarkets, and/or choosing a certain department store, eg Rackhams rather than another, eg Debenhams. It is used in a number of circumstances. If customers are willing to exert some effort in searching for the product or service then exclusive distribution is possible. There may be an aim to restrict outlets providing your product to encourage a high quality image. This can be beneficial for the supplier and the store which sells the product. The producers may adopt exclusive distribution if there is a high degree of service or after sales support required from the product. Exclusive distribution allows the producer more control of the marketing mix at the point of sale and minimises channel conflict. There is necessarily a close relationship between channel members in an exclusive distribution system.

Intensive distribution is the opposite of exclusive distribution. Here the aim is to cover the market as intensively as possible. Many intermediaries are used to bring the products to as many people as possible, both within one geographical area and throughout many areas. This coverage method is often used for goods and services that either consumers or organisational buyers purchase frequently. It can be typified by convenience goods that the buyer will not want to put any effort into purchasing. Examples include food, washing powder, tobacco and in organisational markets, office supplies. Outlets for these goods have to be easily accessible and to have a choice of readily available brands.

Selective distribution is somewhere between exclusive and intensive distribution. It is suitable for products that consumers are willing to put some effort into purchasing. This method is chosen when brands are important to consumers or the outlets are important to consumers (for example Harrods). The reasons for adopting this type of channel strategy are similar to those outlined in our discussion of exclusive distribution.

There are four main factors that determine the choice of distribution strategy.

(a) *Customers*

Target customer groups have a major impact on market coverage decisions. Social class, income and geographic area are important market segmentation variables that have an influence on channel decisions. Consumer behaviour also plays an important part in market coverage decisions. How consumers view stores and products will influence the most appropriate distribution strategy to undertake.

(b) *Products*

The actual product characteristics are important in determining appropriate market coverage. A relatively cheap, frequently bought product will be better suited to intensive distribution. An expensive product that is purchased infrequently may be better distributed exclusively or selectively.

(c) *Outlets*

Too few or too many outlets in an area may affect the choice of distribution strategy. If an organisation has too few outlets in an area then sales targets will be difficult to achieve. If the organisation has too many outlets, this may not be efficient. When a reseller is unable to perform some marketing functions, for example after sales service when an intensive strategy has been adopted, then this will determine the future of the distribution strategy.

(d) *Control*

The level of desired control over how the product is presented to the public is a major determining factor in formulating a distribution strategy. If an intensive distribution strategy is adopted, then the supplier usually gives up some of its control over the marketing of the product. For instance, if the product is sold in nationwide supermarket chains then display and final pricing is usually determined by the supermarket. If an exclusive distribution strategy is adopted then control is less likely to be relinquished.

7 MAIL ORDER SELLING

Mail order shopping has developed from small beginnings in the nineteenth century to a major industry. It grew substantially in the early twentieth century because in the Depression consumers wanted to spread the cost of purchases over time. Traditional mail order shopping has four key characteristics.

(a) *Commission.* The company pays a certain percentage of sales (often 10%) to agents.

(b) *Convenience.* Shopping in the home is promoted as more convenient than spending time and energy visiting stores.

(c) *Comprehensive.* Catalogues have a great variety of products available.

(d) *Credit.* Payment can be spread over a period of time.

In the 1950s and 1960s mail order shopping extended rapidly, although by the early 1980s it was suffering from a slowdown in growth, mainly due to a staid and downmarket image. In the late 1980s, however, mail order shopping underwent a transformation and correspondingly grew in profitability and popularity. The main reason for the growth in recent times has been the adoption of marketing principles. This includes the adoption of market segmentation techniques, customer service and image building.

The five main mail order companies in the UK at present are Great Universal Stores (GUS), Littlewoods, Freemans, Grattan and Empire Stores. These have a 97% share of the market. The rest of the market is made up of specialist mail order companies that have developed niche markets. Many companies have developed mail order services to increase the number of customers they can serve without expensive store expansion. Examples include Habitat, Selfridges and Lakeland Plastics. In the past, catalogues were run on an agency level, but this has now developed into direct catalogues (shorter than agency catalogues) and 'specialogues'. The agency networks have become less effective over the past decade with many 'agents' using catalogues only for themselves and their immediate family rather than a wider network of family, friends, neighbours and colleagues.

Until recently mail order companies were being left behind by high street retailers in marketing techniques. One of their main competitive advantages was the availability of credit but this was eroded by the high street retailers developing credit systems. There has recently been a blurring of the distinctions between mail order and traditional store retailing. Charge cards have aided the stores in developing mail order services. Retailer involvement has helped the image of mail order companies, as this has increased the perceived quality of products. For example, Next merged with Grattan, Freemans with Sears and there are close links between Top Shop and Empire Stores. The 'Direct' catalogues have increased significantly. Examples of these include 'You and Yours' (Grattan) and 'Family Album' (GUS). 'Specialogues' have been developed to break away from the traditional downmarket image. They are excellent examples of how mail order companies have taken on board the theory and practice of market segmentation. Consumers have been segmented into the different groupings according to whichever basis of market segmentation is used. These consumers can be targeted by providing certain types of products and promotion that appeals to them. The positioning of new products and services can then be implemented using the media and other promotional tools suitable for this segment.

Computerised databases can be used to increase efficiency, reduce paperwork and, perhaps most importantly, to profile customers. Mail order companies have vast amounts of information on each customer and these can be used to target potential customers of the 'specialogues'. In addition to the general demographic information that can be found in databases, such as age, profession, sex and location, there is a whole history of past products purchased and products returned. So, for example, if a customer has purchased a number of items of clothing in a large size, then they may be suitable candidates for a 'specialogue' in this area.

The introduction in the late 1980s of the Next Directory certainly made mail order companies rethink their marketing strategies. The glossy catalogue with fabric samples and 48 hour delivery was aimed at the AB social groupings, rather than CDs. Many mail order companies responded by improving their catalogue presentation and introducing 'specialogues' aimed at higher social classes. For example, Freemans introduced 'Bymail' which had clothes designed by Jeff Banks.

There are a number of new developments in the industry. There is increased internationalisation of the market with many European retailers now having significant shares in the UK mail order companies. Home shopping services have been developing. These include teleshopping which most mail order companies undertake to some degree. Orders can be placed by telephone, customers can be told immediately if goods are in stock and so these orders can be processed much quicker than those placed by mail. In the future there may be more home shopping facilities developed in this area, for example, videotext sales.

The main reason for the growth of mail order is the response to competitive pressures from the high street. They have used their technology to become closer to the consumer, tailored products and promotions to certain customer groups, rethought their image and replaced the traditional USP of credit with a new emphasis on convenience and customer service.

8 PHYSICAL DISTRIBUTION MANAGEMENT

In order that goods move from producer to consumer efficiently and effectively the movement of these goods need to be managed. To get products to the right place at the right time in the right quantities takes a good deal of management skill. The physical flow of goods and materials coming into the company and going out of the company to the final consumer is usually termed 'logistics management'. *Logistics management* comprises materials management and physical distribution. *Materials management* is the flow of goods and materials into the company. This includes all the raw materials that go into the production of the final goods. *Physical distribution* on the other hand concerns the movement of finished goods to the customers. We will concentrate on the physical distribution aspect of logistics.

SUGGESTED SOLUTIONS

The output of a distribution system is a level of customer service. Physical distribution managers have to balance the desired level of service with their decisions on transport, warehousing and inventory management.

It is usual in manufacturing that the most cost effective means of production is centralised. Warehousing is therefore very important to store finished goods. Managers need to keep an adequate stock of goods to allow for market fluctuations. They also need to calculate how many warehouses are needed, the type of warehouses required and the positioning of warehouses in the most efficient locations. Warehousing provides two important functions. The first concerns the movement of goods. Large amounts of products flow into the warehouse, then they are broken down in to smaller units and go out of the warehouse. The second main function of warehousing is the storage of goods to cope with demand fluctuations. There are two main types of warehousing facilities: *private,* that is owned by the firm, and *public.* Public warehouses are often categorised by the type of goods they store, for example cold storage warehousing. Distribution centres have developed from private warehousing and are used primarily for the movement of goods and not their storage. These are often used by large supermarket chains who want an efficient movement of many goods at frequent intervals. Private and public warehousing systems have advantages and disadvantages and need to be assessed for the individual firm.

Inventory management involves finding a balance between keeping inventory costs as a whole as low as possible and providing customers with a good service. Costs come from the holding of inventories, ordering inventory and the risks that stocks will run out. So the main management roles concerning inventory management are to decide how many goods to order, when to order and how to balance keeping adequate stocks without running out of the goods. How much to order can be assessed using specific formulae and/or the skill and experience of management. Sales forecasts can be used in order to ascertain when to reorder stocks. Sales forecasts are, of course, subject to some amount of error. If this was not so there would never be occasion to run out of goods. An estimate of this error can be used to provide the company with a buffer stock to use if demand is greater than expected.

Physical distribution management is often thought of in simple transportation terms. Although we have seen that there is much more to this management task, transportation is still a very important aspect. If transportation is not handled efficiently then stocks can build up and inventory costs soar, in addition to the adverse effects on customer service. There are many ways in which goods can be transported from one place to another. Management must choose the most suitable method for the product in question according to:

(a) speed;
(b) dependability;
(c) availability;
(d) frequency;
(e) capability;
(f) cost.

There are five main transportation methods available to management: rail, road, sea, air and pipeline. Each of these can be assessed according to the six criteria outlined above. The 'best' method of transporting goods will depend on the product characteristics. For example, oil is suitable for pipeline transportation whilst coal is suitable for rail transportation.

In conclusion, successful physical distribution management is a key factor in the success of a company. It is one of the most obvious ways in which marketing management can build a high level of customer service into their product offering as it concerns the actual delivery of the product to the consumer. The desired level of customer service needs to be balanced against the costs of physical distribution management. An effective physical distribution system should be developed by management and incorporated into the overall logistics management of the business.

9 THE PRODUCT LIFE CYCLE

Product sales and profitability change over time. The pattern of development can be divided into distinct sections. The diagram below shows the typical product life cycle representation.

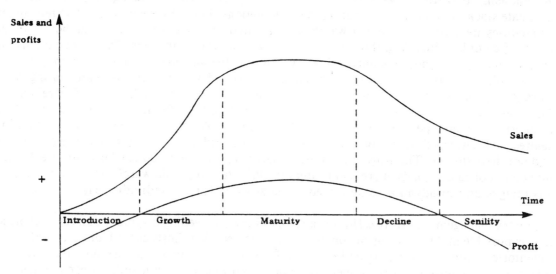

The classic representation of the product life cycle

For different types of products and services the length of the life cycle will vary, as will the level of sales at each stage. In the development stage ideas of new products are generated and screened for viability. The new product's profit potential can then be assessed and the decision taken on whether the launch of the product would fit current company strategic objectives. The initial concept can be tested by consumer research, and then a few prototypes of the products can be produced and tested by consumer panels. Before the launch of the product on a nationwide scale test marketing is often used, commonly using a TV region to launch the product in a limited area. Most discussions of the product life cycle concentrate on the four stages after the product has been launched: introduction, growth, maturity and decline.

Introduction

In the introductory stage the product takes time to be accepted by consumers so sales growth is slow. Only a few firms sell the product so competition is slack, costs are high because of low output. Camcorders are in their introductory stage in the consumer market. The price for the product will depend on product strategy. A high price can be charged in order to recover high development costs if demand for the product is not thought to be particularly price sensitive. This is *price skimming*. A low initial price strategy is known as *price penetration*. This strategy is suitable when demand is price sensitive and there is a need to stimulate demand for the product. Promotion in the introduction stage will concentrate on building awareness of the product. In consumer markets this is often done by above the line advertising and the use of free samples to encourage trial of the product. The distribution method chosen needs to be carefully assessed if products are to succeed. In this stage of the PLC only a few distribution channels are commonly used. The product itself may go through a period of refinement to match consumer preferences. There is usually a limited variety of product features. Word of mouth recommendations of the product are very important in this stage, and sales are often made to consumers who are willing to take a risk buying a new product. These consumers can be described as *innovators*.

SUGGESTED SOLUTIONS

Growth

In the growth stage more competitors enter the market with similar products, sometimes with extra features. There is an overall expansion of the market. Competitors learn from the original producer's mistakes. Customers who purchase in this stage are *'followers'* rather than *'leaders'*. Dishwashers are in their growth stage of the PLC. There are more product varieties, styles, colours and options available to the market. Distribution networks often become much wider in the growth stage. As competitors enter the market the price is likely to fall. Marketers try to create a unique selling proposition (USP) in order to maintain a price premium. This is often achieved by creating a brand image. Promotion in this stage will highlight the differences between the product and competitors and build brand awareness.

Maturity

In the maturity stage the market becomes saturated. Demand becomes more stable so producers can match production and consumption more easily. A small number of competitors are left, with fewer new entrants into the market. Consumers are usually buying the products as a replacement rather than for the first time. An example of a product in the mature stage is refrigerators. Prices become more stable, with temporary price promotions boosting sales in the short term. Promotions will remind consumers of the product, brand image and its USP. Established relationships exist in the distribution of the product. Brand image will be well established and hopefully has encouraged consumers to be loyal to the brand. The maturity stage can be the longest of all four stages. In order to extend it as long as possible managers seek to:

(a) find new users for the product;
(b) develop new market segments for the product;
(c) refine the product design.

Decline

The final stage of the product life cycle is the decline stage. Demand falls as customers purchase new products that fulfil their needs better. An example could be black and white televisions. The product can still be profitable if enough loyal customers remain. If these customers are not particularly price sensitive then price can remain relatively high. Advertising can be used to remind consumers about the product. One of the main problems is that as sales fall distributors may reduce the allocated shelf space or stop stocking the product. Product improvements do not usually occur at this stage. The decision has to be made whether to withdraw the product from sale.

The discussion above looks at the stages of a 'typical' product life cycle. There are, however, failed products that do not go through all the stages and products that are fads or fashions that do not follow the typical shape. Product life cycle analysis can be used on product categories (eg coffee), product forms (eg instant coffee) and brands (eg Nescafe). In the main brands have shorter life cycles. There have been many criticisms of the PLC concept as a marketing tool. One of the main ones is that the course of the PLC can be affected by marketing strategy so products may be discontinued when they could have been revived.

10   SCREEN, POSITION, MIX AND ELIMINATE

Product screening

This involves the screening process in new product development. Ideas for new products can be generated from a number of sources by the firm. These include internal sources such as a formal research and development department or other management of external sources, such as competitors or customers. Not all the new product ideas that a company has can be developed as it would be too costly. Product screening aims to sort out the ideas that are viable from those that are not. First of all an initial review of the product ideas can be carried out. The following questions should be raised.

(a)   What is the sales potential of the product?
(b)   Does the product idea fit in with the current products?
(c)   What costs are involved?
(d)   Will customers accept the product?
(e)   Is the product technically feasible?
(f)   Is there a customer need for the product?

Some companies have a formal assessment procedure for idea screening, others take a more *ad hoc* approach. After product ideas are screened, an initial concept test can be undertaken asking consumers about their opinions of the product idea. If the product idea passes this stage then a working prototype of the product can be produced and this can then be tested on consumers. Some products will then be test marketed in a particular area of the country to gauge their likely success in a nationwide launch. So from initial idea to product launch a product screening process is vital for the success of new products in the marketplace.

Product positioning

Product positioning involves the use of the marketing mix variables to communicate the USP of the product to the consumer. Positioning of a product or service involves positioning it in the mind of the consumer. In target marketing segmentation is used to divide the market into homogeneous clusters, then one or more of these clusters are targeted and finally the product is positioned to reflect the target market's needs. There are three main ways in which products are positioned. Companies can use an informational approach to the target market where product characteristics are emphasised in marketing communications. This approach is often used in detergent advertising. Products can also be positioned by using imagery, for example in perfume advertisements. Comparative advertising is not practised in the UK as much as elsewhere although it has been on the increase. Competitors are used either implicitly or explicitly in these types of advertisements to communicate comparative superiority.

Product mix

The product mix of a company comprises all the products that it markets. The product mix strategy will depend on strategic business unit or corporate management. One of management's main concerns will be the allocation of resources to each product in the mix. An evaluation should be made as to the appropriateness of the product mix given the strategic objectives of the firm. Important decisions will need to be made as to the elimination of products and the addition of products to the product mix. Product mix decisions are made in the context of strategic planning because of their importance to the firm's long-term survival. Product mix concerns the combination of product lines that a firm offers. Product lines are products in the same product category. The *breadth* of a product mix is the number of product lines it offers consumers so this is really a measure of the diversity of the business. The *depth* of the product mix can then be described as narrow but deep if the firm produces a small number of product categories but a large number of lines within each category. The relationship between products a company markets can be described as product 'consistency'. This looks at the similarities or diversity of product offerings.

Product elimination

Product elimination occurs when the decision has been made to stop producing a product. It is important to delete products that are not performing well and do not appear to be profitable in the future. However, product elimination should be considered carefully as the wrong decision can be costly in terms of profits and customer satisfaction. The product's performance should be evaluated to ascertain whether it is fulfilling objectives. If the product is failing to meet these objectives then an assessment should be made of the future potential of the market. If there is little growth in the market then the effect of the product's elimination on other products will have to be analysed. There are often strong links between products and the elimination of one may have a detrimental effect on another. If there were to be no effect on other products then a decision has to be made as to the product's profitability if marketing costs can be kept to a minimum. If this analysis indicates that it is not going to be profitable then the product should be withdrawn.

11 PRICING

(a) *Cost plus pricing*

Costs are the most important influence on pricing decisions. Many firms base their pricing policy on simple cost plus rules. This means that costs are estimated and then a profit margin is added to arrive at the price. This method of pricing is relatively easy for management to implement and affords some degree of stability over pricing. There are two main types of cost based pricing. The first is *full cost*. Although it is not appropriate to go into this in detail here it is worthwhile pointing out the differences between full and cost plus pricing. Full cost pricing takes account of the full average costs of production including an allocation for overheads. The profit margin is then added to determine the price. The problem with full cost pricing is that if the company produces many brands the allocation of overheads costs can be difficult to determine. *Cost plus pricing* on the other hand only uses the direct cost components; for example, labour and raw materials are used to calculate unit costs. An additional margin is then added that includes profit and an overhead charge. Cost plus pricing is used extensively in the UK retailing sector, where the mark up price includes a fixed margin that varies between product classes. The percentage margin may also vary according to demand factors. The problems of cost plus pricing arise out of the difficulties in calculating direct costs and the allocation of overhead costs. The cost plus approach leads to price stability because in the main prices change due to cost changes.

(b) *Market skimming pricing*

Market skimming involves setting a high initial price for a new product. If a new product has a high value to consumers then a high price can be charged. The strategy is initially to command a premium price and then gradually to reduce the price to penetrate the more price sensitive segments of the market. One advantage of this method of pricing is that it is easier to reduce prices if a mistake has been made than it is to increase prices. A high price also creates an image of a quality product, especially if other aspects of the marketing mix reflect this. In order for this strategy to be successful there must be enough consumers who are not price sensitive. The costs of producing the small volumes of premium price products should not be greater than the advantage gained by charging the higher price. The strategy will only work if the higher price does not stimulate competition, so is suitable for markets that have high entry barriers, for example, high development costs or high promotional costs.

(c) *Marginal cost pricing*

Marginal cost pricing is the setting of the price of one unit at the cost of producing an extra unit (marginal cost). From an economics viewpoint marginal cost pricing is the most efficient pricing method. This is because when price is equal to marginal cost it is allocatively efficient. In a perfectly competitive market the market mechanism ensures that price does equal marginal cost if profits are maximised. However, perfect competition never occurs in the real world. Profits are maximised instead when price is greater than the marginal cost of producing the good. If this is the case it is allocatively inefficient; that is, too little of a good is being produced to keep the price high, so consumption is below the optimum level. In theory nationalised industries were supposed to set their price equal to marginal costs but have recently been under instruction to price in a more commercial manner. In practice, marginal cost pricing is difficult because of problems in calculation. Again, there will be problems in the allocation of overheads and the additional problem of whether to set prices equal to long run or short run marginal costs.

(d) *Market penetration pricing*

In a market penetration pricing strategy the company sets a low price for the product in order to stimulate growth in the market or to obtain a larger market share. This strategy is only successful if demand is price sensitive and economies of scale can be achieved. That is, unit costs of production and distribution fall with increased output. So companies set a low price in the belief that consumers will value this and their market share can then increase. The low price strategy should also deter competitors from entering the market. The low price approach is often used with heavy promotional effort to penetrate mass markets and take market share. If the firm needs to recoup high development costs in a short time this may not be the most appropriate pricing strategy. If there are high barriers to entry, including a high degree of branding, the market may not be suitable for penetration pricing. Low prices, however, are not likely to be effective if the product is in the decline stage of the PLC, as customers are usually changing to substitute products.

12 SALES PROMOTION

Recommendations on appropriate sales promotions

To support the launch of Chico it will be necessary to use some form of sales promotion to support our above the line advertising campaign. The main objective of the sales promotions recommended is to stimulate trial of Chico by our target consumers.

The first sales promotion recommended is a free sample of Chico attached to a monthly magazine. The use of impregnated paper in the pages of the magazine could be considered but this is usually the approach of the higher priced perfumes in glossy magazines. It is recommended that a phial of Chico be attached as a free gift to the full circulation of a monthly woman's magazine that is read by our target market. The magazine 'Essentials' has been chosen because the readership is from our target group social class and age bracket. The magazine has also run this type of promotion before and would be willing to co-operate.

The aim of this promotion is to enable potential customers to try our product without having to ask to test it in a store. This can also be combined with advertising copy within the magazine describing the type of woman that wears Chico.

In addition to the free phial of Chico on the outside of the magazine it is recommended that we include a competition inside the magazine. The first 200 postcards to be drawn on a certain date win a full sized bottle of Chico.

The timing of this sales promotion will be crucial. Stores must already have adequate stocks of Chico so that as sales have been stimulated consumers are actually able to buy the product. It should also coincide with the above the line advertising campaign. This method of promotion should only be used once, preferably in the November issue of the magazine as this might encourage purchases for Christmas. A special Christmas promotional offer could be run in the stores at this time. This could be a special gift pack of perfume, talcum powder and body lotion in Chico.

This sales promotion method will stimulate trial of Chico without any adverse effects on the image. Care has to be taken that the image we present during sales promotion does not conflict with the image from our media advertising. The image we want to build for Chico is elegant, sophisticated yet at the same time fun loving and young. Any direct price promotions would 'cheapen' the image of Chico and should be avoided. The promotion method chosen for the launch should get over the buying inertia many women feel towards buying perfume and take the risk out of purchasing the product. As perfume can only really be tested on an individual's skin and then should be allowed to develop for a while before testing this method would be ideal in the circumstances.

After the initial launch further sales can be stimulated using another method of sales promotion. This could take the form of a competition, the details on a leaflet given with purchase, backed up of course with advertising. An appropriate prize would be an exotic holiday.

To evaluate the sales promotion effectiveness a number of methods can be used. Firstly the number of responses to the free draw for Chico should be analysed. Sales data before the promotion should be noted and compared with sales data during and after the promotion. As perfume is not purchased frequently there may be a drop in sales after the sales promotion. The market share Chico has gained needs to be monitored. It may also be necessary to hold consumer panels to see if people responded to the promotion and in what way. A survey could be carried out to evaluate the impact of the promotion on consumer purchase behaviour.

13 NOTES ON PROMOTION

(a) *Unique selling propositions*

The unique selling proposition theory says that consumers remember one main point from advertising. If advertising tries to tell consumers too much then it may fail. Another approach to unique selling propositions is the idea of building a strong brand image. Companies can identify an appropriate USP by analysing the reasons why goods are purchased and then focusing their marketing communications on one of the benefits associated with buying the product. Many marketers favour the approach of one message. Common USPs are 'lowest price', 'best service', 'highest technology' or 'quickest service'. This message can then be incorporated throughout the company's marketing communications. Advertising, sales promotion and public relations can all reinforce the chosen USP. A company's USP can also be thought of as the bundle of messages that combine to make the image of the company. For example the Halifax Building Society's USP can be thought of as large, safe, traditional, market leader. When designing the message in marketing communications there are three main approaches. The first is the rational approach that tries to appeal to consumers' best interests: for example, an advert that says 'if you can buy cheaper we will refund the difference' will be promoting a low price USP in a rational way. The emotional approach uses emotional stimuli to motivate purchase. For example, toothpaste is often advertised to stimulate fear of tooth decay, stained teeth or bad breath. The moral approach tries to appeal to the consumer's sense of right and wrong. A recent example of this type of campaign is the promotion of the environmental benefits of using certain products.

(b) *The promotional mix*

The promotional mix is the combination of marketing communication strategies. It is one of the 'Four Ps' of the marketing mix and includes advertising, sales promotion, publicity and personal selling. Through its promotional mix companies communicate product benefits and the reasons why consumers should purchase the product. The most important aspect of the promotional mix is communication. An effective promotional mix should take into account the suitability of each aspect of the mix in fulfilling promotional objectives. Advertising is paid, ongoing non-personal communication that uses mass media such as television, press or radio. Advertising's main function is to create awareness, stimulate purchase and keep consumers aware of the product in the long term. Sales promotions are usually short term and are inducements for consumers to purchase the product. Sales promotional tools include the use of coupons, competitions, money off packs and free samples. It can be used to stimulate interest from consumers who do not usually purchase the product or to increase sales to existing consumers. Personal selling is the face to face communication between the company's employees and the consumer and is an important element of the promotional mix. Publicity is the unpaid communication about the company, so press articles concerning the company come under publicity. Marketing managers must decide on the overall objectives of the promotional mix and allocate resources for each element depending on the promotional mix chosen.

(c) *Point of sale display*

Point of sales displays include the displays for the product in the store, for example, advertising signs, window displays or in-store displays. Within the promotional mix they come under sales promotion. They are used at the point of purchase and are most effective when combined with advertising. Retailers are often unwilling to co-operate with point of sales displays that are bulky and take up valuable floor space. Smaller stores may be more co-operative than large supermarket chains regarding the siting of point of sales displays. The main point of sale displays in supermarkets are at the checkouts (where confectionery and magazines are displayed in racks) and occasionally at the end of aisles. Smaller stores may be more co-operative in the placing of window displays and advertising posters because they may see this as a way to promote themselves. This can be used in conjunction with other sales promotion techniques. For example, if a competition is running then the point of sales display can promote this. In industrial markets in store displays can be given to dealers, for example display items in car showrooms. If the company owns the point of purchase or if it is more powerful than the channel member at the point of purchase then there is much more control over this element of the promotional mix.

(d) *Publicity*

Publicity is an important aspect of the promotional mix. Although it is essentially non-paid for communication in the media, this does not mean to say the company has no control in this area. It is an effective means of communication for positive news about the company and can also be of use in lessening the effects of negative news. The main advantage of publicity over advertising is that it is seen as a truthful and credible source of information. It is also inexpensive, because of the non-paid nature. There are some costs involved in the successful management of publicity though, such as the production of press releases, or recruiting staff in the area of public relations. It can also support other elements of the marketing mix. However, there are problems in using publicity. A company may give information to the press but the press can do as they wish with it. They may or may not print a story, and it may be presented in either a positive or a negative light. The timing of publicity is also difficult to control. Company communications and press releases are not the only elements in publicity. Special events such as the sponsorship of events are reported in the press or seen on television. The effectiveness of publicity can be assessed by the amount of publicity it receives and the number of people it reaches.

14 PUBLIC RELATIONS

Public relations is the planned and sustained effort to encourage goodwill between an organisation and its publics. A company's publics include shareholders, customers, government and other businesses. The aim of public relations is to present a positive image of the company to these publics or at least to promote some form of understanding. Public relations is a long-term effort by the firm to improve or sustain this image and should be a two way communication between the company and its publics.

The way in which public relations can be seen to reduce the effects of a corporate crisis on the publics can be looked at in terms of the transfer model below.

Transfer model

The corporate crisis causes	*If public relations has been successful then this will change to*
Hostility	Sympathy
Prejudice	Acceptance
Apathy	Interest
Ignorance	Knowledge

As can be seen above in the face of a corporate crisis the company can achieve understanding through public relations rather than a positive image. In order for public relations to work, trends must be monitored so that PR management is prepared if a problem arises. Here we will concentrate on how public relations can help to change the four negative aspects in the above model to the positive achievements.

We will assume that the company is a chemical factory and the crisis a chemical spillage into a local river. The publics involved will be the local community, local anglers, employees, customers, suppliers, government (the Department of the Environment), the local authority, the National Rivers Authority, shareholders, the money markets, distributors and environmentalist groups. As can be seen the list of publics the company must address can be extensive.

Some assessment has to be made about the scale of hostility present in the various publics. Some of this may be based on a lack of information or a misunderstanding of information. However, there may be in this case a very urgent need to satisfy the publics' desire for information. Direct communication should be made with all official bodies concerned with, of course, complete honesty. If there is false information given out at the beginning of the incident then this makes the matter much worse for public relations managers in the future. Misinformation will mean that credibility will be damaged if, or more probably when, it is found out. Other publics can be reached by holding a press conference or a public meeting.

Converting prejudice into acceptance is more difficult in this type of crisis, as many people will think their prejudices have been confirmed. If, however, the situation is handled well and communicated through effective PR then this prejudice might be lessened. Changing apathy to interest will not be as applicable in this example of a crisis. The organisation itself may be accused of apathy. The change from ignorance to knowledge will be more important. Publics will want to know exactly what has been leaked into the river, how it happened, could it happen again, where it was leaked, how much was leaked, what the effects might be and whether there are long-term implications. The role of public relations will be to answer these questions. In the event of the leakage the media should be given the opportunity to discuss with the company the effects of the pollution. If a question cannot be answered reasons should be given. The company should do all in its power to speak with one voice and avoid conflicting statements.

The various general techniques that public relations management can use include:

(a) Open days or organised visits to the company
(b) Sponsorship
(c) Community projects
(d) Company publications including annual reports
(e) Videos
(f) Press releases
(g) Community meetings.

Many of these techniques would not be appropriate to manage the crisis the company faces in the short term. However, as stated earlier, PR concerns the long term and in the future after the initial crisis has been handled these tools and techniques can be used to help the image and understanding of the company. For example, having open days for the local community will help alleviate fears of the incident recurring.

However, we have discussed public relations here in a reactive role, that is, reacting to a crisis that has already occurred. There is also a role for public relations in the prevention of, and preparation for crises. The PR manager is responsible for the goodwill felt towards the company and so should in some respect act as watchdog regarding the practices of the organisation. The preventative role in PR should concentrate on what could possibly go wrong in the organisation. Then some preparation needs to be undertaken for crises. A committee should be set up of interested parties in the organisation, perhaps including top management, safety officers, works manager and the PR manager. This committee need to agree on the responses to any incident that would be desirable by the firm. The provision of information needs to be discussed and adequate information needs to be kept up to date and close to hand.

15 AGENCY/CLIENT RELATIONSHIPS

When developing an advertising programme the advertising objectives should be assessed. These can vary but common ones are outlined below.

(a) To create awareness of a new product.
(b) To create awareness of new features of a product.
(c) To ensure exposure.
(d) To increase sales and profits.
(e) To increase response, for example for a charity.
(f) To improve the company image.
(g) To change attitudes or behaviour, eg the AIDS prevention campaign.
(h) To generate enquiries from potential customers.

SUGGESTED SOLUTIONS

Advertising can have long or short term effects. The above objectives are rather general. Specific objectives of an advertising campaign might be to communicate certain information about a product, or to highlight a particular Unique Selling Proposition.

Advertising also plays a role in industrial markets. It can be used to promote the corporate image, to communicate technical specifications or to make the company more 'legitimate' in the eyes of its buyers. The advertising campaign should be planned through the following stages.

ADVERTISING OBJECTIVES

THE MESSAGE

MEDIA SELECTION

THE FREQUENCY OF DISPLAY

STYLE OF THE MESSAGE

BUDGET

EVALUATION

Most large scale advertising does not simply concern the advertiser and the media owner. In many cases an advertising agency is involved. The role of the advertising agency is to advise the client on the various media forms on behalf of the client. There are a number of different types of agencies. Creative agencies specialise in the more creative side of advertising, for example designing television advertisements. There are also media buyers who specialise in buying air time and media space and smaller agencies who specialise in industrial advertising.

There are many advantages of using an agency. The media owners find it more efficient if they only deal with a small number of organisations. For the organisation advertising, it is cheaper to employ the services of an agency than to set up a specialist advertising department and recruit highly skilled staff. Agencies also have close links with services such as printers and their employees usually have a wide experience of advertising. When choosing an agency the company can either approach an agency whose work it likes or ask for a competitive presentation. This is where one or more agencies give a presentation on either the market generally or a specific campaign proposal.

In order that the campaign is effective, that is, that it fulfils the objectives stated at the beginning of the advertising planning process, there must be good communications between the agency and client. If the client is vague about the objectives of the campaign or the agency misinterprets the aims, then the success of the campaign is doomed from the start. The advertising manager of the company that is going to advertise (client) must be familiar with the techniques and workings of advertising. He must also give the agency as much information about the company as is required, for example on the future objectives of the company. The advertising manager should be involved with all the negotiations between in house specialists and the advertising agency. In house specialists include individual product managers or brand managers.

The relationship between the agency and client varies to a great degree. As stated earlier some agencies' main role is to sell advertising space. However, the agencies that have extended their role look upon their clients as partners in a long-term relationship. One aspect of this is that if a client wishes to get the most from the agency it must disclose a certain amount of confidential information. The relationship between agency and client can therefore be very close and be of mutual benefit. Advertisers are known by the agency and over time the agency knows the type of approach the client likes and the type it dislikes.

16 THE CONSUMER MOVEMENT

One of the main challenges in recent years to marketing management has come from the consumer movement. The consumer movement or *consumerism*, as it is sometimes termed, is concerned with increasing the power of consumers. In the past abuses of power by firms were commonplace. Now, however, the consumer is more likely to get a fairer deal due to consumerism. There are six main areas that have been influenced by consumerism.

(a) *Health and safety*. Recent examples include developments in the storage of cook chill foods, the destruction of cows with BSE and warning signs in shops when cleaning is being undertaken.

(b) *Information*. There has been a substantial increase in the amount of information that can be found on product labels. Some of this information has been criticised as misleading, such as foods described as 'low fat' or products without certain additives, when in fact these were never included.

(c) *Customer complaints*. The Sale of Goods Act states that goods sold must be of a merchantable quality. Many companies go further than the legislation states to bring added value to their products in terms of customer service.

(d) *Government policy*. Government legislation policy has had a considerable impact on consumer's rights. The Sale of Goods Act, the Weights and Measures Acts, Consumer Protection Act, Trade Descriptions Act and the Office of Fair Trading have all affected the way in which companies can trade with the public.

(e) *Promotional constraints*. These can be imposed by the government, by the industry or by a standards body. The most well known standards are imposed by the Code of Advertising Standards and Practice and the Advertising Standards Authority. The latter covers both advertising and sales promotion.

(f) *Environmental factors*. As society in general has become more aware of the environment and the impact consumption has upon it, so business has had to become more aware. Sceptics say this is simply an indication of companies seeking a new 'unique selling proposition'. There have been occasions where promotion has been misleading in this area.

Customer protection is not at the same stage in all industry sectors. In the service sector there are still problems due to inadequate and complex legislation. The Financial Services Act attempted to give consumers more power but it has been very difficult for consumers to get redress from this system. How much information consumers need and want is one problem managers must face. This is especially difficult if the company wishes to protect itself from competitors copying products. At one end of the consumerist spectrum is protection against obvious abuses of power, such as misleading information, while at the other end there is the still controversial view that consumer protection should take a wider perspective. For example, it is suggested that consumers should be protected from products that may not be in their best interests. So tobacco products have government health warnings attached to them and mortgages are advertised with a warning that non-payment may mean repossession.

Businesses can develop customer care programmes and public relations departments in order to meet the challenge of consumer pressure. The industry itself may impose self-regulation by means of a trade association.

In the UK the most important general organisation for consumer rights is the Consumers' Association. It was founded in the 1950s, has seven million members and publishes the 'Which?' magazine. Unorganised individual consumers are also a powerful force. Individual boycotting products or firms with links in South Africa have made many companies rethink their policy in this area.

If firms are practising the marketing concept, they are then consumer oriented and this should go a long way towards enforcing customer rights. Customer satisfaction induces brand or company loyalty. Drucker has stated that consumerism is a sign that marketing management has failed. Kotler goes further by stating that management deliver customer desires, rather than interests, so goods are produced that are not in the long-term interests of the consumer. The major challenge to marketing management is the matching of consumer desires, long-term consumer interest and the company's profit objectives. This has led to the development of the societal marketing concept that takes into account long-term consumer welfare. This marketing concept would rely upon government policy (eg a ban on smoking in public places) and/or consumer education.

In conclusion it has been shown that the consumer movement has a major influence on the activities of companies. Within marketing this influence is on a strategic level, for instance, what products to produce, what legislation is important and quality control procedures. It can also influence the tactical decisions, for example, the copy in an advertisement, customer complaints procedures and product labels.

17 SALES REPS AND SALES MANAGERS

The sales manager's job is difficult and the transition from sales representative to manager can be traumatic. Sales representatives are used to working alone for a good deal of their time. Becoming a sales manager requires the acquisition of a new set of skills. It is of course important that a sales representative communicates well but different communication skills are required by a successful sales manager. The sales manager has to communicate effectively with the sales team, which can be difficult when he was one of the representatives a short time ago. Sales representatives are often widely dispersed throughout the country so communication with them is often a problem of logistics. The sales manager needs written as well as verbal communication skills, in effect to sell the company to the representatives instead of products to customers. As a sales representative he would not normally have many administrative duties. As a sales manager he needs to become more administratively and organisationally minded. It can be frustrating for an ex-salesperson to become more office bound but to be effective he must believe that his co-ordinating role is as valuable as being out on the road. In order to explore what skills a sales manager requires and how their acquisition can be less traumatic we will discuss the role and responsibilities of sales management.

Setting sales objectives and strategies

The sales manager as part of a team will be responsible for formulating sales objectives and strategies. This team might include higher management and marketing. In this role the ex-salesperson will have an objective insight into potential future sales figures and perhaps be able to give a realistic opinion of objectives and strategies. After consulting individual sales personnel, sales targets for territories can be established. One problem that could arise here is the sales manager being seen as the 'boss' and sales representatives either feeling resentful or not taking the person's authority seriously. It is quite easy to over-react in this instance, by being too lenient and not wanting to give the impression that promotion has made the new manager less friendly. Or the sales manager can go the other way, deciding that he has to make his authority clear, and so he becomes too dogmatic. Usually in time a happy medium can be reached if the sales manager sees the initial months of the job as a time for learning and he listens to criticisms. Sales managers who have been sales representatives in the same company are also in a good position to suggest sales strategies. A manager may suggest, for example, improving the quality of service to improve sales, because this was an area his customers appreciated when he was a sales representative.

Recruitment

This is an area where the inexperienced sales manager may need some training. He will probably have a good idea of the characteristics of a good salesperson. He will also be knowledgeable about the product awareness prospective sales personnel need. What he may find problematic is the interviewing and selection process. It would probably be a good idea for the newly appointed sales manager to discuss these aspects with the personnel department of the firm (if there is one). Inexperienced interviewers tend to talk about the job that is on offer rather than eliciting appropriate information from the interviewee. If the sales manager cannot discuss interviewing techniques and selection with personnel then he should himself formulate a checklist of selection criteria. During the interview he should cover all aspects of these criteria to enable a rational selection to be made.

Motivation

One key aspect of the sales manager's role is to motivate sales personnel. It will probably be the case that the way in which representatives are paid has been decided so we will not discuss the relative merits of salary and commission payments. There are many other ways in which sales representatives are motivated which involve the sales manager. With some commission payments sales targets are set. The sales manager's job is to set these targets so they are fair and attainable. If they are not seen as being either fair or attainable then this will demotivate the sales representatives. Meetings between the sales manager and the sales representatives can be a motivation force. The sales manager will be better able to understand the sales personnel as individuals. It may be the case that the sales manager knows these employees already but there are other reasons to hold the meetings. They can be used to assess the need for training, which in itself motivates employees, and for communicating company objectives. They can also be used for all staff to air their opinions. Simply listening and showing understanding can motivate sales personnel.

Organisation

The organisation of the sales team is one area where the newly appointed sales manager may have problems. The basic sales structure will probably be already in place, and will usually be either a geographical, a product or a customer based structure. The ambitious sales manager may have lots of ideas to change the structure for the improvement of the sales function. This would probably cause too much upheaval in the first few months of employment. Instead the sales manager should 'learn the ropes' of the existing structure and perhaps change this later when he has more experience and has been accepted by members of staff.

Evaluation and control

Results should be compared with the original objectives in order to make an assessment on performance. There are many quantitative and qualitative ways in which to measure sales performance. Quantitative measures include sales revenue, new accounts and profits; qualitative may be customer service levels. Sales managers are responsible for evaluating the sales effort as a team and for individual sales representatives.

In conclusion, although the transition from sales representative to sales manager is traumatic it should be remembered that there are many advantages to being a sales representative in a company before becoming a sales manager. New skills however have to be learnt and to make the transition as smoothly as possible the sales manager should accept this and get as much training and advice as possible. It is also the case that the newly appointed sales manager should not make too many changes whilst still learning what the job actually entails.

18 SALES FORECASTING

In order that a company can plan adequately for the future it needs to make some assessment regarding future sales. Factory contraction or expansion will depend on forecasts of future demand for the products. Companies have objectives they wish to fulfil. At the same time they also have resources such as plants, employees and financial resources. In order that objectives are met, resources must be managed accordingly. These resources can be allocated in many different ways, and the basis of this planning is sales forecasting. Forecasts are, of course, only as good as the assumptions on which they are based. Forecasts have to take account of both the controllable and the uncontrollable factors which surround the business environment. Controllable elements include the marketing mix variables of product, price, place and promotion. Uncontrollable elements are not within the company's control and include legal and political changes, consumer tastes and competitors' actions. From these forecasts decisions must be made as to the strategy of the firm. Within a company sales forecasting is used to determine the actions of a number of departments. In the marketing department sales forecasts are used to plan the marketing mix requirements. Production will require sales forecasts to determine future product types and specifications. It can therefore produce the products in an efficient manner and keep stocks at appropriate levels. Personnel departments need to assess the future staffing needs of the company, so sales forecasts will be very important. The finance department will want to have sales forecasts on which to base forecasts of future profit.

Three methods of sales forecasting will now be discussed.

(a) *Time series models*

Time series models take historical data and project trends in to the future. The basic reasoning behind this is that what has happened in the past will affect what will happen in the future. This of course will be more likely in the short term than in the long term when changing customer tastes or technological innovation will change sales dramatically. For this reason it is suitable as a method of forecasting short-term sales so that an accurate assessment of production needs can be made. It also requires that there is an adequate amount of historical data available to base predictions on. It is therefore not very appropriate to use in the early stages of the product's life.

There can be many different types of time series trends. The first task of the forecaster is to plot the data and look at the shape of the trend in sales, often taking moving averages to view the sales. If there is not much fluctuation and the data plotted is more or less horizontal this usually indicates the product is in the maturity stage of the product life cycle and is relatively well established. If the data shows short-term fluctuations this is often due to seasonal aspects. Seasonal data can indicate climatic changes in demand, or changes due to seasonal celebrations such as Christmas or Easter. This can allow management to plan production and staffing levels that take into account fluctuating seasonal demand. Cyclical fluctuations are similar to seasonal changes but last longer. Data that shows a trend of growth or decline can often be related to these stages in the PLC. Inflation needs to be taken into account when analysing time series data, as otherwise this distorts sales value figures upwards. It is also worth noting that data can show seasonality at the same time as the business cycle is affecting the data, although if needed some of the trends can be 'smoothed' so the important data can be analysed.

(b) *Causal models*

Causal models, like time series, use quantitative data. Equations relating the dependent variable (future sales) to a number of independent variables are calculated. For example, sales could be said to be a function of relative price, complementary goods sales and advertising. Each of the independent variables are weighted to take account of their importance. Variables can also be lagged, so last year's sales figures can be incorporated. This method also uses historical data so enough of this type of data is necessary to make an accurate forecast. As this method looks for causal relationships statistical measures and tests can be applied to the results and regression analysis applied. Causal models are longer term than time series and therefore can be used to predict the future needs of plant size and/or workforce. However, although these models are easier to formulate with the increased used of computers they are still expensive and difficult to construct and analyse. They are very useful, though, because they analyse what the determinants of sales are and the impact of changes to these variables can be measured. They are only as good as the variables that have been incorporated, however, and if a major variable has been omitted then this can ruin the analysis.

(c) *Qualitative models*

If there is little quantitative data on which to base sales forecasts then qualitative methods can be used. Lack of historical data can be caused because the product is new on the market or because of a major social or technological change that makes past data obsolete. Qualitative models are usually used for long-term forecasts, and they have the advantages of being relatively cheap and easy to understand. However, they are not very accurate because of the uncertainty associated with long-term forecasts. Examples of the type of forecasts that can be made using this method are forecasts of technological and social changes. These type of forecasts rely on expert opinions to predict the future. There are two main types of techniques available. The first is *explorative*, which starts at the present date with current knowledge and then tries to predict the future from this. The second is *normative* which looks at an innovation at a future date (eg a commercially viable electric car) and investigates the stages that are required to fulfil this change.

As can be seen from the descriptions of some of the available techniques outlined above the 'best' technique will depend entirely on what it is desired to forecast.

19 OBJECTIVES, STRATEGIES AND CONTROL

The product chosen to illustrate the annual marketing plan is washing powder.

The annual marketing plan is the operational plan that is based on the longer term strategic marketing plan. Annual plans explain the way in which the company is aiming for the objectives of the strategic marketing plan. There are a number of reasons why it is important to formulate annual marketing plans.

SUGGESTED SOLUTIONS

(a) They explain what the present situation is and what is expected in the year ahead.
(b) They indicate the resources that are necessary to fulfil the objectives.
(c) They specify expectations so that the company can anticipate where it will be in a year's time.
(d) They describe the course of action over the next year.
(e) They allow performance to be monitored.

The basic marketing planning process can be shown in diagrammatic form for a given year.

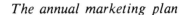

The annual marketing plan

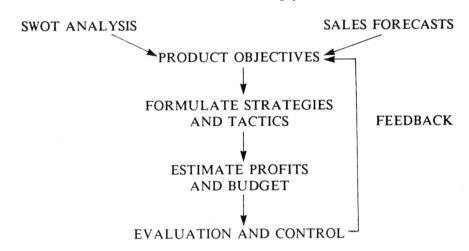

Here, we will concentrate on three areas of the planning process using washing powder as an example. Firstly, objectives. Objectives in the annual plan concentrate on product rather than strategic applications. The SWOT (strengths and weaknesses/opportunities and threats) analysis would indicate a number of implications for the washing powder manufacturer. There may be a new competitor in the market, or new product attributes sought by the consumer, for example more environmentally 'friendly' powders. The objectives for the brand of washing powder over the next year can now be defined. One could be to improve market share by a certain percentage, but with a new competitor the company might be pleased if it maintains market share for this year. A certain sales volume may be specified depending, of course, on the company's assessment of opportunities in the market. Profits will be another objective of the company and are often stated in terms of return on investment (net profits divided by total investment). The company may have to decide whether the return on investment is substantial enough or whether it could do better investing elsewhere. The annual marketing plan should also set objectives for the marketing mix variables. These objectives are necessary in order to satisfy the broader objectives of market share etc. For example, if the washing powder manufacturer wishes to increase market share by 5% over the year, then this will have implications for the marketing mix objectives. Promotional effort will probably have to be increased in order to take market share from other companies, as there would be few new users to target.

There are many levels in the organisation where strategies can be developed. *Corporate strategy* deals with the overall development of an organisation's business activities whilst *marketing strategy* looks at the organisation's activities in the markets served. This can be long term or short term as in the case of annual marketing planning. Going back to the above model, when product objectives have been formulated then the marketing strategy that should allow these objectives to be met can be developed. There may be refinements to be made as to the target market the company is aiming for. Perhaps the washing powder brand has slipped downmarket over time. A decision has to be made whether to fully address this target market or to reposition the powder. Marketing mix variables can then be developed to accomplish these objectives. If the objective is to increase sales by a certain percentage then a promotion of a money off coupon may be used to increase sales. If the objective is to build brand awareness then an extensive advertising campaign can be used. Different objectives will have different implications for the marketing mix strategy that is most appropriate.

The purpose of *control* of the annual marketing plan is to examine whether the objectives have been achieved. Control of marketing planning should not simply be left to the end of the year evaluation of the success of the product, but be reviewed throughout the year. The results of evaluation and control should be included in the formulation of the annual plan in the following year. If sales of the washing powder are below those that were indicated in the objectives then reasons for this should be analysed. It may be that during the year the introduction of liquid detergents for washing clothes and heavy promotion of these products detracted from the company's brand. In this case a decision should be made whether to sit back and see if this was just a short-term phenomenon or whether to promote the powder aggressively. One way in which control can be managed by a company is through 'management by objectives'. Management set short-term goals (monthly or quarterly), performance against these goals is analysed, and if these are not met then the reasons are analysed and corrective action taken. Usually sales analysis, market share analysis, marketing expenses to sales analysis, financial analysis and customer attitudes are used to control the annual marketing plan. The main responsibility for annual marketing plan control is with top or middle management.

20 OVERSEAS EXPANSION

The company firstly has to research markets carefully in order to make an assessment of the viability of their products' success in the overseas market. A selection of target markets should then be made. The question that must then be addressed is 'In what way should we enter the overseas market?' The way in which goods are delivered to overseas customers will include the method of entry into the market and the distribution channels used in the foreign country. Here we will concentrate on the main methods of entry that are open to the company.

The most basic decision regarding foreign market entry is whether to produce the goods in the home country or in the foreign country or indeed both. If goods are produced in the home market then direct or indirect exporting methods can be used. In *indirect exporting* the firm is not undertaking any special overseas activities. Products can be sold in the domestic market, then resold in the foreign market, without any special effort from the company. International trading companies can be used as an indirect exporting method. The largest of these are Japanese and European. Export management companies perform a similar function to that of a specialist export department in a company. There is usually more control over products exported using an EMC rather than a trading company. Another way in which the company can export indirectly is 'piggybacking'. This is when one company with an overseas distribution system allows another company to use its facilities.

Direct exporting takes more commitment from the company considering this option. In direct exporting the company does not delegate exporting to another company. Sales are usually greater, and there is better control of the marketing function and exporting experience with this form of market entry, although of course the costs are higher. There are more decisions to be made in this form of exporting than in indirect exporting. Management have to choose the foreign market(s) they will enter, its representatives in the market, the physical distribution method and export documentation. The company can accomplish this by using an agent or distributor or setting up an overseas marketing subsidiary.

The third main way in which an overseas market can be reached is through manufacturing abroad. There are a number of reasons why firms may decide to manufacture overseas. Transportation costs may be prohibitive, or host governments encourage firms to set up production facilities (or discourage imports into their country). Production in the host country will also mean that there are closer links with the target market. There are a number of options available for the company considering this option. Assembly plants can be set up to assemble components; many car manufacturers do this. Companies can also authorise other companies to produce goods for them. This is termed *contract manufacturing*. If there is a longer term arrangement and the foreign company has greater responsibility, this usually takes the form of a *licensing agreement*. If the company (domestic) has invested in the foreign firm this is often classed as a *joint venture*. Choosing to set up wholly owned foreign production demonstrates the greatest commitment the company can make to the foreign market. It can be achieved either through establishing new production facilities or by acquisition. Obviously this is the most expensive option of foreign market entry for the company to consider, but it allows the most control.

Before choosing a method of market entry the company should look at the following questions and consider the answers before making the decision.

(a)   What are the investment requirements of the particular method of entry? The amount of finance needed varies greatly with the method of market entry.

(b)   What are the administrative requirements of the market entry method? Again these vary according to entry method.

(c)   How many extra personnel would be required?

(d)   How much risk is attached to the method of market entry?

(e)   How flexible is the market entry method? Would management be able to change the method easily?

(f)   How much control will the company have over its marketing mix variables in the market entry method?

(g)   What are the profit possibilities?

(h)   Will the entry method enable the company to learn the skills of international marketing?

(i)   How many countries are to be targeted?

(j)   What level of market coverage is required?

These ten questions should be asked concerning each overseas market entry method being considered. When the answers are analysed management should be able to make an informed decision that matches overseas opportunities with organisational objectives and capabilities. There is no 'best' method of entering foreign markets. Each foreign market entry method has advantages and disadvantages and their appropriateness depends on the matching of company and products with market entry method.

INDEX

CIM – FUNDAMENTALS AND PRACTICE OF MARKETING (9/93)

Name: _____

How have you used this Text?

Home study (book only) ☐   With 'correspondence' package ☐

On a course: college_____ ☐   Other _____

How did you obtain this Text?

From us by mail order ☐   From us by phone ☐

From a bookshop ☐   From your college ☐

Where did you hear about BPP Texts?

At bookshop ☐   Recommended by lecturer ☐

Recommended by friend ☐   Mailshot from BPP ☐

Advertisement in _____ ☐   Other _____

Your comments and suggestions would be appreciated on the following areas.

Syllabus coverage

Illustrative questions

Errors (please specify, and refer to a page number)

Presentation

Other